The Idea of Latin America

Blackwell Manifestos

In this new series major critics make timely interventions to address important concepts and subjects, including topics as diverse as, for example: Culture, Race, Religion, History, Society, Geography, Literature, Literary Theory, Shakespeare, Cinema, and Modernism. Written accessibly and with verve and spirit, these books follow no uniform prescription but set out to engage and challenge the broadest range of readers, from undergraduates to postgraduates, university teachers and general readers – all those, in short, interested in ongoing debates and controversies in the humanities and social sciences.

Already Published

Forthcoming

The Idea of Latin America

Walter D. Mignolo

Blackwell
Publishing

© 2005 by Walter D. Mignolo

BLACKWELL PUBLISHING
350 Main Street, Malden, MA 02148–5020, USA
9600 Garsington Road, Oxford OX4 2DQ, UK
550 Swanston Street, Carlton, Victoria 3053, Australia

First published 2005 by Blackwell Publishing Ltd

5 2007

Library of Congress Cataloging-in-Publication Data

Mignolo, Walter.
The idea of Latin America / Walter D. Mignolo.
p.   cm.—(Blackwell manifestos)
Includes bibliographical references and index.
ISBN 978-1-4051-0085-4 (hardcover : alk. paper)
ISBN 978-1-4051-0086-1 (pbk. : alk. paper)
1. Latin America—Name.   2. Latin America—History—Philosophy.   3. Latin
America—Civilization—European influences.   4. Latin America—Race
relations.   5. Latin America—Colonization.   I. Title.   II. Series.

F1406.M54 2005
982—dc22
2005006595

A catalogue record for this title is available from the British Library.

Set in 11.5 on 13.5 pt Bembo
by SNP Best-set Typesetter Ltd, Hong Kong
Printed and bound in Singapore
by Markono Print Media Pte Ltd

The publisher's policy is to use permanent paper from mills that operate a sustainable forestry policy, and which has been manufactured from pulp processed using acid-free and elementary chlorine-free practices. Furthermore, the publisher ensures that the text paper and cover board used have met acceptable environmental accreditation standards.

For further information on
Blackwell Publishing, visit our website:
www.blackwellpublishing.com

To Andrea and Alexander Wylie Mignolo,
tireless interlocutors

Contents

Acknowledgments

Without the invitation of Andrew McNeillie to write a monograph for the "Manifestos" series, this book would have never come into existence. And without the continuous work of the modernity/coloniality project, the narrative and argument would have not been what they are now. Participant members of the project, with whom I have met many times during the past two years, are Enrique Dussel (Argentina and Mexico), Anibal Quijano (Peru), Boaventura de Sousa Santos (Portugal), Catherine Walsh (Ecuador), Libia Grueso (Colombia), Marcelo Fernández Osco (Bolivia and USA), Zulma Palermo (Argentina), Freya Schiwy (USA), Edgardo Lander (Venezuela), Fernando Coronil (Venezuela and USA), Javier Sanjinés (Bolivia and USA), José D. Saldívar (USA), Ramón Grosfoguel (Puerto Rico and USA), Nelson Maldonado-Torres (Puerto Rico and USA), Agustín Lao-Montes (Puerto Rico and USA), Marisol de la Cadena (Peru and USA), Arturo Escobar (Colombia and USA), Eduardo Restrepo (Colombia and USA), Margarita Cervantes-Zalazar (Cuba and USA), Santiago Castro-Gómez (Colombia), and Oscar Guardiola (Colombia).

I am particularly indebted to Catherine Walsh for facilitating access to and conversations with members of the Indigenous and Afro-Ecuadorian social movements; to Javier Sanjinés for opening many doors in Bolivia; and to Nelson Maldonado-Torres for facilitating contact with members of the Caribbean Philosophical Association and for sharing with me – verbally and in written forms – his path-breaking "Fanonian Meditations." Beyond their

generosity with facilitating contacts, we spent hours of tireless conversations that contributed – indirectly – to shaping my arguments
and to decolonizing the idea of Latin America. At Duke University,
I have benefited from the conversation and advice of Leo Ching and
Ralph Letzinger regarding the idea of Asia, and Roberto Dainotto
taught me to rethink the idea of Europe from the Italian South. The
professional advice of the three of them has been enhanced and
complemented by many friendly and intellectual conversations, most
of the time evolving toward shifting the geo-politics of knowledge
and undoing (rather than rethinking) area studies.

My debt to V. Y. Mudimbe for his insightful studies on the idea
and the invention of Africa goes back to 1993, when I moved from
the University of Michigan to Duke. At Duke also I have benefited
from working with graduate students, with whom I share the effort to
understand from the perspective of people who have been reduced,
by official histories in South America and imperial histories in Europe
and the US, to being "understood." Ground-breaking research is
being done by Michael Ennis in the literature program and Silvermoon
in the history department on Nahuatls co-existing and struggling
with imperial institutions in the sixteenth and seventeenth centuries;
and by Gonzálo Lamana in the department of cultural anthropology,
exploring the first twenty years of Spaniards being in Tawantinsuyu
from the perspective of both Inca rulers and Spanish conquistadores.
The three projects and researchers are shifting the geo-politics of
knowledge and teaching us how to read the Spanish documents from
the perspectives of Aztecs and Incas during the conquest and during
colonial times. And I owe to Marcelo Fernández Osco, an Aymara
intellectual and graduate student at Duke, his perceptive views on
Bolivian history and society and his continuing interventions in
Andean scholarship and politics, which bring together in insightful
ways the geo-political and body-political epistemic shift. It is this
shifting that informs my decolonial archeology of the idea of Latin
America. Last but not least, I am grateful to Lía Haro for her editorial
skills and infinite patience; she read and re-read the last versions of the
manuscript several times and did not stop asking questions, suggesting
deletions and additions, moving paragraphs up or down. As the
dictum goes, none of my advisors and collaborators is accountable for
the final version of my argument.

Preface: Uncoupling the Name and the Reference

An excess of confidence has spread all over the world regarding the ontology of continental divides.[1] While it could be debated whether there are four, six, or seven continents, it is unquestionable that the count of six or seven includes the basic four-way subdivision of Asia, Africa, America, and Europe. That undisputed division underlies not only debates over continental divides but also ideas of East and West, North and South, and explicitly hierarchical categories such as first, Second, Third, and Fourth Worlds (the last a term invented to accommodate Indigenous people in the Americas, New Zealand, and Australia). It may be common practice to buy a plane ticket to "Australia" or "sub-Saharan Africa" as opposed to "north Africa," but the wide acceptance of those geographical designations hides the fact that the division of continents and the geo-political structures imposed upon them are all imperial constructions of the past five hundred years. A god did not create the planet earth and divide it, from the very beginning, into four continents. "America," the fourth, was appended to the three that had been imagined in Christianity, which St Augustine articulated in *The City of God*, as we will see in chapter 1.

The narrative and argument of this book, then, will not be about an entity called "Latin America," but on how the "idea" of Latin America came about. One of the main goals is to uncouple the name of the subcontinent from the cartographic image we all have of it. It is an excavation of the imperial/colonial foundation of the "idea" of Latin America that will help us unravel the geo-politics of knowledge from the perspective of coloniality, the untold and unrecognized historical counterpart of modernity. By "perspective of coloniality" in this case, I mean that the center of observation will be grounded in the colonial history that shaped the idea of the Americas. I refer to the process as an excavation rather than an archeology because it is impossible to simply uncover coloniality, insofar as it shapes and is shaped by the processes of modernity. After all, the Americas exist today only as a consequence of European colonial expansion and the narrative of that expansion from the European perspective, the perspective of modernity.

You can tell the story of the world in as many ways as you wish, from the perspective of modernity, and never pay any attention to the perspective from coloniality. I am here referring to something important and much more than a mere "conflict" of interpretations. To illustrate, consider that a Christian and a Marxist analysis of a given event, say the "discovery of America," would offer us different interpretations; but *both would be from the perspective of modernity.* That is, the "discovery of America" would be seen in both cases *from the perspective of Europe.* A Fanonian perspective on "the discovery of America," however, would introduce a non-European perspective, the perspective grounded on the memory of slave-trade and slave-labor exploitation, and its psychological, historical, ethical, and theoretical consequences. In this case, it would be a *perspective from coloniality and from the Afro-Caribbean rather than from Europe.* Readers will be more familiar with Christianity and Marxism than with Fanonism – a critical current of thought (parallel with and complementary to, but not reducible to, "Marxism") that is producing a decolonial shift in the domain of knowledge and action, inspired by the twentieth-century Martinican intellectual and activist Frantz Fanon, discussed in the following chapters – which should already point to an important aspect of the issue that structures my entire argument. Of course, I could have organized my argument from a European perspective, even if I was born and educated in South America. All I would need to do would be to embrace the philosophical frame of reference that is already in place and locate myself within a paradigm of knowledge that, in spite of conflicting interpretations within it, is based on the geo-historical location of Europe.

Instead, I situate my argument within the decolonial paradigm of knowledge and understanding enacted by Waman Puma de Ayala (see chapter 3), as well as other intellectuals after him belonging to the sphere of society that anthropologist Eric Wolf identified as "people without history."

From the sixteenth-century Spanish missionary Bartolomé de Las Casas to G. W. F. Hegel in the nineteenth century, and from Karl Marx to the twentieth-century British historian A. J. Toynbee, all we can read (or see in maps) about the place of the Americas in the world order is historically located from a European perspective that passes as universal. Certainly, every one of these authors acknowledged that there was a world, and people, outside Europe. Indeed, both people and continents outside of Europe were overly present as "objects," but they were absent as subjects and, in a way, out of history. They were, in other words, subjects whose perspectives did not count. Eric Wolf's famous book title, *People without History*, became a metaphor to describe this epistemic power differential. By "people without history," Wolf did not mean that there were people in the world who did not have memories and records of their past, which would be an absolutely absurd claim. He meant that, according to the regional concept of history as defined in the Western world from ancient Greece to twentieth-century France, every society that did not have alphabetic writing or wrote in a language other than the six imperial languages of modern Europe did not have History. In this view, History is a privilege of European modernity and in order to have History you have to let yourself be colonized, which means allowing yourself, willingly or not, to be subsumed by a perspective of history, life, knowledge, economy, subjectivity, family, religion, etc. that is modeled on the history of modern Europe, and that has now been adopted, with little difference, as the official model of the US. Perspectives from coloniality, however, emerge out of the conditions of the "colonial wound," the feeling of inferiority imposed on human beings who do not fit the predetermined model in Euro-American narratives.

To excavate coloniality, then, one must always include and analyze the project of modernity, although the reverse is not true, because coloniality points to the absences that the narrative of modernity produces. Thus, I choose to describe the modern world order that has emerged in the five hundred years since the "discovery of America" as the modern/colonial world, to indicate that coloniality is constitutive of modernity and cannot exist without it. Indeed, the "idea" of Latin America cannot be dealt with in isolation without producing turmoil in the world system. It cannot be separated from the "ideas" of Europe and of the US as America that dominate even today. The "Americas" are the consequence of early European commercial expansion and the motor of capitalism, as we know it today. The "discovery" of America and the genocide of Indians and African slaves are the very foundation of "modernity," more so than the French or Industrial Revolutions. Better yet, they constitute the darker and hidden face of modernity, "coloniality." Thus, to excavate the "idea of Latin America" is, really, to understand how the West was born and how the modern world order was founded.

The following discussion is, thus, written within the frame of what Arturo Escobar has called the modernity/coloniality research project.[2] Some of the premises are the following:

1 There is no modernity without coloniality, because coloniality is constitutive of modernity.
2 The modern/colonial world (and the colonial matrix of power) originates in the sixteenth century, and the discovery/invention of America is the colonial component of modernity whose visible face is the European Renaissance.
3 The Enlightenment and the Industrial Revolution are derivative historical moments consisting in the transformation of the colonial matrix of power.
4 Modernity is the name for the historical process in which Europe began its progress toward world hegemony. It carries a darker side, coloniality.
5 Capitalism, as we know it today, is of the essence for both the conception of modernity and its darker side, coloniality.
6 Capitalism and modernity/coloniality had a second historical moment of transformation after World War II when the US took the imperial leadership previously enjoyed at different times by both Spain and England.

Following these presuppositions, I organize the narrative and the argument of this book around three heterogeneous historico-structural moments that link the empires and the colonies. The first is the entry of America into the European consciousness (the Renaissance). The second (the Enlightenment) is the entry of "Latinidad" – "Latinity," "Latinitée": see chapter 2 – as a double identity, imperial and colonial. In the third moment (after the Cold War), I change gears to focus on radical shifts in the geography of knowledge that we are witnessing now around the world and that, in the Americas, are questioning the ontology and the ideology of a continental divide between "Latin" and "Anglo" Americas.

Chapters 1 and 2 tell the story of the silences created by the entangled narratives that begin in the sixteenth century and cross the five hundred years since then to make modernity appear as the innocent point of arrival (the secular translation of Paradise in Christian cosmology) toward which History flows. Given this, I attempt a decolonial shift in the domain of history. Chapter 1 describes the building of the colonial framework and the invention of the idea of "America," while Chapter 2 follows the emergence of the specific idea of "Latin" America.

Chapter 1 examines the consequences of the various narratives that underlie the "idea of America," which subsumed the histories and cosmologies of the people living in Tawantinsuyu and Anáhuac, the territories of the Aztecs and Incas, when Europeans arrived. Christian Europeans could imagine the "discovery and conquest" of America as the most outstanding event since God created the world (a widely accepted view that even free-trade theorist Adam Smith and radical critic of capitalism Marx could agree on), but the Aymara of what is now Bolivia and Peru saw it as a *Pachakuti*, a total disruption of space and time – a revolution in reverse, so to speak, that did not yield the "progressive" consequences of the American, French, and Industrial Revolutions. We could say, metaphorically, that a *Pachakuti* has been taking place in Iraq since March of 2003. Christian cosmology, as we will discuss, organized the world into continents revolving around Europe. The fact that those in Cuzco or Tenochtitlan, capitals of the Inca and Aztec Empires, conceived of themselves as living in the center of space would have no bearing on the maps that were drawn.

The geo-politics of continental division are also of key importance for understanding the way that "Latin" America could subsequently be imagined as part of the West and yet peripheral to it. America, as a continent and people, was considered inferior in European narratives from the sixteenth century until the idea was refashioned in the US after the Spanish-American War in 1898, when "Latin" America took on the inferior role. Chapter 2, therefore, goes on to explore the divisions within "America" after the revolutions of independence (North/South, Anglo/Latin), in which "Latin" America would come to be seen as dependent on and inferior to the United States. The concept of "Latinidad," an identity asserted by the French and adopted by Creole elites to define themselves, would ultimately function both to rank them below Anglo Americans and, yet, to erase and demote the identities of Indians and Afro-South Americans. These are, in a nutshell, the history, meaning, and consequences of the "idea of Latin" America that I explore in more detail in the next two chapters.

Many secular scholars, intellectuals, World Bank officers, state functionaries, and journalists believe that "modernity is an incomplete project." In my view, coming from the perspective of coloniality, to complete the incomplete project of modernity means to keep on reproducing coloniality, which is our current reality at the beginning of the twenty-first century. While we no longer have the overt colonial domination of the Spanish or British models, the logic of coloniality remains in force in the "idea" of the world that has been constructed through modernity/coloniality. Examining the evolution of the "idea of Latin America" should show that while its materialization belongs precisely to the manifestation of that logic in particular moments of imperial/colonial restructuring, the perspective of those who have been silenced by it can open up possibilities for radical change. Chapter 3, then, will focus on movements among Indigenous people and Afro descendants in "Latin" America, as well as among Latinos/as[3] in the US who are unfolding new knowledge projects and making the "idea of Latin America" obsolete.

I did not write chapter 4 because of the limited length of the books in the "Manifesto" series. If I had had the chance to write another chapter, it would have dealt in more depth with the tense opposition between the idea of "Latin" America and the ideas of "nature" and "culture." To look briefly at their evolution now, however, should provide a good overview of the ways such European categories shape the "idea" of Latin America both from inside (the Europeanized component of its population) and from outside (the "othering" to which Latin America has been subjected by the Western European and US gaze), and of how they are being changed today by emerging perspectives. In the sixteenth century, there was a sense of admiration for the novelty and the exuberance of "nature." Spanish Jesuit José de Acosta, who spent several decades in the Andes, wrote in 1590 that to know and understand "nature" was to understand its creator. However, a few decades after Acosta, Frances Bacon changed gears and conceived "nature" as something men have to conquer and dominate. The opposition was settled between nature and humanity. "Latin" America has been conceived on both sides of that opposition. Thus, Creole intellectuals in the nineteenth century, like Domingo Faustino Sarmiento in Argentina and Euclides Da Cunha in Brazil, used the "nature" versus "civilization" paradigm to define the Creole elite against the "barbarian" indigenous inhabitants of South America. As we will see in chapter 2, however, the Creole elites were simultaneously self-colonizing by taking on a French idea of themselves as "Latin," which opposed them to the Anglo, who represented civilization, and located them more on the side of "nature." At the same time, intellectuals from the French naturalist Georges comte de Buffon to the German philosopher Hegel, and including the US president Thomas Jefferson, were articulating an opposition between "nature" and civilized man that put all of America on the "nature" side of the opposition. These debates saw the New World as younger and immature; therefore, the American population was expected to evolve accordingly to a state of civilization.[4]

Toward the end of the eighteenth century and through the nineteenth, nature, as God's creation, was opposed to culture as man's creation. Consequently, the opposition between nature and humanity was not abandoned but simply redrawn. "Culture" (from Latin *colere*, "to cultivate or to inhabit") surfaced as a necessary concept during the process of secularization because "culture" meant "to cultivate" in the sense of human production and creation. In the sense of inhabiting, "culture" is the dwelling place, the inhabitation of what is created. "Culture" was needed to replace "religion" as a community bond. *Religio* comes from the Latin *re-ligare*, "to unite." In ancient Rome, *re-ligare* was conceived as both temporal, insofar as *religio* also meant *traditio* ("tradition"), and spatial, as *religio* united those with common beliefs in a given area. When a term was needed to designate a new type of community not based on faith, it was necessary to conceive and put into practice a new institution, "the community of birth" or the nation-state, which was defined in conjunction with "national culture" in order to create subjects with "national identity." Imperial national identities, in their turn, established a measuring stick to rank and (de)value the national identities of the "independent states" from the nineteenth century until today. Imperial national identities managed by the state have served to redraw, since the nineteenth century, the colonial difference, and the "idea" of Latin America was part of such imperial redrawing.

"Culture," in other words, created national unity: national languages, national literature, national flag and anthem, etc. were all singular manifestations of a "national culture." It served to name and institute the homogeneity of the nation-state. However, insofar as the term emerged in the nineteenth century when England and France were embarking on the second wave of colonial expansion, "culture" also served the colonial purpose of naming and describing those alien and inferior "cultures" that would be under European "civilization." While European civilization was divided into national cultures, most of the rest of the population of the world would be conceived as having "culture" but not civilization. "Latin" Americans had a culture, created in part in complicity with the French ideologues of "Latinidad," but not a civilization, since the ancient Aztec, Inca, and Maya civilizations were already consigned to a forgotten past. Consequently, "Latin" Americans were considered second-class Europeans who lacked the science and sophisticated history of Europe. During the Cold War that image was still in place and it was extended to the entire Third World.

Yet these macro-narratives elide the fact that in Indigenous cosmology, nature and humanity do not necessarily oppose each other, and "civilization" is nothing more than a European self-description of its role in history. For the Indigenous, oppositions can co-exist without negation. "The Andean world is supported by *complementary*

xvii

dualisms," writes intellectual Kichua activist Ariruma Kowii from Otavalo, Ecuador.[5] This simple logical difference is crucial to performing a decolonial shift in knowledge and understanding (e.g., looking at the world from the perspective of Kichua and not from that of Greek and Latin, although with the "imperial" presence of European principles of knowledge since the Renaissance). Such a shift is fundamental in changing the perception of the world and society as we know them through the categories of knowledge of modern/imperial European languages rooted in Greek and Latin. Kowii dismantles the above oppositions in the very title of his article "Barbarie, civilizaciones e interculturalidad" ("Barbarians, civilizations and 'interculturalidad' ['interculturality']").[6] Today, then, the category of "barbarie" is being questioned by an Indigenous intellectual, whom Sarmiento would have considered a barbarian Indian. Next, "civilizaciones" (in Kowii's title) is plural, which affirms the historical civilization of Indians that was disqualified by the singular model of the European civilizing mission. The *terms of the conversation, and not just the content without questioning the terms*, are redressed in a civilizational dialogue that opens the monologue of civilization and the silence of barbarism. Once the terms are reconceived as dialogical instead of based on a logic of contradictory terms (civilization vs. barbarism), barbarism is put on hold and relocated: the civilization that Creoles and Europeans had in mind has been genocidal and, therefore, barbarian. If X and non-X co-exist, the question becomes how different civilizational structures can put barbarism aside. That is precisely the work of intercultural struggles and dialogues, which we will discuss further in chapter 3.

There is one proviso: at this point in time, the colonial difference must be kept in view, because Creoles in the Americas of European descent (either Latin or Anglo), as well as Creoles of European descent around the world, may still see civilization and barbarism as ontological categories, and therefore they may have trouble accepting Indian (or Islamic, for that matter) civilizational processes and histories when entering into dialogue. There are no civilizations outside of Europe or, if there are, like those of Islam, China or Japan (to follow Huntington's classification: see chapter 1), they remain in the past and have had to be brought into the present of Western civilization. That is the colonial difference that should be kept in mind. The future can no longer be thought of as the "defense of Western civilization," constantly waiting for the barbarians. As barbarians are ubiquitous (they could be in the plains or in the mountains as well as in global cities), so are the civilized. There is no safe place to defend and, even worse, believing that there is a safe place that must be defended is (and has been) the direct road to killing. Dialogue, properly speaking, cannot take place until there are no more places to be defended and the power differential, consequently, can be redressed. Dialogue today is a *utopia*, as we are witnessing in Iraq, and it should be reconceived as *utopistic*: a double movement composed of a critical take on the past in order to imagine and construct future possible worlds. The decolonial shift is of the essence if we would stop seeing "modernity" as a goal rather than seeing it as a European construction of history in Europe's own interests. Dialogue can only take place once "modernity" is decolonized and dispossessed of its mythical march toward the future. I am not defending "despotism" of any kind, Oriental or Occidental. I am just saying that "dialogue" can only take place when the "monologue" of one civilization (Western) is no longer enforced.

This book can be read in two different, but complementary, ways. Readers not familiar with current academic debates can enter through the argument that America was not discovered but invented, and from there follow the path that made of "Latin" America an extension of the initial imperial/colonial invention. Those who are familiar with conversations in the humanities could see the argument itself as an attempt to shift the geography, and the geo-politics of knowledge, of *critical theory* (as introduced by the Frankfurt School in the 1930s) to a new terrain of *decoloniality*. The first reading can still be performed within the paradigm of modernity that emphasizes the linear evolution of concepts and, above all, newness. The second reading, however, demands to be performed within the paradigm of (de)coloniality that implies modernity but emphasizes "co-existence" and simultaneity instead. I will introduce a concept of *historico-structural heterogeneity* at the end of chapter 1 to locate the argument in that paradigm of co-existence and to critique the paradigm of newness and historical progression. Within the limits of European local histories, *critical theory* pushed humanists and critical social scientists toward critical explorations of the conditions that make events and ideas possible, instead of taking ideas for granted and seeing events as carrying their own, essential, meaning. A critical theory *beyond* the history of Europe proper and *within* the colonial history of America (or Asia or Africa; or even from the perspective of immigrants *within* Europe and the US who have disrupted the homogeneity) becomes *decolonial theory*. That is, it is the theory arising from the projects for decolonization of knowledge and being that will lead to the imagining of economy and politics *otherwise*. By going to the very roots of modern coloniality – the invention of America and of "Latin" America – this book is a contribution to that decolonization of knowledge and being; an attempt to rewrite history following an-other logic, an-other language, an-other thinking.[7]

1

The Americas, Christian Expansion, and the Modern/ Colonial Foundation of Racism

America has been discovered, conquered and populated by the civilized European races, who were carried forward by the same law that moved Egyptian people from their primitive land to bring them to Greece; later on, the same law moved the inhabitants of Greece to civilize the Italian peninsula; and finally the same law motivated the Greeks to civilize the barbarous inhabitants of Germany who changed with the remains of the Roman world, the virility of its blood illuminated by Christianity.

Juan Bautista Alberdi, *Bases y puntos de partida para la organización nacional*, 1852[1]

One of the foremost differences separating white and Indian was simply one of origin. Whites derived predominantly from Western Europe . . . Conversely, Indians had always been in the western hemisphere. Life on this continent and views concerning it were not shaped in a post-Roman atmosphere . . . The western hemisphere produced *wisdom*, western Europe produced *knowledge*.

Vine Deloria, Jr, *Custer Died for Your Sins: An Indian Manifesto*, 1969 (italics added)

The "Americas" on the Colonial Horizon of Modernity

Before 1492, the Americas were not on anybody's map, not even on the map of the people inhabiting Anáhuac (the territory of the Aztecs) and Tawantinsuyu (the territory of the Incas). The Spanish and Portuguese, as the sole and diverse European occupants in the sixteenth century, named the entire continent that was under their control and possession. It may be hard to understand today that the Incas and the Aztecs did not live in America or, even less, Latin America. Until the early sixteenth century, America was not on anybody's map simply because the word and the concept of a fourth continent had not yet been invented. The mass of land and the people were there, but they had named their own places: Tawantinsuyu in the Andes, Anáhuac in what is today the valley of Mexico, and Abya-Yala in what is today Panama. The extension of what became "America" was unknown to them. People in Europe, in Asia, and in Africa had no idea of the landmass soon to be called the Indias Occidentales and then America, or of all the people inhabiting it who would be called Indians. America came, literally, out of the blue sky that Amerigo Vespucci was looking at when he realized that the stars he was seeing from what is now southern Brazil were not the same stars he had seen in his familiar Mediterranean. What is really confusing in this story is that once America was named as such in the sixteenth century and Latin America named as such in the nineteenth, it appeared as if they had been there forever.

"America," then, was never a continent waiting to be discovered. Rather, "America" as we know it was an *invention* forged in the process of European colonial history and the consolidation and expansion of the Western world view and institutions. The narratives that described the events as "discovery" were told not by the inhabitants of Anáhuac or Tawantinsuyu, but by Europeans themselves. It would be four hundred and fifty years until a shift in the geography of knowledge would turn around what Europeans saw as a "discovery" and see it as an "invention." The conceptual frame that made possible this shift in the geography of knowledge, from discovery to invention, came from the Creoles' consciousness, in the Spanish- and Portuguese-speaking world.

Of course, we should briefly note that Indigenous and Afro frames of mind in continental South America had not yet intervened in these public debates from their own broken histories. The idea of "America" and subsequently of "Latin" and "Anglo" America was an issue in the minds of European and Creoles of European descent. Indians and Creoles of African descent (men and women) were left out of the conversation. Afro-Caribbeans had been working toward a similar and complementary shift in the geography of knowledge, but in English and French. For Creoles of Afro descent, the European arrival in the islands that today we call Caribbean was not of primary concern: African slaves were brought to the continent that was already called America many decades after it was discovered or invented. In the Indian genealogy of thought, whether America was an existing continent discovered or a non-existing entity that was invented was not a question.

Mexican historian and philosopher Edmundo O'Gorman strongly and convincingly argued many years ago that the invention of America implied the appropriation and integration of the continent into the Euro-Christian imaginary.[2] The Spanish and Portuguese, as the sole and diverse European foreign intruders in the sixteenth century, claimed for themselves a continent and renamed it at the same time as they began a process of territorial organization as they had it in Spain and Portugal. Vespucci could pull America out of the sky when he realized that, navigating the coasts of what is today Brazil, he was in a "New World" (new for Europeans, of course), and not in "India," as Columbus thought about ten years before him. The story is well known that since Vespucci conceptually "discovered" (in the sense of "discovering for oneself" or "realizing") that Europeans were confronting a New World, the continent was renamed "America" after Amerigo Vespucci himself, with a slight change to the ending to make it fit with the already existing non-European continents, Africa and Asia.

"Discovery" and "invention" are not just different interpretations of the same event; they belong to *two different paradigms*. The line that distinguishes the two paradigms is the line of the shift in the geo-politics of knowledge; changing the terms and not only the

3

content of the conversation. The first presupposes the triumphant European and imperial perspective on world history, an achievement that was described as "modernity," while the second reflects the critical perspective of those who have been placed behind, who are expected to follow the ascending progress of a history to which they have the feeling of not belonging. Colonization of being is nothing else than producing the idea that certain people do not belong to history – that they are non-beings. Thus, lurking beneath the European story of discovery are the histories, experiences, and silenced conceptual narratives of those who were disqualified as human beings, as historical actors, and as capable of thinking and understanding. In the sixteenth and seventeenth centuries the "wretched of the earth" (as Frantz Fanon labeled colonized beings) were Indians and African slaves. That is why missionaries and men of letters appointed themselves to write the histories they thought Incas and Aztecs did not have, and to write the grammar of Kechua/Kichua and Nahuatl with Latin as the model. Africans were simply left out of the picture of conversion and taken as pure labor force.

Toward the end of the seventeenth century, a new social group surfaced, and when they surfaced they were already outside of history: the Creoles of Spanish and Portuguese descent. Although their marginalization was far from the extremes to which Indians and Africans were subjected, the Creoles, between the limits of humanity (Indians and Africans) and humanity proper (Europeans), were also left out of history. The geo-political configuration of scales that measured the nature of human beings in terms of an idea of history that Western Christians assumed to be the total and true one for every inhabitant of the planet led to the establishment of a colonial matrix of power, to leave certain people out of history in order to justify violence in the name of Christianization, civilization, and, more recently, development and market democracy. Such a geo-political configuration created a divide between a minority of people who dwell in and embrace the Christian, civilizing, or developing missions and a majority who are the outcasts and become the targets of those missions.

Max Weber has been credited, after Hegel, with having concep-tualized "modernity" as the direction of history that had Europe as a model and a goal. More recently, since the late 1980s, Peruvian sociologist Anibal Quijano unveiled "coloniality" as the darker side of modernity and as the historical perspective of the wretched, the outcasts from history told from the perspective of modernity. From the perspective of modernity, coloniality is difficult to see or recognize, and even a bothersome concept. For the second set of actors, the wretched, modernity is unavoidable although coloniality offers a shifting perspective of knowledge and history. For the first actors, modernity is one-sided and of single density. For the second, modernity is double-sided and of double density. To understand the coexistence of these two major paradigms is to understand how the shift in the geo-graphy and the geo-politics of knowledge is taking place. My argument is straightforwardly located in the second paradigm, in the double density of modernity/coloniality.

How do these two entangled concepts, modernity and coloniality, work together as two sides of the same reality to shape the idea of "America" in the sixteenth century and of "Latin" America in the nineteenth? Modernity has been a term in use for the past thirty or forty years. In spite of differences in opinions and definitions, there are some basic agreements about its meaning. From the European perspective, modernity refers to a period in world history that has been traced back either to the European Renaissance and the "discovery" of America (this view is common among scholars from the South of Europe, Italy, Spain, and Portugal), or to the European Enlightenment (this view is held by scholars and intellectuals and assumed by the media in Anglo-Saxon countries – England, Germany, and Holland – and one Latin country, France). On the other side of the colonial difference, scholars and intellectuals in the ex-Spanish and ex-Portuguese colonies in South America have been advancing the idea that the achievements of modernity go hand in hand with the violence of coloniality. The difference, to reiterate, lies in which side of each local history is told. O'Gorman's "invention of America" theory was a turning point that put on the table a perspective that was absent and not recognized from the existing European and imperial narratives. Let's agree that O'Gorman made visible a dimension of history that was occluded by the partial "discovery" narratives, and let's also agree that it is an example of how things may look from the varied experiences of coloniality.

America, as a concept, goes hand in hand with that of modernity, and both are the self-representation of imperial projects and global designs that originated in and were implemented by European actors and institutions. The invention of America was one of the nodal points that contributed to create the conditions for imperial European expansion and a lifestyle, in Europe, that served as a model for the achievements of humanity. Thus, the "discovery and conquest of America" is not just one more event in some long and linear historical chain from the creation of the world to the present, leaving behind all those who were not attentive enough to jump onto the bandwagon of modernity. Rather, it was a key turning point in world history: It was the moment in which the demands of modernity as the final horizon of salvation began to require the imposition of a specific set of values that relied on the logic of coloniality for their implementation.

The "invention of America" thesis offers, instead, a perspective from coloniality and, in consequence, reveals that the advances of modernity outside of Europe rely on a colonial matrix of power that includes the renaming of the lands appropriated and of the people inhabiting them, insofar as the diverse ethnic groups and civilizations in Tawantinsuyu and Anáhuac, as well as those from Africa, were reduced to "Indians" and "Blacks." The idea of "America" and of "Latin" America could, of course, be accounted for within the philosophical framework of European modernity, even if that account is offered by Creoles of European descent dwelling in the colonies and embracing the Spanish or Portuguese view of events. What counts, however, is that the need for telling the part of the story that was not told requires a shift in the geography of reason and of understanding. "Coloniality," therefore, points toward and intends to unveil an embedded logic that enforces control, domination, and exploitation disguised in the language of salvation, progress, modernization, and being good for every one. The double register of modernity/coloniality has, perhaps, never been as clear as it has been recently under the administration of US president George W. Bush.

Pedagogically, it is important for my argument to conceptualize "modernity/coloniality" as two sides of the same coin and not as two separate frames of mind: you cannot be modern without being colonial; and if you are on the colonial side of the spectrum you have to transact with modernity – you cannot ignore it. The very idea of America cannot be separated from coloniality: the entire continent emerged as such in the European consciousness as a massive extent of land to be appropriated and of people to be converted to Christianity, and whose labor could be exploited. Coloniality, as a term, is much less frequently heard than "modernity" and many people tend to confuse it with "colonialism." The two words are related, of course. While "colonialism" refers to specific historical periods and places of imperial domination (e.g., Spanish, Dutch, British, the US since the beginning of the twentieth century), "coloniality" refers to the logical structure of colonial domination underlying the Spanish, Dutch, British, and US control of the Atlantic economy and politics, and from there the control and management of almost the entire planet. In each of the particular imperial periods of colonialism – whether led by Spain (mainly in the sixteenth and seventeenth centuries) or by England (from the nineteenth century to World War II) or by the US (from the early twentieth century until now) – the same logic was maintained; only power changed hands.

Some would say (mainly before the 9/11 attacks on the US) that the US was not an imperial country because it has no colonies like those of Spain or England. This opinion, however, confuses "colonialism" with having "colonies" in the sense of maintaining the physical presence of institutions, administrators, and armies in the colonized country or region. And it confuses also "colonialism" with "coloniality." Coloniality is the logic of domination in the modern/colonial world, beyond the fact that the imperial/colonial country was once Spain, then England and now the US. Modern technology, alongside political and economic restructuring in the second half of the twentieth century, has made it unnecessary to colonize in the old, more obvious, manner. Still, the US does in fact maintain military bases in strategic parts of the world (e.g., the Middle East and South America). Likewise, the occupation of Iraq and consequent pressure by the US for the appointment of a government favorable to imperialist power[3] reflects a clear method of colonial*ism* today. After 9/11, liberal voices in the US began to recognize that imperialism was necessary; but, being liberals, they called it "reluctant"

7

or "light" imperialism. No matter what it is called, imperialism implies colonialism in some form, as it is difficult to imagine any empire without colonies, even if colonies take different shapes at different points in history.[4]

The idea of America, therefore, is a modern European invention and limited to Europeans' view of the world and of their own history. In that view and in that history, coloniality, naturally, was (and still is) ignored or disguised as a necessary injustice in the name of justice. Coloniality names the experiences and views of the world and history of those whom Fanon called *les damnés de la terre* ("the wretched of the earth," those who have been, and continue to be, subjected to the standards of modernity). The wretched are defined by the *colonial wound*, and the colonial wound, physical and/or psychological, is a consequence of *racism*, the hegemonic discourse that questions the humanity of all those who do not belong to the locus of enunciation (and the geo-politics of knowledge) of those who assign the standards of classification and assign to themselves the right to classify. The blindness toward histories and experiences lying outside the local history of Western Christianity, as shown by secular Europeans, grounded in the Greek and Latin languages, and unfolded in the six vernacular imperial languages (Italian, Spanish, Portuguese, French, German, and English), has been and continues to be a trademark of intellectual history and its ethical, political, and economic consequences.

The shift in the geo-politics of knowledge (the perspective of modernity is also geo-politically grounded, although it is disguised as the natural course of universal history) began with the recognition that even the postmodern endorsement of pluralities of interpretations cannot be celebrated as long as it is restricted to a *diversity of interpretations within the one Eurocentric frame of knowledge*, which has been shaped and governed over time both by theology, in the sixteenth and seventeenth centuries, and by "egology" (a frame of knowledge having "ego," instead of "theo," as the center and point of reference), the growing European consciousness since René Descartes.[5] To account for experiences, feelings, and world views beyond the center of European narratives and its philosophical frame of reference, it is necessary to shift from a conception of knowledge grounded in theology and egology, which hides its geo-political

8

underpinning, to a decentered one that is geo-politically rooted in the histories of the borders, and not in territorial histories created by European and US expansionism.[6]

As a matter of fact, the geo-politics of knowledge emerged already in the sixteenth century as a decolonial attitude (countering the implicit "Roman attitude" that Rémi Brague attributes to the history of Europe; see chapter 2) when men of wisdom and officers of the state, in and from Anáhuac and Tawantinsuyu, needed to deal with the question of how to accommodate their system of knowledge, accumulated information, and organization of memory to a system that was alien to their lived experience and collective shared past. They needed to think in a double framework that revealed a differential in power relations. One of the frameworks was introduced by Europeans who spoke vernacular imperial languages and grounded their thoughts in Greek and Latin. Europeans, in general, did not have to incorporate Indigenous languages and frameworks of knowledge into their own. For Indigenous people (and for Africans transported to the New World), the situation was different. They had no choice but to incorporate European languages and frameworks of knowledge into their own. One of the unavoidable consequences of modern/colonial expansionism is that the conditions for *border thinking* were created, and the theo-politics of knowledge (in sixteenth-century Tawantinsuyu and Anáhuac) and the ego-politics of knowledge (in nineteenth-century British India and French and British Africa) were thereby decentered. Thus, the events that led to the idea of "America" led, simultaneously, to the appearance of a new type of thinking and understanding that could not be suppressed by theology (or later on by egology) – border thinking. The only way possible was to control it by suppressing the materiality of its manifestations (e.g., not publishing Indigenous writings), demonizing it, or making impossible any kind of diffusion. However, thoughts and ways of thinking survive with bodies; they are part of life. Border thinking is exploding now in the Andes under the name of *inter-culturalidad* and all over the world as well, including the parts of Europe that are becoming the dwelling place of African, Asian, South American, and Caribbean migrants. Border thinking, which was the historically unavoidable condition for Indigenous people, surfaced in its own way among African slaves and Creoles of African descent, as well as among Creoles of Spanish and Portuguese descent. The name here is less important than the phenomenon I am trying to describe, which is a new way of thinking prompted by modern imperial expansion and the necessary colonial matrix of power that modern expansionism implies.

The geo-politics of knowledge (the local historical grounding of knowledge) goes hand in hand with the body politics of knowledge (i.e., the personal and collective biographical grounding of understanding). The view of events and the conception of the world provided by a Spanish Jesuit or soldier (or later on, by a French or British traveler or philosopher) were geo- and bio-graphically grounded in languages, memories, and histories not shared in the views and conceptions of the world experienced by Aymara- or Nahuatl-speaking intellectuals whose geo- and bio-graphies were grounded in other memories and histories. There is a *difference* in this apparent symmetry: the Spanish missionary and the French philosopher did not have to incorporate Indigenous languages and experiences into their theological or egological frame of thinking. The Aymara or Nahuatl intellectuals of what are now Bolivia, Mexico, and Central America had no choice, because Spanish and French institutions were set up in their territory, on top of and around their dwelling places. For that material reason, border thinking is the consequence of the power differential under modern/colonial conditions, a power differential that constitutes the *colonial difference*.

It is not easy to explore the idea of "Latin" America beyond the rhetoric of modernity (celebratory of the discovery) and to enter the logic of coloniality. To enter the logic of coloniality means to think from what *Pachakuti*[7] meant within Indigenous people and their own conceptual memories; and what "invention" meant for O'Gorman within the Creole tradition of thought. The map of knowledge and understanding has to be redrawn. The question is not simply that of a name (America, Latin America) and a reference (the pear-shaped form, plus the stem connecting Mexico), but that of the naming agents involved in the process. The idea that "America" was a continent discovered by European navigators belongs to the rhetoric of (European) modernity. *Pachakuti* and "America" as *invention* reveal the logic of coloniality (the colonial matrix of power) hidden beyond the rhetoric of modernity.

The logic of coloniality can be understood as working through four wide domains of human experience: (1) the economic: appropriation of land, exploitation of labor, and control of finance; (2) the political: control of authority; (3) the civic: control of gender and sexuality; (4) the epistemic and the subjective/personal: control of knowledge and subjectivity. The logic of coloniality has been in place from the conquest and colonization of Mexico and Peru until and beyond the war in Iraq, despite superficial changes in the scale and agents of exploitation/control in the past five hundred years of history. Each domain is interwoven with the others, since appropriation of land or exploitation of labor also involves the control of finance, of authority, of gender, and of knowledge and subjectivity.[8] The operation of the colonial matrix is invisible to distracted eyes, and even when it surfaces, it is explained through the rhetoric of modernity that the situation can be "corrected" with "development," "democracy," a "strong economy," etc. What some will see as "lies" from the US presidential administration are not so much lies as part of a very well-codified "rhetoric of modernity," promising salvation for everybody in order to divert attention from the increasingly oppressive consequences of the logic of coloniality. To implement the logic of coloniality requires the celebratory rhetoric of modernity, as the case of Iraq has illustrated from day one. As capital and power concentrate in fewer and fewer hands and poverty increases all over the word, the logic of coloniality becomes ever more oppressive and merciless. Since the sixteenth century, the rhetoric of modernity has relied on the vocabulary of *salvation*, which was accompanied by the massive appropriation of land in the New World and the massive exploitation of Indian and African slave labor, justified by a belief in the dispensability of human life – the lives of the slaves. Thus, while some Christians today, for example, beat the drum of "pro-life values," they reproduce a rhetoric that diverts attention from the increasing "devaluation of human life" that the thousands dead in Iraq demonstrate. *Thus, it is not modernity that will overcome coloniality, because it is precisely modernity that needs and produces coloniality.*

As an illustration, let us follow the genealogy of just the first of the four domains and see how the logic of coloniality has evolved in the area of land, labor, and finance. Below I will complement the brief sketch of this first quadrant by going deeper into the fourth one (knowledge and subjectivity) to show how knowledge transformed Anáhuac and Tawantinsuyu into America and then into Latin America and, in the process, how new national and subcontinental identities were created. But, first, think of the massive appropriation of land by the Spanish and Portuguese, the would-be landlords of the Americas during the sixteenth century, and the same by the British, French, and Dutch in the extended Caribbean (from Salvador de Bahia in Brazil to Charleston in today's South Carolina, and including the north of Colombia and Venezuela in addition to the Caribbean islands). The appropriation of land went hand in hand with the exploitation of labor (Indians and African slaves) and the control of finance (the accumulation of capital as a consequence of the appropriation of land and the exploitation of labor). Capital concentrated in Europe, in the imperial states, and not in the colonies. You can follow this pattern through the nineteenth century when England and France displaced Spain and Portugal as leading imperial countries. The logic of coloniality was then reproduced, and, of course, modified, in the next step of imperial expansion into Africa and Asia.

You can still see the same projects today in the appropriation of areas of "natural resources" (e.g., in the Amazon or oil-rich Iraq). Land cannot be reproduced. You can reproduce seeds and other "products" of land; but land itself is limited, which is another reason why the appropriation of land is one of the prime targets of capital accumulation today. The "idea" of Latin America is that of a large mass of land with a wealth of natural resources and plenty of cheap labor. That, of course, is the disguised idea. What the rhetoric of modernity touted by the IMF, the World Bank, and the Washington consensus would say is that "Latin" America is just waiting for its turn to "develop." You could also follow the exploitation of labor from the Americas to the Industrial Revolution to the movement of factories from the US to developing nations in order to reduce costs. As for financial control, just compare the number and size of banks, for example, in New York, London, or Frankfurt, on the one hand, versus the ones in Bolivia, Morocco, or India, on the other.

Thus, if we consider "America" from the perspective of coloniality (not modernity) and let the Indigenous perspective take center

12

stage, another history becomes apparent. The beginning of the Zapatista "Manifesto from the Lacandon Jungle" gives us a blueprint:

> We are a product of 500 years of struggle: first against slavery, then during the War of Independence against Spain; then to avoid being absorbed by North American imperialism, then to promulgate our constitution and expel the French empire from our soil; later the dictatorship of Porfirio Diaz denied us the just application of the Reform laws and the people rebelled and leaders like Villa and Zapata emerged, poor men just like us. We have been denied by our rulers the most elemental conditions of life, so they can use us as cannon fodder and pillage the wealth of our country. They don't care that we have nothing, absolutely nothing, not even a roof over hour heads, no land, no work, no health care, no food or education. Nor are we able to freely and democratically elect our political representatives, nor is there independence from foreigners, nor is there peace or justice for ourselves and our children.[9]

The "Manifesto from the Lacandon Jungle" precedes a long history rewritten from an Indigenous perspective (as opposed to the perspective of Mexican Creoles and Mestizos/as or French or US "experts" on Mexican and "Latin" American history). You may wonder whether the Indigenous people had a perspective because you imagine that *history* is *history* and what happened just happened, and argue that there are of course "different interpretations" but not "different perspectives." Different interpretations presuppose a common and shared principle of knowledge and of the rules of the game, while different perspectives presuppose that the principles of knowledges and the rules of the game are geo-historically located in the structure of power of the modern colonial world. To show how this works, we need something such as "dependency theory" for the epistemological domain.[10] "Dependency theory" showed the differential of power in the economic domain insofar as it described a certain structure of differential power in the domain of the economy. But it also proved the epistemic differential and the distribution of labor within an imperial geo-politics of knowledge in

13

which political economy moved in one direction: from First to Third World countries and to contain Second World communism. In this sense, dependency theory is relevant in changing the geopolitics of knowledge and in pointing toward the need for, and the possibility of, different locations of understanding and of knowledge production.

The first part of the "Manifesto from the Lacandon Jungle" is a history and a description of the current economic and social situation in Chiapas, subdivided into the "First Wind" and the "Second Wind" in emulation of sixteenth-century Spanish chronicles of the New World. Cast in terms familiar to those conversant with globalization, the first wind is the wind from above and the second that from below. The declaration, then, outlines the direction of a project to rewrite the colonial history of modernity from the perspective of coloniality (instead of writing the history of coloniality from the perspective of modernity). This framing is subject to questions and criticisms by critical and inquisitive readers. Professional historians could argue that there is little historical rigor in this "pamphlet" and that what we need is serious and rigorous histories of how things "really" happened. Again, that argument assumes that the events carry in themselves their own truth and the job of the historian is to discover them. The problem is that "rigorous historiography" is more often than not complicitous with modernity (since the current conceptualization and practice of historiography, as a discipline, are a modern rearticulation of a practice dating back to – again – Greek philosophy). In that respect, the argument for disciplinary rigor turns out to be a maneuver that perpetuates the myth of modernity as something separate from coloniality. Therefore, if you happened to be a person educated in the Calmemac in Anáhuac and were quite far away from the legacies of the Greeks, it would be your fault for not being aware what civilized history is and how important it is for you.

Other criticisms may stem from the fact that the division of above and below still originates in the concept of the "above." Indeed, it was the Dominican friar Bartolomé de Las Casas who first described (but did not enact himself) the perspective now being enacted by the Zapatistas. The most suspicious reader would add that it is Sub-Comandante Marcos (a Mexican Mestizo who studied anthropology at the Universidad Autónoma de México) who narrates. Legitimate and interesting objections, these. However, such objections remain entangled in the web and the perspective of modernity; that is, in the *expectations* created by the hegemonic perspective of modernity itself. To unfold this last statement, let's take another step and perhaps a detour and come back to the inception of the logic of coloniality implied in the very idea of both "America" and "Latin" America.

The First "Barbarians" were not "Latin" Americans: The Invention of Racism in the Modern/Colonial

The complex articulation and disarticulation of diverse histories for the benefit of one, the history of the discoverers, conquerors, and colonizers, left to posterity a linear and homogeneous concept of history that also produced the "idea" of America. But in order for one history to be seen as primary, a system of classification to marginalize certain knowledges, languages, and beings needs to be in place. Thus, colonization and the justification for the appropriation of land and the exploitation of labor in the process of the invention of America required the simultaneous ideological construction of racism. The emergence of the Indians in the European consciousness, the simultaneous expulsion of the Moors and Jews from the Iberian peninsula in the late fifteenth century, and the redefinition of the African Blacks in slavery prompted a specific classification and ranking of humanity. The presumptuous "model" of ideal humanity on which it was based was not established by God as a natural order, but according to the perception of Christian, White, and European males. *The geo- and body politics of knowledge were hidden and sublimated into an abstract universal coming from God or from the transcendental ego.* Consequently, the geo-politics and body politics of knowledges that unfolded from the borders of imperial experiences in the colonies (that is, imperial/colonial experiences) offer not only a new and distinct epistemology (i.e., border epistemology), but also a perspective from which to analyze the limits of the regional universalizing of understanding based on both theology and egology (i.e., theo- and ego-politics of knowledge). The overall

15

classification and ranking of the world do not just reveal a reality out there, in the world, that they reflect, like in a mirror. They also hide the fact that such classification and ranking are valid only from a "given perspective" or locus of enunciation – the geo-historical and bio-graphical experience of the knowing subject of the philosophical principles of theology, the historical experiences of Western Christians, and the way of looking at the world as a male.

Of course, the hierarchy depends on who is in a position of power to decide the model and where one is located in relation to it. In the case at hand, Incas, Aztecs, or Mayas were not in a position to classify people around the planet, or were not interested in doing so, because they did not have that kind of understanding. That was in the hands of the Portuguese and Spaniards. Thus it happened that the European Renaissance model of humanity became hegemonic and the Indians and African slaves were considered second-class human beings, if human beings at all. We are talking here about the historical, demographic, and racial foundation of the modern/colonial world. "Race," of course, at this level is not a question of skin color or pure blood but of categorizing individuals according to their level of similarity/proximity to an assumed model of ideal humanity. "Race" would become interchangeable with "ethnicity," as race itself refers only to a genealogy of blood, of genotypes, or of skin color, while "ethnicity" includes a language, memories, and shared past and present experiences; that is, it also refers to a cultural sense of community, what people have in common. That is precisely what "ethnos" mean and why it is also equivalent and complementary to the concept of "nation" (from Latin *natio*, "a community of birth"). After the merging of politics and religion (which originally meant tradition and community) in the Roman Empire under Constantine (third century AD), religion became a word to designate communities of faith, while nation (*natio*) designated communities of birth. With secularization in the eighteenth century and the emergence of the modern state, "nation" replaced "religion" to bring about a new kind of imagined community. The concept of "culture" was resignified to express "national culture" (language, literature, flag, history). People began to identify themselves as members of a nation-state and, secondarily, as members of a given religion.

16

Ethnicity referred to communities not necessarily defined by physical attributes.

When "race" (mainly in the nineteenth century) replaced "ethnicity" and, thus, placed the accent on "blood" and "skin color" instead of other attributes of community, "race" became synonymous with "racism." "Racism" emerges when members of a given "race" or "ethnicity" have the privilege of classifying people and power in the words and concepts of the given group. "Racism" was and still is a classifying matrix that not only encompasses the physical characteristics of the human (blood, skin color, etc.) but also extends to the interpersonal realm of human activities like religion, languages (ranked with Greek, Latin, English, German, and French first; Italian, Spanish, and Portuguese second; Arabic, Russian, and Bengali third; and then the rest), and geopolitical classifications of the world (e.g., East–West, North–South; First, Second, and Third Worlds; Axis of Evil; etc.). The complex "racial" matrix continues to be in place today, as we can see if we look around or listen to the rhetoric of neo-liberalism that has been advanced most recently by President Bush's administration. What is important to remember is that racialization is applied not only to people, but to language, religions, knowledge, countries, and continents as well.

To be more specific about the formation of race as part of the idea of "America" and of "Latin" America, let's look at one of the foundational moments of the racial classification of the world. Confronted with previously unknown groups of people, the colonizing Christians in the Indias Occidentales (or simply the Indias) began determining individuals on the basis of their relation to theological principles of knowledge, which were taken as superior to any other system around the world. Las Casas offered, toward the middle of the sixteenth century, a classification of "barbarians" which was, of course, a racial classification, although not based on skin color. *It was racial because it ranked human beings in a top-down scale assuming the ideals of Western Christians as the criteria and measuring stick for the ranking.* Racialization does not simply say, "you are Black or Indian, therefore your are inferior." Rather, it says, "you are not like me, therefore you are inferior," which in the Christian scale of humanity meant Indians in America and Blacks in Africa were inferior. Las Casas made a key contribution to the racialized imaginary of the modern/colonial world when he defined, at the end of his *Apologética Historia Sumaria* (c.1552), four kinds of "barbarians." Using Aristotle as a basis and point of departure, Las Casas proposed the following categories in order to have a clear sense of how a nation or part of it could be properly considered "barbarous."[11]

The first of the four kinds of "barbarians" could be identified when a human group showed signs of strange or ferocious behavior and could be proven to have a degenerate sense of justice, reason, manners, and/or human generosity (*benignidad*). The term "barbarous" could thus be applied to a person or a people who acted on the basis of opinions that were not clear or that were attained in a quick, not altogether rational manner, or who showed tumultuous and unreasonable behavior. In the same vein, Las Casas believed that some peoples, once rational rules and generosity were forgotten, would fall into ferocious behavior and forget the generous and cordial manners (*blandura y mansedumbre*) that should characterize all civilized human social behavior. They would "become in some way ferocious, hard, rough, and cruel because barbarous means a strangeness and exorbitance or novelty that does not accord with human nature and common sense" (II, p. 637).

The second meaning of "barbarous" or "barbarian" is narrower: all those people who lacked a "literal locution that responds to their language in the same way that our locution responds to the Latin language" are "barbarous" (II, p. 638). What Las Casas implied, then, was that "the Latin language" is the ultimate condition for the true warranty of any statement. On the basis of such principles, Spaniards would be able to assert, for instance, that the Indigenous people of the New World "lacked" the proper words to name God, an entity that was properly and truly named in and through the Latin language. By extension, Arabic and Hebrew would also be languages that "lacked literal locution." Similarly Las Casas considered "barbarous" all those people who lacked the practice and study of "letters," of poetry, rhetoric, logic, history, and every aspect of knowledge called "literature" in the broadest sense of the word, meaning anything written in alphabetic writing; that is, every "writing with letters" of the Latin alphabet. Las Casas nuanced his characterization by saying that it should be clear that a person or people could be *sabio y pulido* ("sage and sophisticated"), not ferocious or cruel, and still be considered "barbarous" because they lack "literal locution."

The third kind of barbarians were those who lacked basic forms of governmentality. This third type was closely related, then, to the first with its requirement for rational forms of thought and organization. The third kind, though, specifically lack the law and the state, and live in what Thomas Hobbes or John Locke would later theorize as the state of nature. The fourth criterion for "barbarians" captured all those who were rational and had a structure of law but were considered infidels and pagans because they "lack true religion and Christian faith," even when they are "sage and prudent philosophers and politicians" (II, p. 645).

For Las Casas, then, "there is no nation (with the exception of Christian nations) that does not lack something or that is exempt from major defects such as in their law, costumes, life style and public policy" (II, p. 645). Take his example of the Turks and Moors as barbarians of the fourth type. Remember that at the end of the fifteenth century the Moors had been expelled from the south of the Iberian peninsula to the north of Africa, and those who remained in the peninsula became "moriscos"; that is to say, Moors in Castilian and Christian lands. The situation was similar to what happened to Mexicans in 1848 when the frontier of the US moved south – the Mexicans who remained in their place became Mexicans in the territory of the US. Regarding the Turks and Moors, Las Casas wrote:

> The Turks and the Moors, in our times, are undoubtedly people whose lifestyle is urban and settled. But how many and what kind of defects do they, in their urbanity, carry with them? And how irrational are their laws and what kind of flaws or shortcomings do they have? How barbarous are their habits? And how much sin and unreasonable ugliness is among them? The Moors are known for their tendency to let go and engage in base and lascivious pleasures; the Turks are inclined to the abominable vice [sodomy] as well as other ignominious vileness, although it is said that they surpass us in every thing related to justice and government. (II, p. 646)[12]

19

Briefly, then, Las Casas recognized that the Turks and the Moors were above the Castilian Christians in matters of law and statehood, although for him they (Moors and Turks) failed miserably in terms of Christian morals and were to be considered inferior. Las Casas's conclusion was that the first, second, and fourth kinds of "barbarians" are *secundum quid barbaros* ("next to barbarians") because they lack something – mainly, they "lack our Christian faith" (II, p. 653). The proper "barbarians" are those who fall under the third type, who are without the rule of law. As for the fourth type, Las Casas insists that this corresponds to the infidels and that there are two kinds of infidels: those who lived peacefully and owe nothing to the Christians, and those who are enemies and persecutors of the Christian faith.

After he defined the four kinds of barbarians, Las Casas came up with an unannounced fifth one that he called *barbarie contraria*. While the four types of barbarism responded to specific criteria, *barbarie contraria* ("enemy barbarism") could refer to anyone. *Barbarie contraria* identified all those who (like today's "terrorists") actively worked to undermine Christianity. It was called "enemy barbarism" because of the "barbarians'" hatred of the Christian faith. It would apply to all those infidels who resisted and refused to accept the Gospel. They resisted evangelical preaching, Las Casas concluded, "out of the pure hatred they have toward our faith and to the name of Christ; and they not only refuse to receive and to hear the Christian faith but they mainly impugn and persecute it; and if they could – just to elevate and expand their own sect – they would destroy it" (II, p. 647). Las Casas did not clarify who "they" were, beyond examples taken from Thomas Aquinas. Las Casas wrote, "Barbarous are all those who are outside the (Christian) Roman Empire; all those, that is to say, who are beyond the Universal Church, since beyond the Universal Church there is no Empire" (II, p. 648). The genealogy is here established in retrospect. The empire is defined as coterminous with the universal church, while *barbarie contraria* encompasses every act against the church or against the empire. Thus *barbarie contraria* subsumes the imperial and colonial differences, insofar as both non-Christian empires, Indians and Black Africans, are "barbarous." Throughout the centuries and throughout the making of the modern colonial world, "negative barbarism" has been redefined and expanded to refer to those who fight against the West and its ideals: democracy, freedom, and modernity.

But Las Casas's major goal in introducing these criteria was to be able to decide what kind of barbarians the Indians of the New World were, because he had already demonstrated their rationality. The Indians, particularly those of the Aztec and Inca Empires, were "rational."[13] They governed themselves and were "sage and sophisticated." They were not "negative barbarians" either, since they did not know about the church of Christ until the Spanish arrived to the New World. Thus, he positioned them in the banal fourth type, those lacking Christianity, and in the second type, those lacking "literal locution." The first "barbarians" of the modern/colonial world, then, were certainly not "Latin." Aymara and Kichua/Kechua histories were, of course, different from the stories that could be told in Latin. But little by little, after 1500, the only and true story was written in Latin and in European imperial languages. All other stories were buried and denied "authenticity," the authenticity that European stories were endowed with. The "conquest and colonization of America" was, among other things, a conquest and colonization of existing knowledges that, of course, were coded in languages of "non-literal locution." Indian languages became obsolete in epistemic terms. The epistemic domains and practices of Indians and Afros were subsumed into the universal history conceived from the perspective and experiences of Western Christians, later secularized by Hegel at the inception of the imperial dominance of England and France.

You may be wondering at this point what all of this has to do with the "idea" of America and of Latin America. Let's try to move in that direction. The "idea" of America was indeed a European invention that took away the naming of the continent from people that had inhabited the land for many centuries before Columbus "discovered" it. This phenomenon has been described as "deculturation," as "dispossession" (both material and spiritual), and more recently as "colonization of knowledge" and "colonization of beings." When the first and second generation of Creoles of European descent in what are today the two Americas, Latin and Anglo, came into power, the Creoles appropriated the name of the continent for themselves, labeling themselves "Americans" or "Americanos."

Indians and Blacks were definitively put out of the game. Today, the continental Indigenous movements, from the Antarctic to the Arctic pole, are claiming "Abya-Yala" as the name of the continent they inhabit (see chapter 3).[14] This means that "Latin" America is the name of the continent inhabited by people of European descent. This may be difficult to understand, because of the success of the logic of coloniality in making it seem that "Latin" America is at once a subcontinent and the idea in the consciousness of everybody who dwells in the territory thus named. There is no claim yet, as far as I know, being made generally by Afro-Americans (that is, in North and South America and the Caribbean) as to how they will locate themselves in relation to a subcontinental name that was invented by Europeans and appropriated by Latin and Anglo Creoles. In Ecuador and Colombia, though, the term *la gran co-marca* – the idea of a large, shared (*co-*, as in co-operation), marked territory with a common root – is being used by Afro-Andeans. The moral is that the "idea" of Latin America is, ontologically, the "idea" in the consciousness of the Creoles and Mestizos/as identified with European descent and histories. It may have been assumed at some point in the past by Indians and people of Afro descent that they too inhabited "Latin" America – but this is no longer the case (see chapter 3). "Latin" America is not their dwelling place, although their daily life grew, changed, and unfolded over a mass of land identified as Latin America. The mass of land could be renamed any time, but the *consciousness* of being "Latin" American cannot be changed or renamed that easily. The first is a question of naming that requires *consensus* in international law. The second is a question of consciousness that requires *self-examination* by the people who identify themselves (or are identified) as "Latin" Americans.

Occidentalism and the "Americanity" of America

But how did we get to this point of universal acceptance of the ideas of America and Latin America? What was the geo-political and geo-historical framework in which this idea of America came to life? Behind the apparently neutral description of the "discovery"

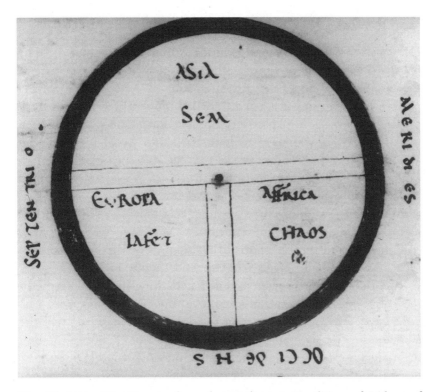

The Christian T-in-O map, from the ninth-century edition of Isidore of Seville's Etymologies. The complicity between geography and epistemology is already at work in this map: the partition of the world is from the privileged position of an observer who is, at once, located in Europe and above and beyond the three continents. (Courtesy of the Newberry Library, Chicago.)

there is a logic of continental racialization, whose definitive form was set up (obviously without a clear design and road map for its future) in the sixteenth century with the drawing of the first maps of the modern/colonial world. How can continents be racialized, you may ask. At the time of the "discovery," Christian cosmology incorporated America as a fourth arm in a world previously conceived as tripartite and divided into Asia, Africa, and Europe. To understand the world into which America would be integrated, observe the famous "T-in-O" map shown on p. 23, which was published in the ninth-century edition of Isidore of Seville's *Etymologies* (originally compiled in the early seventh century).[15] The tripartite division is obvious, with Asia occupying the top part of the circle and Europe and Africa dividing among themselves the bottom half. You might ask who divided the world into these three continents before the "discovery" of the fourth one. If, prompted by that question, you were to look back into world histories, you would realize that no other of the existing sixteenth-century civilizations (China, India, Arabo-Islam, Japan, Inca, Maya, Aztec) divided the world into three continents and identified them as Asia, Africa, and Europe. It would become apparent that only Western Christians had divided the world into three parts. Moreover, Western Christians had assigned each of the parts to one of the three sons of Noah: Asia to Shem, Africa to Ham, and Europe to Japheth.

Two questions arise from Isidore's map: how did this imaginary, the correspondence between continents and Noah's sons, get to be articulated? And, more important for our discussion, what were the consequences of such an imaginary? The idea of "America" cannot be understood without the existence, previous to the discovery/ invention, of the tripartite division of the world, with the corresponding Christian geo-political connotations. It is not excessive to remind the reader that there was no reason why people in China, in Islam, in the empires of Tawantinsuyu and Anáhuac would believe that the world was divided into three and that each division has to be related to a son of Noah! This reminder is necessary because after the discovery/invention and from the sixteenth century onward, there would be an overwhelming belief in the fact that *the planet was actually and naturally divided into four continents* – Asia, Africa, Europe, and America.

When we look at the world maps of Gerardus Mercator (1542) and Abraham Ortelius (c. 1575),[16] we see, for the first time in the history of the human species, the world now divided into the four major continents recognized today. ("Australasia," which includes Australia, New Zealand, and Papua New Guinea, doesn't have in the imaginary the force of one of the four major continents. Of course, Papua New Guineans do not see the world in those terms.) And we see the mass of lands and water in Ortelius' map not

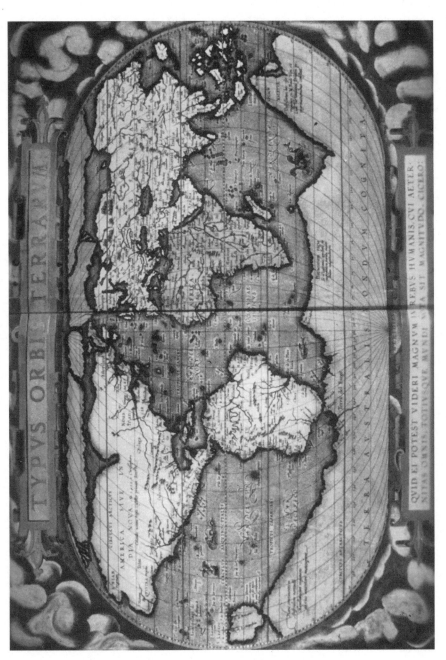

Ortelius' "Orbis Universalis Terrarum," the "Universal World" (c.1575). Without the T-in-O map it would be impossible to "see" four continents in Ortelius' map. However, the complicity between geography and epistemology has been maintained: the observer of the planet is located in Europe, but at the same time beyond and above it. (Courtesy of the Newberry Library, Chicago.)

because the planet is divided into four continents, *but because the T-in-O map has been invisibly imposed upon Ortelius' "Orbis Universalis Terrarum."*

The shift from the three continents in Isidore's map to the addition of a fourth one at the end of the fifteenth century is interesting for several reasons. First and most obviously, the division of the world into continents according to Christian cosmology was simply an isolated Christian invention that was applied and later accepted globally. Next, when America was invented and appended to the triad, Tawantinsuyu and Anáhuac disappeared. It was as if they had not existed before, and only began to do so at the very moment of their disappearance (invasion). That is to say, they lost their autonomous history. From the beginning of the sixteenth century onward, the histories and languages of Indian communities "became historical" at the point where they lost their own history. They became, in other words, museum cultures as they ceased to be human history. When Gerardus Mercator drew his world map in 1542 and represented the New World as an independent continent, he contributed to an "American" identity that ignored and suppressed Anáhuac, Tawantinsuyu, and Abya-Yala. This kind of suppression would become conceptualized as "modernity," as if modernity was a necessary historical force with the right to negate and suppress everything that did not fit a model of world history that is seen as "an essential historical process."

Be that as it may, Mercator labeled the two landmasses as North and South America (*pars Sept(entrionalis)* and *pars Merid(ionalis)* respectively) and separated the Americas from the other three continents (Asia, Africa, and Europe), following the already existing idea of the Old and the New Worlds. America, because of the colonial differential effect, has always been conceived as a continent that did not coexist with the other three but came into being late in the history of the planet. For that reason it was called the "New World" and, by the eighteenth century, Buffon and Hegel really saw its nature and culture as "young." History – that is, official and canonical narratives of a chronological successions of events and their location in space – placed a similar gulf between the history of Europe and that of its colonies, as if they were independent entities always "trailing behind" the triumphal march of European, supposedly universal, history.

St Augustine, writing in the early fifth century, contributed significantly to continental racialization. Although the *term* "race" in today's sense is from the eighteenth century, the *idea* of superiority imbedded in the Christian classification of people by continent was already implicit in the T-in-O map. The geographical distribution of Noah's three sons (Shem, Ham, and Japheth), one in each continent, speaks to the ways in which Japheth was considered in relation to Shem and Ham. There should be no surprise, therefore, in the fact that seventeenth-century world maps have Europe in the upper left, Asia in the upper right, and Africa and America at the bottom (usually represented by naked or semi-naked women). If that is not racialization of people and continental divisions, I do not understand what racism is. Before Augustine such a link had not been clearly established. In other words, there were obviously no natural connections whatsoever between Asia and Shem, Africa and Ham, and Europe and Japheth, as Isidore would have it in his T-in-O map. In *The City of God*, Augustine (book XVI) wanted to ask whether the holy city could be traced in "a continuous line from the flood or was so interrupted by intervening periods of irreligion that there are times when not one man emerges as worshipper of the one true God" (book XVI, 1, 649). Thus, Augustine speculates:

In fact, from the time of Noah, whom with his wife and his three sons and their wives was found worthy to be rescued from the devastation of the Flood by means of the ark, we do not find, until the time of Abraham, anyone whose devotion is proclaimed by any statement in the inspired Scriptures – *except for the fact that Noah commends his sons Shem and Japheth in his prophetic benediction, since he knew, by prophetic insight, what was to happen in the far distant future.* Hence it was that he also cursed his middle son, that is the one younger than the first-born and older than the last, because he had sinned against his father. He did not curse him in his own person, but in the person of his son, Noah's grandson; and he used those words: "A curse on Canaan! He shall be a slave, a servant to his brothers." Now Canaan was the son of Ham, who had not covered the nakedness of his sleeping father, but instead had called attention to it. This is also why Noah went on to add a blessing on his two sons, the eldest and the youngest, saying, "Blessed be the Lord God of Shem, and Canaan shall be his slave; may God enlarge Japheth, and may he dwell in the houses of Shem." In the same way the vineyard planted by Noah, the drunkenness resulting from its fruit, the nakedness of the sleeping Noah, *and all the other events recorded in this story, were laden with prophetic meanings and covered with prophetic veils.*[17]

At this point, Augustine begins a hermeneutic argument (that is, an argument about meaning, not about causes) by which the meaning attributed to each of the names of Noah's sons will be the "prophetic insight" that illuminates "the distant future," a future that was in fact Augustine's present. He argues: "Now that the historical fulfillment of these prophecies has come about in the posterity of these sons, the things which were concealed have been abundantly revealed" (book XVI, 2, 650). So what were the "prophetic meanings" covered with "prophetic veils" in each of the names?

The name Shem, as we know, means "named" and it was in Shem's line that Christ was born in the flesh. Japheth means "enlargement" and "in the houses of Christ"; that is, *the "enlargement" of the nations dwells in the church.* The name Ham means "hot" and Noah's middle son was separated from the other two and, by keeping his position between them, was included neither in the first fruits of Israel nor in the full harvest of the Gentiles. He could only stand for the hot breed of heretics: *"They are hot, because they are on fire not with the spirit of wisdom, but with the spirit of impatience; for that is the characteristic fervor in the heart of heretics; that is what makes them disturb the peace of the saints."*

To understand the implications of Augustine's argument, let's remember that he was following the line of descent from Shem to show the unfolding of the City of God after the Flood (book XVI, 10, 665). A second important moment after Shem's is the "development of the City of God from the epoch marked by Father Abraham" (book XVI, 12, 670). Abraham was born, Augustine informs us, in the territory of the Chaldeans, "a land which formed part of the Assyrian Empire" (book XVI, 12, 670). Now, this information is relevant in that section 17 of book XVI is devoted to "the three outstanding Gentile empires." And here is where we find, several centuries before Isidore of Seville, the explanation of the continental division in the T-in-O map.

My extended review of the famous, and yet forgotten, history of the tripartite continental division has two ultimate purposes. One is to underscore the fact that the planet was not ontologically divided into continents, but that the continental triad was a Christian invention. Second, I want to show that the meaning of *America* (and the Indias Occidentales) can't be understood outside the Christian continental divide. If, in a hypothetical revision of history (an exercise in the logic of "possible worlds"), the lump of land into which Columbus bumped had been "discovered" instead by the Moors, the Turks, or the Chinese, you can be absolutely sure that there would be no "America" today, and even less likely would be the existence of a "Latin" America. Of course, history is based on what happened and not on what could have happened. Philosophy, though, is based on possible worlds and on always asking about the alternatives that have been left out by that which "really" happened. In other words, "historical reality" is not only what happened but also the possibilities that the sheer facts of what happened negate.

What happened has much to do with the increasing complicity of Christianity (and Christian knowledge) with the force of developing capitalism and its consequences in the cultural industry: map making, book publishing and circulation, the authority of the printed book, etc. Without that partnership, the outcome of capitalism and the world in which we are living in today, with the Americas, would have certainly been different. History is an institution that legitimizes the telling of stories of *happenings* simultaneously silencing other stories, as well as stories of the silence of histories.[18] How did Christianity and capitalism come together in America? Indeed, Christianity and *capital* came together before, more clearly toward the middle of the fifteenth century. But America propelled *capital into capitalism*. How come? Again, the massive appropriation of land, massive exploitation of labor, and massive slave trade came together with a common goal (to produce the commodities of a global market, from gold to tobacco and sugar) and a dramatic consequence (the expendability – dispensability – of human lives in the pursuit of commodity production and capital accumulation). Capital turned into capitalism when the radical changes in land appropriation, labor exploitation, and massive commodity production were conceived in the rhetoric of modernity as an advancement of humanity (in the eighteenth century, Adam Smith would be the first in theorizing political economy starting from the Atlantic commercial circuits). The consequences of the conversion of capital into capitalism were the devaluation of human lives and and the naturalization of human expendability. *That is the beginning of a type of racism that is still well and alive today* (as evidenced in the treatment of immigrants in Europe and the US, as well as the expendability of people's lives in Iraq).

The commercial circuits in the expanding mercantile economy had been forming between 1250 and 1350.[19] But a new dimension – the justification of the possession of land, ports, and places – appeared with the *Romanus pontifex* bull of 1455, the bull *Inter caetera* of 1493, the Tratado de Tordesilla of 1497, in which the pope distributed the "new" discovered lands between Spain and Portugal, and the *Requerimiento* of 1512. These declarations foreshadow the constitution of the modern/colonial world. For example, the early *Romanus Pontifex* bull responds to the "discoveries" made by the Portuguese prince Henry the Navigator (1395–1460) and states:

> And so it came to pass that when a number of ships of this kind had explored and taken possession of very many harbors, islands, and seas, they at length came to the province of Guinea, and *having taken possession* of some islands and harbors and the sea adjacent to that province, sailing farther they came to the mouth of a certain great river commonly supposed to be the Nile, and war was waged for some years against the peoples of those parts in the name of the said King Alfonso and of the prince, and in it very many islands in that neighborhood were subdued and *peacefully possessed*, as they are *still possessed* together with the adjacent sea. Thence also many Guineamen and other negroes, taken by force, and some by barter of unprohibited

articles, *or by other lawful contract of purchase*, have been sent to the said kingdoms. *A large number of these have been converted to the Catholic faith*, and it is hoped, by the help of divine mercy, that if such progress be continued with them, either those peoples will be converted to the faith or at least the souls of many of them will be gained for Christ.[20]

These bulls clearly linked the Christian church with mercantilism and added a new and important element: the right of the Christians to "take possession." Experts in modern/colonial history and the "discovery" of America are familiar with the famous *Requerimiento*[21] that officers of the Castilian crown and the church read to the Indians in order to enact possession of their land. The combination of an expansive ideology (that of Western Christianity), on the one hand, with the transformation of the mercantile trade by the emphasis on land possession and the massive exploitation of labor to produce commodities for a newly global market, on the other, engendered the colonial matrix of power.[22] The point here is that the emergence of the Atlantic commercial circuit (in the "discovery and colonization" of America) established the links between faith, land possession, and the massive exploitation of labor (serfdom, slavery) in the Americas, in mines as well as in plantations producing for the global market.

The thirteenth-century mercantile world-system economy was different. First, it was not driven in conjunction with a global design, such as the one Christians began to envision and implement toward the middle of the fifteenth century. Abu-Lughod has remarked:

Indeed, what is noteworthy in the world system of the thirteenth century is that a wide variety of cultural systems coexisted and cooperated, and that societies organized differently from those in the West dominated the system. Buddhism, Confucianism, Islam, Zoroastrianism, and numerous other smaller sects often dismissed as "pagan" all seem to have permitted and, indeed, facilitated lively commerce, production, exchange, risk-taking and the like. And among these, Christianity played a relatively insignificant role.[23]

We cannot account in detail here for the radical transformation that in two centuries led to the assumption of imperial control of the modern/colonial world by Christianity, and the design to convert by force and by possession all barbarians outside it. What is relevant for us is a second observation made by Abu-Lughod. She notices and analyzes a decline of naval and commercial control by China and India, toward the end of the fourteenth century:

> The withdrawal of the Chinese fleet after 1435, coupled with the overextension into the two easternmost circuits of the Indian Ocean trade of the Arab and Gujarati Indian merchants, neither protected by a strong navy, left a vacuum of power in the Indian Ocean. Eventually, this vacuum was filled first by the Portuguese, then by the Dutch, and finally by the British . . . What decisively transformed the shape of the *"modern" world* system was not so much the Portuguese take-over of the "old world" but the Spanish incorporation of the "new world." This geographic reorientation displaced the center of gravity in a decisive manner and, if Marx's *contention is accepted, provided through primitive accumulation, the windfalls of wealth that eventually were spun into industrial gold.* This perhaps, is *why European scholars* have in the last analysis been fixated on the sixteenth century.[24]

Confronting Abu-Lughod's narrative with the perceptions that emerged in and from the colonial history of the Americas will help us understand the co-existence and the conflict of interpretations not only within one paradigm but across paradigmatic frameworks of thought and across the epistemic colonial difference. We will see later that this general philosophical problem has serious implications for power relations and, more specifically, for one particular kind of power relations, the "coloniality of power" (i.e., imperial appropriation of land, exploitation of labor, and control of finance; control of authority; control of gender and sexuality; and control of knowledge and subjectivity). "Discovery" is the dominant, imperial version of what happened (the version that became "reality," the ontological dimension of history that blends what happened with the interpretation of what happened), while "invention" opens the window of possibility for decolonizing knowledge. That is, if "discovery" is an imperial interpretation, "invention" is not just a different interpretation but a move to decolonize imperial knowledge. Which one is the true one is a moot question. The point is not which of the two interpretations better "represents the event" but, rather, what the power differential in the domain of knowledge is. And what we have here are two interpretations, one offering the imperial vision of the event, and the other the decolonial vision. Both co-exist in different paradigms: the imperial paradigm imposes and maintains the dominant view (which all students learn from elementary to high school and which is disseminated in popular culture and the media). The decolonial paradigm struggles to bring into intervening existence an-other interpretation that brings forward, on the one hand, a silenced view of the event and, on the other, shows the limits of imperial ideology disguised as the true (and total) interpretation of the events.

The idea of America that complemented the idea of "discovery" came into being at the intersection of Christian cosmology, the emerging capitalist economy, and the decolonial responses of Indigenous populations in Anáhuac and Tawantinsuyu, who tried first to expel the invaders and later to find strategies of survival mixed with rejection of the invaders and preservation of their own language, beliefs, and ways of social and family life. The initial tensions between the diversity of Spaniards and Portuguese and the diversity of Indians was complicated later on by the arrival of African slaves and, still later, by the emergence of the Creole consciousness by the mid-seventeenth century. That sixteenth-century intersection was also marked by the fact that, then and there, Christianity gained ground over Moors and Jews and became "the" religion of the capitalist world, which turned into liberalism in the eighteenth century and neo-liberalism (that is, political conservativism) in the second half of the twentieth and the first part of the twenty-first centuries. The complicity between the US and the state of Israel since its inception cannot be detached from the long history of the modern/colonial world, which includes the expulsion of the Jews from Spain at the very moment in which Spain was becoming the imperial foundation of the modern/colonial and capitalist word, as well as the changing faces of the idea of America, from the fourth continent in Christian cosmology to the exceptionality of America-as-US to save the world from the axis of evil.

O'Gorman's thesis is located within the Creole decolonial genealogy of thought. As we will see in chapter 3, similar decolonial discourses grounded in the "colonial wound," and in the genealogies of thoughts and experience of Indians and Afro descendants, surfaced more or less at the same time as O'Gorman's. The Afro-descendant decolonial genealogy of thought was clearly and loudly manifested in and for the Americas by Aimé Césaire in *Discours sur le colonialisme* (1950) and *Retour au pays natal* (1956), and by Frantz Fanon in *Peaux noires, masques blancs* (1952). In parallel with decolonial discourses articulated after World War II, Aymara intellectual and activist Fausto Reinaga, in *América India y Occidente* (1974), was also articulating a decolonial discourse embedded in Indigenous and Andean colonial experiences and genealogy of thoughts. Observing the colonial history of the Americas, then, helps us understand the co-existence and the conflict of interpretations across paradigmatic frameworks and across the epistemic colonial difference;. that is, the decolonial epistemic shift means understanding modernity from the perspective of coloniality, while, for instance, postmodernity means understanding modernity from within modernity itself.

The Historical Foundation of Occidentalism and its Epistemic, Political, and Ethical Consequences

The "idea" of America came into being deeply rooted in the "idea" of Occidentalism. After all, "Indias Occidentales" was the name attributed by the Spaniards to their newly possessed lands. America, as a name, co-existed for three centuries with "Indias Occidentales" before that name fell into desuetude after the Creoles gained independence from Spain. O'Gorman's thesis on the "invention of America" and "the universalism of Western culture" revealed not only that the idea of discovery is an imperial interpretation but also that America as the extreme West is rooted in Christian cosmology, in which the destiny of Japheth, the son located in the West, was to expand. "Occidentalism" was one of the consequences of the

colonial revolution and the condition that made possible, three
centuries later, the invention of "Orientalism" in the imperial expansion of Britain and France into Asia and Africa. "Occidentalism," as
O'Gorman's thesis on the "universalism of Western culture" suggests,
has two interrelated dimensions: First, it served to locate the geo-
historical space of Western culture. But, less obviously, it also fixed
the privileged locus of enunciation. It is from the West that the rest
of the world is described, conceptualized, and ranked: that is, modernity is the self-description of Europe's role in history rather than
an ontological historical process. Without a locus of enunciation
self-conceived as Occidental, the Oriental could not have been
thought out.[25]

Hegel's philosophy of history is a striking example in which the
West is both a geo-historical location and the center of enunciation.
History moves from East to West. In that move, the very idea of
Western civilization became the point of reference for the rest of
the world, and the goal as well. How was it that the "West" came
to occupy the "center" in terms of political theory, political economy,
philosophy, arts, and literature? And when? Up to the fifteenth
century, Western Christendom (or Europe in Greek mythology) was
literally the "West" – but "West" of what? Of Jerusalem, of course,
as it was the center of the Christian world. Athens and Rome were
construed as the part of the "West" that offered the foundation of
knowledge, social organization, and the consolidation of the church
and the state under Emperor Constantine, three centuries AD. Thus,
"Western Europe" did not begin to occupy the "center" until the
emergence of the "Indias Occidentales" (later called America and,
even later, Latin and Anglo America) in the Christian European
consciousness. The very idea of a West (Occidentalism) and the
ideology of Western expansion since 1500 also began with the identification and invention of America. From that moment on, the
Indias Occidentales defined the confines of the West and, as its
periphery, were part of the West nonetheless. Those confines were
traced from a locus of observation that placed itself at the center of
the world being observed, described, and classified. This allowed
Western Europe to become the center of economic and political
organization, a model of social life, an exemplar of human achievement, and, above all, the point of observation and classification of

the rest of the world. Thus the idea of "West" as "center" became dominant in European political theory, political economy, philosophy, arts, and literature, in the process by which Europe was conquering the world and classifying the world being conquered. The hubris of the zero-point became the legitimate and naturalized point of observation in cartography (as in Ortelius' map) and in theology. The sixteenth is the century in which the eye of God is in complicity with empirical observations provided by navigations around the globe. Theology provided the authority of the locus of observation and cartography the truth of the world being observed.[26]

"Occidentalism," more than a field or domain of study like "Orientalism" in the hands and pens of French and British intellectuals since the late eighteenth century, is itself the perspective from which the Orient can be conceived. For how could "Orientalism" become a geo-political concept without the presupposition of an "Occident" which was not only its counterpart, but also the very condition for the existence of "Orientalism"? Furthermore, "Occidentalism" was both a geo-political concept and the foundation of knowledge from which all categories of thought emerged and all classifications of the rest of the world were determined. "Orientalism" did not have this privilege. Western people have disciplines and Eastern people have cultures to be studied by Western disciplines. The West was, and still is, the only geo-historical location that is both part of the classification of the world *and the only perspective that has the privilege of possessing dominant categories of thoughts from which and where the rest of the world can be described, classified, understood, and "improved."*[27]

The enchanting power of Occidentalism resides in its privileged geo-historical location, a privilege that was self-attributed by the growing hegemonic belief in its own racial, religious, philosophic, and scientific superiority. One of the most devastating consequences of such a system of belief is that the world seems to be what European (and later US) categories of thought allow you to say it is. The rest is simply wrong and any attempt to think otherwise opens one up to harassment, demonizing, and, eventually, elimination. The idea of America (and subsequently of Latin and Anglo America) is a product and a consequence of this Occidentalist ideology of Western expansion and civilization. The Occidental is, primarily, the place of hegemonic epistemology rather than a geographical sector on the map. Samuel Huntington demonstrated as much when he placed Australia in the First World and in the West while leaving Latin America out.[28] For, after all, "(Latin) America" is not an "entity" that can be observed and experienced, but an "idea" that arises in the conflicts of interpretation across the colonial difference. The "differences" between Latin America and Europe and the US are not just "cultural"; they are, well and truly, "colonial differences." That is, the *links* between industrial, developed, and imperial countries, on the one hand, and could-be-industrial, underdeveloped, and emerging countries, on the other, *are* the colonial difference in the sphere where knowledge and subjectivity, gender and sexuality, labor, exploitation of natural resources, and finance, and authority are established. The notion of cultural differences overlooks the relation of power while the concept of colonial difference is based, precisely, on imperial/colonial power differentials.

We can deepen our understanding of the functions and implications of the idea of Occidentalism by contrasting it with the formation of the ideas of other areas that were constructed vis-à-vis a hegemonic idea of Europe. The contrast between Asia or Africa and the Americas can also illuminate the importance of the emergence of "Occidentalism" as part of the ideology of colonization during the Renaissance, and of "Orientalism" as its counterpart to justify the later expansion of England and France. Both rely on the image of the world put in place in the sixteenth century when "America" emerged in the European consciousness and in the global designs of capitalist empires.

In "How Does Asia Mean?" Sun Ge presents a compelling argument that from the beginning Asia:

is not only a political concept, but also a cultural concept; it is not only a geographical location, but also a measure of value judgment. The Asia question itself does not bear any necessary relation to the question of hegemony and counter-hegemony, although the attempts to tackle this question have brought into play considerations of hegemony of the East and the West.

More specifically, Sun Ge frames the problem as follows:

> For a long historical period, Asia has not been treated as a self-contained geographical concept, *but has only been put forward ideologically in opposition to Europe.* The discussion of Asia involved not only the question of Eurocentrism, but also the question of hegemony within the East. As difficult as it is to sort out the question of Asia, it remains an underlying thread running through the intellectual history in the *modern world*. Hence, we still have to grapple with the question of Asia as one that constitutes a totality in itself.[29]

The general statement that Asia has "been put forward ideologically in opposition to Europe" already reveals the fact that "Asia" surfaced out of the political project of European agents more than from the spirit imbedded in the ontology of a continent. In the same way as the people living in Tawantinsuyu and Anáhuac did not know that they inhabited a continent named America, the people of China, Japan, and India did not know that they were living in a continent named Asia (and, of course, the equivalent holds for Indigenous people in what later came to be called New Zealand and Australia). *Who really knew* that Incas and Aztecs were living in America and that Chinese and Japanese were in Asia? *The Western Christians, who drew the maps and named the areas, were the only ones who knew.* And how and when did Chinese and Japanese and other people in "Asia" know that they inhabited a continent named Asia? To determine the precise moment or period in which the different people and institutions in China, Japan, India, etc. accepted the idea that they were living in a continent named "Asia" and began to associate a particular territory with that specific name, we would need to do further investigation. One answer, however, can be taken as a given: *not before 1582*. Why? Because it was in the decade of 1580 that Italian Jesuit Mateo Ricci presented a world map (presumably Ortelius' "Orbis Universalis Terrarum") to the intellectuals and officers of the Ming Dynasty.[30] We can be almost certain that it was only then that people inhabiting China and Japan "learned" for the first time that they were living in a space called Asia, just as the Indigenous people and African slaves transported to

America learned, also in the sixteenth century, that there was a continent named "America." And what about Africa? A similar "learning" curve can be traced. People from the Maghrib, the empire of Mali, the kingdoms of the Niger Bend and of Chad, etc. began to learn, in the fifteenth and sixteenth centuries, that they belonged to a continental unit called "Africa." *There was no good reason for the different people of "Africa" to spontaneously conceive of themselves as they were conceived of by the European Christians!* The adoption of an image, Africa, which belonged not to their memories but to the memories of Christian Europe, accompanied the increasing force of the colonial matrix of power, which as we have seen came into the picture with the "discovery of America" and the Christian maps locating the "barbarians" of the world.

The political project subjacent to and invisible under the continental division has important consequences for contemporary intellectual debates. Sun Ge appropriately brings to the forefront the need for a radical revisiting of Edward Said's concept of Orientalism (a revisiting to radicalize the concept, and not to favor the Bernard Lewises of the world that have been attacking Said for his critique both of Orientalism and of Israel). "Asia," writes Sun Ge, is a singular term that "has emerged to name collectively a plurality of countries and regions." However, "in the hands of Asians, Orientalism becomes different from that which Said criticizes, for it is directed against the Asian Occidentalism."[31] Recognizing the fundamental contribution made by Said, she calls for an equally fundamental revision. Sun Ge makes an epistemic geo-political move (that is, a move that shifts the geo-politics of knowledge) "to take a different perspective from that of Western intellectuals on the question of Asia – a question that deserves greater attention from intellectuals in both the East and the West."[32] Sun Ge observes, rightly in my view, that when Said declares:

> To speak of scholarly specialization as a geographical "field" is, in the case of Orientalism, fairly revealing since no one is likely to imagine a field symmetrical to it called Occidentalism. Already the special, perhaps even eccentric attitude of Orientalism becomes apparent. For . . . there is no real analogy for taking a fixed, more or less total geographical position

towards a wide variety of social, linguistic, political and historical realities.[33]

Here, Sun Ge goes on to make a weighty observation:

> what Said fails to understand is that *there is another side to this
> problem. That is, for the Asians engaged in the discussion of the Asia
> question, though one cannot say there is precisely something called
> "Occidentalism"* worked out by them, there indeed exists, and
> not without reason, in abstraction an ambiguous single entity
> named the "West." Although it is no longer meaningful today
> to consider the "West" as a single entity, Occidentalism had, at
> least in the modern history of East Asia, once played a key
> role in mediating the self-knowledge of the nations within
> the East with important questions being stirred up in the
> process.[34]

Sun Ge is correct to point out that Said only saw half of the
problem and did not stop to wonder how Orientalism could have
emerged without a previous notion of Occidentalism. The problem
in Said's argument, which is very clear in the statement just quoted,
is that he takes for granted that the "beginning" of modern history
(and the very idea of modernity) is located in the eighteenth
century. He, along with many others, particularly scholars in postcolonial studies, was blind to the sixteenth and seventeenth centuries
and the consequences of the "discovery" of America. This means,
really, that the emergence and configuration of the colonial matrix
of power of "Orientalism" are but a second round of world-order
transformation.

Asia or (Latin) America are, to paraphrase Sun Ge, mediums
through which *we* are effectively led to *our* history, and it is precisely
because of this historical significance that it is important we keep
asking how Asia (or "Latin America") signifies.[35] I take *we* and *our*
in the previous sentence to refer to the inscription of the geo-
politically identified subject (that is, the geo-politically marked loci
of enunciations). The history of Asia or (Latin) America could be
written by someone for whom it is not "our history" but "theirs."
This is precisely what happened in the sixteenth century when

Spanish missionaries decided that the Indians did not have history while they, the Spanish missionaries, were God-appointed to write the history that Indians did not have. Spanish missionaries could not have said "our" or "my" when they were writing the history of the Mexica people, as they could with the memories and subjectivity of their own past.

And how does "Africa" signify, then? A substantial answer has been advanced in two of Valentin Mudimbe's classic books: *The Invention of Africa* (1988) and *The Idea of Africa* (1994).[36] As we have said, "Africa" was not the name and the spatial image "Africans" had of their territory. It was a growing and changing conceptualization from the times of Strabo and Ptolemy (who used the name "Libya"), and a construction of theirs and other Greek and Latin geographers and historians. Thus, the invention of Africa has its foundation in the "Greek paradigm of thought" (as Mudimbe analyzes it in *The Idea of Africa*). The Greek paradigm was subsequently translated into the "Christian/Latin" one. The legacies of Greek cartography were translated into the T-in-O map with a clear articulation between the three continents and the three sons of Noah, as I described above. However, with the discovery/invention of America, Africa went through a redefinition and this time through the adaptation of the Christian T-in-O map to accommodate the existence of a fourth continent: the invention of America forced a redefinition of the idea of Africa. The "idea" of Africa was transformed due to the emergence of the Atlantic commercial circuits that displaced the "centrality" that the Mediterranean had for the consolidation of Western Christians. From the sixteenth century on, northern Africa became the location of the Moors who had been expelled from European territories, and sub-Saharan Africa became the territory where African slaves could be found and transported to the Americas. One of the consequences of the transformation of the "idea" of Africa was that slavery came to be more identified with Africanness and Blackness. For sure, not every slave was Black; there were Indian and White slaves too, particularly in the early colonial period, but "reality" does not always match the idea or the image that people make for themselves of that "reality." Slaves in Greece and Rome, of course, were not defined by skin color or continental provenance. Rather, they were people who were not

41

considered competent for other kind of labor and roles in the organization of society. The massive slave trade prompted by the colonization of America changed that frame of mind and those assumptions.

Thus, the "West," evolving from its very inception as a marker of the Christian T-in-O map, implied Europe (basically Spain and Portugal at that point) and the New World, the "Indias Occidentales." The fact that a significant sphere of modern history has been silenced is a consequence of the perspective of European modernity (of Occidentalism as a locus of enunciation), from where the history of modernity has been written. When Said says that "no one is likely to imagine a field symmetrical to it [Orientalism] called Occidentalism," many intellectuals thinking from the underside of history – like myself – would remain on Said's side and support his scholarly and political project while disagreeing with this particular statement. And this means, precisely, that decolonial projects had to be pluriversal, not universal like the imperial projects of Western modernity. The issue at stake here is not to make a claim for Occidentalism to be a remembered, symmetrical field of study. To the contrary, Occidentalism is not a field of study (the enunciated) but the locus of enunciation from which Orientalism becomes a field of study (with Said's critique of its Eurocentric underpinning). The idea of "America" was part of "Occidentalism," and the idea of "Latin" America became problematic later when South America and the Caribbean were progressively detached from the increasing identification of Occidentalism as a locus of enunciation with Western Europe and the US. To review, the decisive points for my argument, as well as for the understanding of the colonial matrix of power (i.e., coloniality of power), are that:

1   Occidentalism was the name of the sector of the planet and the epistemic location of those who were classifying the planet and continue to do so.
2   Occidentalism was not only "a field of description" but was (and still is) also and mainly *the* locus of enunciation; that is, the epistemic location from where the world was classified and ranked.

When I say "from where" (both as a location and as a starting point) I am assuming that knowledge is not something produced from a postmodern non-place. On the contrary, knowledge is always geo-historically and geo-politically located across the epistemic colonial difference. For that reason, the geo-politics of knowledge[37] is the necessary perspective to dispel the Eurocentric assumption that valid and legitimate knowledge shall be sanctioned by Western standards, in ways similar to those in which the World Bank and the IMF sanction the legitimacy of economic projects around the world. Here Eurocentrism is equivalent to Occidentalism, as both refer to a centralization and hegemony of principles of knowledge and understanding, even if there are differences within it such as those between Christians, liberals, and Marxists. Of course, it is hardly enough to live in Asia or America to inscribe oneself in a genealogy of thought that implies the language, and also the weight that the language carries in the memory and in the knowledge of people inhabiting that particular language. Of course, physical space does matter, because if you live in Bolivia or in China you will be soaked, so to speak, in the language, the memory, the concern, the television, the everyday life of that particular place. You can certainly make an abstraction of it and devote your life, in Bolivia, to studying Leibnitz. However, whatever you can do with Leibnitz in Bolivia, assuming that you are not a German person living in Bolivia but someone who was born and educated in Bolivia and whose native language was Aymara or Spanish, will differ from what someone who was born and raised in Germany, has a PhD from Heidelberg, speaks German, and has learned Latin since primary school will do.

It should not be taken lightly, then, that the claim for a geo-political reconceptualization of knowledge came, precisely, from one of the imperial/colonial histories, that of the Americas. Argentinian philosopher Enrique Dussel strongly and clearly argued for such an awareness in his *Philosophy of Liberation*.[38] "I am trying to take space, geopolitical space, seriously," stated Dussel in the first chapter, titled "Geopolitics and Philosophy." To be born at the North Pole or in Chiapas is not the same thing as to be born in New York, he observed in 1977 when he laid out a diagram of the world order.

In that diagram, the two Americas are split. The center of economic, political, and epistemic power is located in Europe, supported by the US and Japan. The periphery of economic, political, and epistemic power is located in underdeveloped, dependent, and non-aligned geo-political spaces. Latin America has a place in the underdeveloped and dependent sector of the periphery and next to the non-aligned.

Access to and accumulation of knowledge, like access to and accumulation of economic wealth, are not exactly there to grab on a first-come, first-served basis. Both depend on what part of the globe you were born in and educated in, and what language you speak. You may have been born and raised in a high-class family in Bolivia and studied in Heidelberg. Certainly, your situation and struggles in life will be different from someone born and educated in an Aymara community, whose chances of getting a fellowship to study in Heidelberg are very low. Economy, politics, and social conditions put heavy restrictions on individual intelligence. The chances are still 98 to 2 that you would not have the same possibilities and conditions as a middle-class German who has spoken German from her infancy and studied in Germany (or in England or France or the US, for that matter). I call the uneven distribution of knowledge the *geo-politics of epistemology*, just as I call the uneven distribution of wealth the *geo-politics of economy*. The "idea" of America and of "Latin" America emerged and has been maintained in the field of forces in which knowledge and wealth are unevenly distributed, and where the colonial difference has been silenced by the trumpeting and celebration of cultural differences.

The "Americanity" of America

In the 1950s, intellectuals in South America and the Caribbean began to express – as we have seen in the previous sections – a subcontinental concern about national as well as subcontinental identities. They introduced the "invention of America" theory that we have been expounding here and began to question the imperial foundation of "Latinidad" (discussed in chapter 2). For lack of a better term, "Latin" America continued to be used, not only as an entity described by European scholars and area studies specialists, but as a *critical self-consciousness of decolonization*. From José Martí turning "Latin" into "Nuestra" America – "our" America – at the end of the nineteenth century, to José Carlos Mariátegui in the 1920s locating his discourse in the legacies of Spanish colonialism and the invasion of US imperialism, "Latin" America turned into a critical reflection for intellectual decolonization that departed from its imperial foundations. The awareness (or lack of it) of the colonial differential of power in the geo-political configuration of knowledge brought Creoles of White European descent, some of them Mestizos/as, close to the contemporary critical and decolonizing discourse of Afro-Caribbeans and Andean-Aymaras.

The "invention of America" could be read, then, as closer to the dissenting project of "Nuestra" America than the consenting one of "Latin" America. Nevertheless, Martí's affirmation of an America that is "ours," in contradistinction to the other America, the Anglo, is not just Latin. Afros and Indians left a legacy of struggle and optimism in "our" America. The "Latin" American legacy left, instead, a legacy of despair that was felt in the 1950s when "Latin" America, economically and politically, slid down the scale of expectations that many countries had had from the beginning of the twentieth century to the financial crisis of 1929. Since then, the economic and political decay has awakened feelings of pessimism and inferiority among "Latin" Americans displaced by their not being European. The initial sentence of Hector A. Murena's *El pecado original de América* (1954) reveals an inferiority complex whose seed was planted in the second half of the nineteenth century, when "Latin" America was forged as an identity in confrontation with "Anglo" America and Europe: "These are the facts: there was a time in which we inhabited a land, named Europe, inseminated by the spirit; but all of a sudden we have been expelled from her, and we fell in another land, in a brutish land, void of spirit, that we agree to name America."[39]

What the "invention thesis" actually did after its articulation, however, was something wholly unintended: it offered an epistemic affirmation of something that, half a century later, Peruvian sociologist Anibal Quijano and US sociologist Immanuel Wallerstein would identify as "Americanity."[40] Why Americanity? Because the

45

distinction between Anglo and Latin Americanity is not an essential distinction that somehow emanates from the particular Spirit of Latins and Anglos, since it is something that emerged together with the formation of the modern/colonial world system. *The common history of the Americas, including their own name, lies in their historical foundation: the colonial matrix of power, or capitalism as we know it today, and modernity as the imperial ideology of Western Europe.* In that process, the Americas were shared out in the margins, and the degree of marginality depended on whose sector of Western European population and institutions was making history. Americanity, grounded in the idea of the modern/colonial world, starts from different premises and invites the reader to look for the silences in official histories in books, in encyclopedias, and on the web that assume historical narrative and what happened are one and the same thing. The concept of "Americanity" is one necessary corrective to the excessive belief in one and only one history of the world, which happens to leave out a significant part (what became known as America) that was unknown to those who were writing universal history. Consequently, the idea of "America" belongs to the European historical narrative, since millions of people inhabiting the "land" were not allowed to tell their own stories; they had different narratives about the origin and process of human beings, about the very concept of "human," of knowledge, of social organization etc. But difference was disabled by the colonial matrix of power. Certainly, Christianity and, later on, European secular history and philosophy were successful in eliminating and subsuming the "other histories."

The emergence of America marks three major global economic changes, which are: (1) the expansion of the geographical size of the world; (2) the development of variegated methods of labor control for different products and different zones of the world economy; and (3) the creation of strong state machineries at the imperial end of the colonial spectrum. In their joint article "Americanity as a Concept; Or the Americas in the Modern World System," Quijano and Wallerstein made the following claim:

> The modern world-system was born in the long sixteenth century. The Americas as a geo-social construct were born in the long sixteenth century. The creation of this geo-social entity,

the Americas, was the *constitutive act* of the modern world-system. The Americas were not incorporated into an already existing capitalist world-economy. There could not have been a capitalist world-economy without the Americas.[41]

Americanity and coloniality are mutually imbricated from the beginning. The singularity of the Americas resides in several erasures that European colonial expansion enacted: on the Indigenous territorial imaginary as well as their social and economic organization and concepts of life, justice, and happiness; on the histories, languages, and practices of transplanted Africans; and on the marginalization of the population of Southern European descent, mainly in Hispanic and Luso America, that began in the seventeenth century with the first generation of White Creoles. Yet, even in these perspectives, the singularity of the Americas beyond the US still resides fundamentally in the massive exploitation of labor that was initiated with colonization, and with it the idea of the expendability of human life that, under the concept of inferior human races, justified the demand for increasing productivity in the mines and the plantations. The singularity of the Americas, seen from the perspective of coloniality, also resides in its being the space where a population of Creoles of European descent gained independence from the imperial metropolis, and reproduced the logic of coloniality in the new independent governments in both the North and the South against the Indigenous and the Afro populations. Thus, the Creole population of European descent became, in South America and the Caribbean, the master while remaining the slave with respect to Western Europe and the US.

America is singular insofar as the first structures of *internal* colonialism in the modern/colonial world were put in place there. After World War II, Asian and African countries that gained "independence" from British, French, and German colonialism would follow the example. "Coloniality" is the logic that put in place and held together the hierarchical system in all the spheres of the social, and pushed out of existence the economies previously existing in the would-be America. But what made the system work was, above all, knowledge and the capacity of the system to establish "natural" epistemic principles that legitimized the ruling out of differential economies. The colonial matrix of power, still invisible under the triumphant rhetoric of modernity and modernization, yesterday and today, was and is precisely the capacity of the machine to transform differences into non-existences and racialize (human) life into dispensable entities. To embrace Americanity is to dwell in the erasures of coloniality.

The important observation to make here is not simply whether there are other perspectives about the "same event" but that an-other paradigm emerges across the epistemic colonial difference. The dominant theo- and ego-politics of knowledge is being contested by the emerging shift to the geo-politics and body politics of knowledge: knowledge produced from the geo-historical and bio-historical perspective of racialized locations and people. The deeper problem is that all existing different interpretations about the same event are still within the same overarching paradigm of European modernity and its continuity and transformation in US government, universities, and media. What I have been arguing here is that an-other paradigm (the decolonial, globally diverse one) is at work; and my own argument is intended to be inscribed in it. "America" becomes a "conceptual node" around which not only do different interpretations within the same paradigm come into conflict but, more radically (and I mean here at the roots of the epistemic principles underlying different conceptions of knowledge and understanding), multiple paradigms are at war at the other end of the colonial difference. Once you get out of the natural belief that history is a chronological succession of events progressing toward modernity and bring into the picture the spatiality and violence of colonialism, then modernity becomes entangled forever with coloniality in a spatial distribution of nodes whose place in history is "structural" rather than "linear." Further, since modernity and coloniality are two sides of the same coin, each node, in addition to being structural and not linear, is heterogeneous and not homogeneous. Thus, the point here is not so much "the end of history" as "the end of Hegelian concepts of history." If instead of conceiving of history as a linear chronological process we think instead of "historico-structural heterogeneity" (*heterogeneidad histórico-structural*),[42] of historical processes interacting, we will better understand the role of the "idea" of America and of "Americanity" in it, as well as what it means to talk about modernity and coloniality as two sides of the same coin.

Taking this step moves us away from the Bible's sacred and Hegel's secular narratives and also offers a radical departure from the early Marx's canonization of "historical materialism." Why *heterogeneous historico-structural nodes* instead of *a linear succession of events*? Because history seen as a series of nodes in which historico-structural heterogeneity is deployed provides a theoretical anchor in the perspective of local histories (and languages) instead of grand narratives. Space is made for multiple and contesting perspectives and historical processes. We can then look at history as a set of historico-structural heterogeneities that are the consequence of a given set of events being cast and interpreted both from the rhetoric of modernity (progress, happiness, wealth) and from the *constitutive* logic of coloniality (stagnation, death, poverty). Instead of looking at "modernity" as a triumphal historical process, like Santa Claus bringing happiness to needy children, historico-structural heterogeneity highlights the fact that such dreams of happiness have been achieved at the cost of enormous sacrifices of human lives (Indian and Afro genocides in the conquest of America), and will continue to be so (as in the lives lost in the "miscalculated" war in Iraq) as long as the rhetoric of modernity keeps on convincing and enforcing the idea that history is a linear process, with neo-liberalism now the goal.

Today, as the "idea" of America, as well as of Asia and Africa, is in the process of being transformed through neo-liberal globalization, "Latin" America is a place for the exploitation of natural resources and human labor. The colonial matrix of power continues to be rearticulated, and the appropriation and control of space (not just land) are at the core of the new form of colonialism we have been witnessing developing since the early 1990s. The control of space entails the control of intellectual resources, as capitalism grows now also by the appropriation of knowledge. For example, by patenting every imaginable piece of knowledge possessed through the ancestral accumulation of the people inhabiting the Amazon or the forests of India, "experts" in the area of knowledge become similar to soldiers in the area of war. In controlling space, the appropriation of land and the appropriation of knowledge (two domains of the colonial matrix of power) come together to maintain capital accumulation in particular hands and to increase the marginality and dehumanization of others. "Latin" America, together with Africa and certain sectors of Asia, including South Asia, Central Asia, and the Middle East, form the sector of the globe where the tentacles of imperial expansion continue to be extended under a flourishing rhetoric of modernity, a rhetoric of which Tony Blair has given the world outstanding examples before, during, and after the invasion of Iraq. The above mentioned are significant areas of the planet where human lives become more expendable. They are part of the "rest" – those whom the neo-liberal economy cannot account for as subjects precisely because the survival of neo-liberal economic principles means that more and more people in the planet become disposable.

Today, the "Americas" are divided. One is the temple of neo-liberalism while the other provides the land, natural resources, and cheap labor, as well as emerging, contesting states and myriads of social movements. Let's turn now to the emergence and formation of the idea of "Latin" America on the colonial horizon of modernity, and then move on, in the third chapter, to turn our attention to the consequences of coloniality and the emergence of social actors contesting and transforming the idea of America and of "Latin" America.

2

"Latin" America and the First Reordering of the Modern/Colonial World

I am talking about societies drained of their essence, cultures trampled underfoot, institutions undermined, lands confiscated, religions smashed, magnificent artistic creations destroyed, extraordinary *possibilities* wiped out ... I am talking about millions of [women and] men torn from their gods, their land, their habits, their life – from life, from the dance, from wisdom.

I am talking about millions of [women and] men in whom fear has been cunningly instilled, who have been taught to have an inferiority complex, to tremble, kneel, despair, and behave like flunkies ...

I am talking about natural *economies* that have been destroyed – harmonious and viable *economies* – adapted to the indigenous population – about food crops destroyed, malnutrition permanently introduced, agricultural development oriented solely toward the benefit of the metropolitan countries; about the looting of products, the looting of raw material.

Aimé Césaire, *Discourse on Colonialism*, 1955

The "vital breath" of Western thought is reason; reason of "rectilinear time." From Socrates to Kant and from Hegel to Marx, reason marches in a straight line. This thought organizes Occident. And Occident arrives at the atomic bomb ... Thought in the New World is not "genocidal reason"; it is "cosmic reason," vital reason. . . . Thought in the New World is Maya-Inka, that is to say, is Indian thought.

Fausto Reinaga, *La América India y Occidente*, 1974

The Point of No Return:
From *Pachakuti* to Revolution

A series of unprecedented events occurred in the Atlantic world between 1776 and 1830 that would decide the future of world history – unprecedented because before the sixteenth century the modern/colonial structure that they would shake did not even exist. Thus, the transformations sought by the "revolutions" for "independence" that took place over that span of fewer than sixty years were responding to a historically invisible revolution, a drastic reversal that has been conceptualized among Kechua/Kichwa and Aymara speakers, then and now, as *Pachakuti*.

In chapter 1, I introduced the concept of *Pachakuti*. It is time now to return to it and to enter "Latin" America from the shadow of its negated specter. One of the meanings of *Pacha*, as I registered in chapter 1, is close to "mother earth" (like "Gaia" in the recent Gaia science); but it can also mean "world," since the very conception of the world was grounded on the assumption that "life" is the thread that links "earth" (as "nature" in European languages and the source of life) with all living organisms. *Kuti* means a sudden and dramatic change in the order of things, an extreme turnaround, like what happens when you lose control of your car and it flips upside down several times until it stops with the wheels toward the sky and the roof on the road. That was the experience (still being felt today) of *Pachakuti* for the people of the Americas in the long process of the Spanish conquest and reorganization of life and social fabric.

The conquest and colonization of America have not traditionally been seen as "revolution." From the European perspective, the process was, and continues to be, simply the "foundation" upon which future revolutions would take place. However, if you put yourself in the perspective of people in Tawantinsuyu after the arrival of the conquistador Francisco Pizarro, or in Cemenahuac (today's valley of Mexico) after the arrival of the conquistador Hernán Cortés, or, even earlier, in the place of the Taino population in the Caribbean islands after the arrival of Christopher Columbus, you will witness the arrival of a group of unknown people and, soon after that, see your population dying, killed, raped, and exploited, all of which will be experienced as a massive revolution of disruption and destruction. Thus, the "foundation" that allowed European entrepreneurs, monarchs, and bourgeois to fulfill their supposed destiny was, for people in Tawantinsuyu and Anáhuac, a *Pachakuti*: violent destruction, relentless invasion, and disregard for their way of life – a convulsion of all levels of existence and the moment of *the founding colonial wound of the modern/colonial world*. Indigenous peoples in the Americas have not stopped struggling with that initial wound and are making their presence felt today.

History – official and canonical narratives of chronological successions of events in particular locations in time and space – places a gulf between the history of Europe and that of its colonies, as if they were independent entities with Europe always in front and the colonies trailing. Unlike Hegel, who wrote of universal history as it arrived at his feet in Germany, those of us speaking from the history of the ex-colonies see simultaneous occurrences in time, though not necessarily space, which are interconnected by the structuring power differential. By power differential, as we saw in chapter 1, I mean not only in the accumulation of riches and military technologies of death but in the control of the very conception of life, of economy, of human being and labor. There is no time to dispute Hegel (though we cannot ignore him). The time has indeed arrived to play a different game than the one that makes it possible to believe that the collapse of the Soviet Union hailed the end of history.

In the scale (magnitude and range) of modernity's imaginary, the order of importance of revolutions would begin after the Glorious Revolution, with the French Revolution as the key historical event in the linear unfolding of History. It would be followed by the American Revolution, Spanish-Portuguese independence, and, finally, the Haitian Revolution (with the latter being seen as peripheral events lagging behind in time and following the lead of the locomotive of History). Yet, in the nodes constituted simultaneously by imperial/colonial expansion, by the rhetoric of modernity, and by the logic of coloniality in which those expansions are conceived and justified, there are no ranking priorities of events, since each event has a similar range and magnitude in the historico-structural heterogeneity linking imperial centers with peripheral colonies. After all, the imperial center cannot exist as such without the colonies. The French Revolution can be understood as a phenomenon internal to the history of Europe only if it is read from the perspective of modernity and of empire; that is, as part of the historical narrative that is linear, progressive, limited, and Eurocentric. But, really, how could the Glorious and the French Revolutions be understood independently from the accumulation of wealth in England and France from their plantations in the colonies? Both the Glorious and the French Revolutions "depended" on the colonies.

When "history" is conceived of in the simultaneity of events in the metropolis and the colonies, not only through the national history of the metropolis or the colonial history of the colonies alone (as told by metropolitan historians), we can see the heterogeneous historico-structural links (which are spatially temporal rather than temporally spatial) between the two sides of each event and, consequently, the two sides of modernity/coloniality. Independence in the colonies was, in fact, a consequence of the changing economic and political structures in Europe. The "revolutions" for independence by the Spanish, Portuguese, British, and French colonies in the Americas that took place between 1776 and 1830 should be understood, in their singularities, as part of a socio-economic structure of the Atlantic world with its global implications, in relation with and distinction from European revolutions. For example, the Glorious Revolution brought about the victory of free trade over mercantile monopoly. The Glorious Revolution has been described from the Caribbean perspective by Eric Williams:

One of the most important consequences of the Glorious Revolution of 1688 and the expulsion of the Stuarts was the impetus it gave to the principle of free trade. In 1698 the Royal African Company lost its monopoly and the right of a

54

free trade in slaves was recognized as a fundamental and natural right of Englishmen. In the same year, the Merchant Adventurers of London were deprived of their monopoly of the export trade in cloth, and a year later the monopoly of the Muscovy Company was abrogated and trade to Russia made free. Only in one particular did the freedom accorded in slave trade differ from the freedom accorded in other trades – the commodity involved was man.[1]

Undoubtedly, English merchants and government were not solely responsible for the transformation of certain human lives into commodities. In different periods of intensity, the Spaniards, Portuguese, French, and Dutch also worked from that same template. In fact, the entire Atlantic economy, from the sixteenth century until the dawn of the twenty-first, was founded on the increasing devaluation of whatever did not sustain capital accumulation. Military defense and political institutions were based on the assumption that human life was expendable in the set of global designs. British and French exploitation of the Caribbean was as greedy as the attitude that those same countries attributed to Spanish conquistadores. The "Black Legend" of Spanish corruption, which the British initiated to demonize the Spanish Empire in a ploy to get a grip on the Atlantic economy during the seventeenth century, was part of a European family feud over the economic, political, and intellectual (in the general sense of accumulation and control of knowledge, including science and technology, of course) riches of the "New World." Therein originates the *imperial difference* that would become widespread in the eighteenth century and shape the conception of "Latin" America.

The French Revolution introduced a radical change in the legal and political system of Western Europe that complemented the economic and financial changes that took place in England with the Glorious Revolution. Concepts of rights and of the citizens in France shaped ideas of personal and collective independence, autonomy, emancipation, freedom, etc. which bore directly on the understanding of the "revolutions" in the Americas. Immanuel Kant's conception of Enlightenment as emancipation expresses one such formative idea. In his piece "What is Enlightenment?" Kant explained that:

Enlightenment is man's emergence from his self-imposed
nonage. Nonage is the inability to use one's own understanding
without another's guidance. This nonage is self-imposed if its
cause lies not in lack of understanding but in indecision and
lack of courage to use one's own mind without another's
guidance. Dare to know (Sapere aude): "Have the courage to
use your own understanding" is therefore the motto of the
enlightenment.[2]

You can hear the echoes of Kant's statement today in daily conversations about freedom and democracy and even in the very concept
of the "free" market. Insofar as the statement has become a given
and crucial part of the rhetoric of modernity, it elides the critique
of its self-contradiction. That is, to follow Kant's recommendation
to the limit would require the questioning of Kant's own authority
to "establish guides" that promote "understanding without guidance." In other words, understanding without guidance requires an
acceptance of Kant's guidance. When I talk about decolonizing
knowledge, then, I am doing it *with* and *against* Kant, which is what
critical border thinking as decolonization of knowledge is all about.

As wars of independence spread all over the Spanish and
Portuguese colonies in South America beginning in 1810 (six years
after the Haitian Revolution), republican ideas being discussed and
implemented in France occupied the minds and bodies of Iberian
Creoles as well as African Creoles in Haiti and what later became
the Dominican Republic. However, African Creoles had an extra
burden upon them. It was easier for Creoles of Spanish and
Portuguese descent to be "recognized" as having a right to independence; but it was not so easy or clear, at the time, to accept that
Black people could take their destiny into their own hands. It was
expected that freedom for the Blacks and Mulattos/as, slaves and
ex-slaves, would be "given" by the White man. Kant's dictum apparently only applied selectively. Yet the "revolutions" for "independence" that took place in the Americas demonstrate that Blacks
fighting for freedom didn't need Kant's dictum. In fact, it worked
to the Haitians' disadvantage to rely on it insofar as it pre-empted
their own creativity and originality and replaced it with the legitimacy and authority of White European philosophers.

Emancipation belonged to the rise of a new social class (the bourgeoisie) whose members were mostly White, educated in Christian cosmology and in the curriculum of the Renaissance university, soon to be transformed with the advent of the Kantian-Humboldtian university of the Enlightenment. One of the consequences of such ideas of "emancipation" was that while celebrating the economic and political emancipation of a secular bourgeoisie from the tutelage both of the monarchy and of the church (particularly in France, where the separation of the church and the state was greater than in Germany and England), that same bourgeoisie and its intelligentsia appointed themselves to take into their hands the "emancipation" of non-European people in the rest of the world. In general, these new directions worked in two different manners: colonialism and imperialism, direct or indirect. The emergence of "Latinidad" and of "Latin" America, then, is to be understood in relation to a European history of growing imperialism grounded in a capitalist economy and the desire to determine the shape of "emancipation" in the non-European world.

"Latinidad": From the "Colonial Creole Baroque Ethos" to the "National Creole Latin American Ethos"

Latin America is actually a hyphenated concept with the hyphen hidden under the magic effect of the ontology of a subcontinent. By the mid-nineteenth century, the idea of America as a whole began to be divided, not so much in accordance with the emergent nation-states as, rather, according to their imperial histories, which placed an Anglo America in the North and a Latin America in the South in the new configuration of the Western Hemisphere. At that moment, "Latin" America was the name adopted to identify the restoration of European Meridional, Catholic, and Latin "civilization" in South America and, simultaneously, to reproduce absences (Indians and Afros) that had already begun during the early colonial period. The history of "Latin" America after independence is the variegated history of the local elite, willingly or not, embracing "modernity" while Indigenous, Afro, and poor Mestizo/a peoples get

57

poorer and more marginalized. The "idea" of Latin America is that sad one of the elites celebrating their dreams of becoming modern while they slide deeper and deeper into the logic of coloniality.

The idea of "Latin" America that came into view in the second half of the nineteenth century depended in varying degrees on an idea of "Latinidad" – "Latinity," "Latinitée" – that was being advanced by France. "Latinidad" was precisely the ideology under which the identity of the ex-Spanish and ex-Portuguese colonies was located (by natives as well as by Europeans) in the new global, modern/ colonial world order. When the idea of "Latinidad" was launched it had a particular purpose within European imperial conflicts and a particular function in redrawing the imperial difference. In the six-teenth century, Las Casas contributed to drawing the imperial dif-ference by distinguishing Christians from the Ottoman Empire. By the nineteenth century the imperial difference had moved north, to distinguish between states that were all Christian and capitalist. In the Iberian ex-colonies, the "idea" of Latin America emerged as a consequence of conflicts between imperial nations; it was needed by France to justify its civilizing mission in the South and its overt conflict with the US for influence in that area. France, as a country that joined the Reformation, could count itself in the same camp as England and Germany; but it was, at the same time, predomi-nantly Latin and, hence, in historical contradistinction to the Anglo-Saxon.

In the late nineteenth century, France faced a British Empire that had just colonized India and parts of Africa and was in the process of strengthening its control over the commercial and financial markets in South America. Evidence of the competition posed from Britain can still be seen today in the presence of remnants of its railroad system in Latin American countries. The position officially assumed in France at that moment has endured and it is still present in the conflicts, tensions, and complicities within the European Union and in the European Parliament today. The concept of "Latinidad" was used in France by intellectuals and state officers to take the lead in Europe among the configuration of Latin countries involved in the Americas (Italy, Spain, Portugal, and France itself), and allowed it also to confront the United States' continuing expan-sion toward the South – its purchase of Louisiana from Napoleon and its appropriation of vast swaths of territory from Mexico. White Creole and Mestizo/a elites, in South America and the Spanish Caribbean islands, after independence from Spain adopted "Latinidad" to create their own postcolonial identity. Consequently, I am arguing here, *"Latin"* America is not so much a subcontinent as it is the political project of Creole-Mestizo/a elites. However, it ended up by being a double-edged sword. On the one hand, it created the idea of a new (and the fifth) continental unit (a fifth side to the continental tetragon that had been in place in the sixteenth century). On the other hand, it lifted up the population of European descent and erased the Indian and the Afro populations. *Latin* America was not – therefore – a pre-existing entity where modernity arrived and identity questions emerged. Rather, it was one of the consequences of the remapping of the modern/colonial world prompted by the double and interrelated processes of decolonization in the Americas and emancipation in Europe.

Nineteenth-century Colombian intellectual Torres Caicedo was a key figure in justifying and pushing forward the idea of "Latin" America. In Caicedo's opinion, "There is Anglo-Saxon America, Danish America, Dutch America, etc.; there is also Spanish America, French America and Portuguese America; and therefore to this second group what other scientific name applies but Latin?"[3] Caicedo was a Francophile, spent much time in France, and maintained good relations with governmental and official spheres in that country. If his is one of the names that readily come to mind when "Latin" America is mentioned, the implication is clear. He was not the only one with such interests and he defended a very common geo-political position along the lines of French imperial interests. Of course, he does not "represent" everything that was being thought at the time, but he certainly "represents" a sector of the intelligentsia for whom, until recently, France "represented" the ideal in politics and literary culture. "Latinidad" came to refer to a Spanish and Portuguese government and an educated civil society in America that turned its face to France and its back to Spain and Portugal. In the same way as John Locke and other British thinkers, like David Hume and Thomas Hobbes, are associated with the political culture of the US, Jean-Jacques Rousseau, Montesquieu, and Voltaire are associated with the political culture of "Latin" America.

In the first half of the nineteenth century, after several nation-states originated as a consequence of gaining independence from Spain, the idea of them was not of "Latin" but of "Spanish" America. If "Latinitée-Latinidad" was simply a global design imagined and implemented from France, how did it come to displace and replace Simón Bolívar's "Confederation of Spanish American Nations"? One interpretation, advanced several years ago by eminent Uruguayan intellectual Arturo Ardao, held that the idea of "Latin" America materialized in a triangular complicity between French, Spanish, and Spanish American Creole intellectuals. In his opinion, Latin America came into being as part of the orientation of the Creole elites toward the intellectual leadership of France after Spain missed the train of modernity in the eighteenth century, and France became the model even for Spanish intelligentsia.[4] What has been insinuated but not explored in detail is that the subjective foundation for a "Latin" American identity among the post-independence Creoles of Spanish descent was already being articulated in the colonies in the late seventeenth century. That moment was the *colonial* Baroque in the Spanish colonial possessions, and was different, for sure, from the *continental* Baroque in Spain as well as in France, Italy, and Germany. The idea of a "Spanish American Confederation" was a political and administrative identification, while "Latin" America touched different cords. It touched upon the subjectivity and it became the *ethos* of the emerging Creoles elites: it was the colonial *Baroque ethos* translated into a national *Latin American ethos*.

The Baroque period, in European arts and ideas, is known as a moment of seventeenth-century splendor between the Renaissance and the Enlightenment. If the Renaissance has been characterized by symmetry of forms in the visual arts and humanism in letters and ideas, while the Enlightenment is known for secularism, for the celebration of Reason, for the emergence of a new social class and a new form of government (the nation-state) together with that of the political economy associated with free trade and overcoming mercantilism, the Baroque was a period of the celebration of exuberance. In the history of ideas, it is associated with a consolidation of the autonomy of the subject in relation to the legitimacy of classical authors (Greek and Latin) as well as the church and God. In this sphere, the Baroque was a "rest area" before the era of "revolution" and the call for emancipation launched by Immanuel Kant's paragraph quoted above. In Spain, Miguel de Cervantes's *Don Quixote* is associated with the Baroque. The questioning of authority from the past is debated in the prologue as well as in the second part when Don Quixote reads his own adventure in a narrative recently published. That mirror effect, noted by Michel Foucault, singles out the moment of an epistemic break, in the history of Western thought and culture, in which the relation between the word and its reference is placed in question. For some, the Baroque is also associated with the "birth" of modernity. Economically, Europe in the sixteenth century (and particularly Spain, Portugal, France, and England) was enjoying the enormous wealth generated in its colonies, in the "Indias Occidentales" and the "West Indies" (as England named its Caribbean possessions), and in "les Antilles" (as France named its own). The splendor in arts and ideas in Europe and in the European colonies goes hand in hand with the wealth generated in gold and silver mines, in the plantations of sugar, coffee, tobacco, cotton, in the appropriation of land and the exploitation of Indian and African labor. While the sixteenth century was one in which only Spain and Portugal were the imperial powers in the newly "discovered lands" and wealth was mainly generated by the extraction of gold and silver, the seventeenth was the century in which the slave trade and Caribbean plantations peaked and European Atlantic countries enjoyed fully the benefits of colonial labor.

Above and beyond the colonial exploitation of labor, there was also a Baroque in the colonies, mainly in the viceroyalties of Mexico and Peru. Baroque architecture can be found in other places like Guatemala, or Quito in Ecuador, as well as Salvador de Bahia and Ouro Preto in Brazil. At the surface level, the *colonial* Baroque in the Spanish and Portuguese colonies responded to the general tendencies of the *continental* Baroque in Spain. But there were "two Baroques," really, in the colonies. The state version was basically a "transplantation" of the Spanish and Portuguese elites in power, enjoying for themselves the wealth generated by the colonial economy. The Baroque of the state was also a lifestyle of consumption by the elite in power, from the Iberian peninsula. Spanish and Portuguese dominions in America had created, by the mid-seventeenth century, important urban centers with complex demography. Mexico City was built over the ruins of Tenochtitlan; the colonial city of Cuzco in Peru was built over the ruins of the Inca Empire. Beyond the spaces controlled by the colonial administration and the peninsular elites in power, however, something else was burgeoning in the streets, in the plazas, in the market as well as in the peripheries of centers of intellectual production like monasteries, seminars, and, in the case of Lima and Mexico, universities. A marginal society of displaced Creoles existed alongside Indians and Mestizos/as, Blacks, and Mulattos/as (see the graphic below, p. 73). In the colonies, the Baroque was the expression of protest, complaint, rebellion, and critical consciousness by socially and economically displaced Creoles of Spanish descent.[5] It was indeed the cry of the White Creoles feeling the pain of the colonial wound.

The Baroques of the Indies – at the level of the state and of civil society – cannot therefore be placed together as one more chapter of the European Baroque. They formed a Baroque that emerged out of the *colonial difference* of a displaced Spanish elite in power and of a wounded Creole population. It was a Baroque pretending-to-be for the Spanish elite in the colonies and of anger and decolonial impulses for the White Creoles and some Mestizos/as. It was, properly, a "Baroque Other," a heterogeneous historico–structural moment in the complex structure of the modern/colonial world. It was the moment in which, after the final defeat of the Indigenous elites at the beginning of the seventeenth century,[6] the emerging Creole population felt the colonial wound and took over the conflict of the difference, the colonial difference, racial, political, social, and economic. Of course, and as always, there were Creoles who did their best to assimilate and gain a position among the Iberian elite in power. Assimilation has been and still is a response to the colonial difference, since "you are not one of them" but you want to "become one of them." Dissension is the other type of response to the *colonial wound*. In the first case, the colonial wound is repressed, while in the second case, it offers the starting point not only for acts of rebellion but for thinking-otherwise. The "Barroco de Indias" ("Baroque of the Indies") was precisely the angered expression, in art and ideas (e.g., philosophy), built upon the colonial difference and the colonial wound. It was the sprouting of the Creole critical consciousness.

Ecuadorian philosopher and essayist Bolívar Echeverría explained in detail the appearance of the Creole identity, an identity that was no longer Spanish or Portuguese but properly Spanish American and Luso American. Echeverría observed that:

> There were the Creoles from low social levels, the Indian and Afro-Mestizos, those whom, without knowing it, would end up doing what Bernini did with the classical canon of painting: these mixed groups of lower social strata *endeavored to re-establish the most viable civilization, which was the dominant one, the European.* They intended to wake it up and then to restore its original vitality. In doing so, in invigorating the European code over the ruins of the pre-Spanish code (and with the remainders of the African slaves' codes brought by force into the picture), they would find themselves building something different from their original intention; they would find themselves raising up a Europe that never existed before them, a different Europe, a "Latin American" Europe.[7]

Beyond the fact that "Latin American" here is an anachronism (there was no such a thing as "Latin" America in the colonies, but vice-royalties united in the concept of the "Indias Occidentales"), it must also be noted that this political project in practice as well as in consciousness was still defined by the Spanish and Portuguese Creole elites, who kept their backs to the Indian and African populations co-existing among them. The mixed group of the lower strata, whom Echeverría identified as the main actors of a variegated political project throughout Spanish America and to a certain extent in Brazil, was a demographic reality clearly managed and repressed by Whites/Creoles. Creole consciousness was indeed a singular case of double consciousness: the *consciousness of not being who they were supposed to be* (Europeans). That being as not-being is the mark of the *coloniality of being*. Afro-Creoles and Indians do not have the same problem. Their critical consciousness emerged from not even being considered *human*, not from not being considered *Europeans*.

In the twentieth century the situation got more complicated with the increasing influence of the US. The "Latino/a" identification in the US, as we will see in chapter 3, brings this to the fore: while

"Latin" American Creoles and Mestizos/as do not want or cannot pretend to be "Creoles of US (American) descent," Latinos/as in the US have cut the Gordian knot with Europe. *This is one of the lines cutting across Latinos/as in the US and Latins in South America*: while the first are of European descent, the second are not. Latinos/as in the US cut the umbilical cord that still connects Latins, in South America, to Europe. This tension was reconfigured when, after 1970, "Hispanics" and "Latinos/as" were recognized as a minority (that is, an inferior social group) in the US. Thus, *for the imperial imaginary*, "Latin" Americans are second-class Europeans while Latinos/as in the US are second-class Americans. In short, "Latinidad," from its very inception in the nineteenth century, was an ideology for the colonization of being that Latinos/as in the US are now clearly turning into a decolonizing project (see chapter 3).

But let's not get derailed, and instead return to the formation of the Creole subaltern identity. Bolívar Echeverría's argument, thus, explains how the idea of Latin America became entrenched in Creole/Mestizo/a ideology and subjectivity and, consequently, alien to the Indigenous people and Afros, as well as to the European populations. The diverse communities of Creoles/Mestizos/as (Catholics of different persuasions, liberals of different convictions, socialists of diverse faiths, in different strata of society and of different gender and sexual engagement) were in the position of having to invent themselves after "independence," and they did so by engaging in the restoration of the most viable civilization (said Echevarría) – the European, and not the Indigenous or African. Indian civilizations became ruins, and Afro-creations in the New World took on their own identities. The Afro-based "religions" of Candomblé in Brazil, Santería in the Spanish Caribbean, Voodoo in the French colonies, and, lately, Rastafarianism in the British colonies all reach toward a dense, potent civilizational energy that was tragically erased by the surfacing of the critical Creole consciousness.

The movements for independence took place roughly over one hundred and fifty years after the emergence of the Creole Baroque critical consciousness. After independence, Creoles found themselves in power and no longer subalterns of the Spanish colonial elites. They became, indeed, the postcolonial elite. While theology was the overall framework in which the Baroque ethos materialized, it was already receding in the nineteenth century, and the individual, the ego in Descartes's terminology, was taking center stage along with secular political theories. The "idea" of Latin America came into sight in the process of the transformation of the colonial Creole Baroque ethos into the postcolonial Creole "Latin" ethos. In that transformation, Spain receded and France and England gained ground in the minds and the pockets of postcolonial Creoles. Republicanism and liberalism displaced the colonial ideology under which the Spanish Empire organized, controlled, and sustained its colonies. The "Latin" American ethos was a product and a consequence of the transformation from the dominance of theology and religious spiritualism to the dominance of egology and secular materialism, as much as it was the transformation of the critical and subaltern consciousness of the Baroque ethos into the assenting consciousness of the postcolonial Creole elites. "Postcolonial" here refers to the period following the shift from the colonial regime ruled from the metropolis to a national regime ruled by the Creoles. In that shift, internal colonialism was born. And "Latin" America as a political and ethical project was the ethos of internal colonialism.

When the Creoles moved from being a subaltern group to become a dominant elite, the only anchor they had was the "Baroque ethos" which, at that point, was more a blurred memory than a source of political energy. Closer to their memory was the so-called "debate on the New World" in the course of which the Jesuits had been expelled from South American countries in the second half of the eighteenth century. If the Baroque moment created the conditions for the Creoles to come out of their shell, the expulsion of the Jesuits (all of them Creoles, certainly) inflamed their hatred not only against the Spanish colonial authority but also against the imperial coalition between the Spanish crown and the Catholic church. When military action for independence was followed by the need to put their house in order, the Creole elite put their past in the closet and joyfully looked for political ideals toward France, where they found the republican emphasis on the "res publica" (the state) and the important role of the state in the coordination of a just and peaceful society (with a long history going back to Plato, Machiavelli, Bodin, Hobbes). And they also found liberalism, a newer doctrine or ideology, propagated by Locke and the Glorious Revolution in England and theorized by Adam Smith, that pushed the freedom of the individual and free trade rather than state management.[8] However, for the Creole elite of Spanish and Portuguese descent, France was closer than England, and Montesquieu became the central figure from whom republicans and liberals would draw their ideas.[9]

I am telling these stories for two reasons, mainly. The first is to show the struggle to identify the historical grounding of the Creole consciousness, since Creoles could not claim the past that belonged to the Spaniards, to the Indians, or to the Africans. Creoles of Spanish and Portuguese descent were, indeed, closer than they imagined to African slaves and Creoles of African descent – they were all cut off from their pasts and they were living in a present without history. However, while Blacks invented "religions," Creoles of Spanish and Portuguese descent lived under the illusion that they were Europeans too, although they felt their second-class status. The "Baroque ethos" and the expulsion of the Jesuits from the New World were receding from their consciousness. By the mid-nineteenth century, the British railroad made it clear that a new economic era was dawning. The historical foundation of Creole identity under colonial rules was quickly stored away, and the Creole elite alienated itself in its effort to adopt and adapt republican and liberal projects. Republicanism and liberalism, in Europe, emerged as bourgeois projects against the monarchy and a despotic form of government; they were also against the Christian church, which was curtailing the sovereignty of the individual; and, finally, they were against monarchic control of the mercantile economy, which was holding back the benefits that free trade was promising to the emerging social-economic class, the bourgeoisie. None of these conditions obtained in the ex-Spanish and ex-Portuguese colonies. The Creole elite really missed the point. And instead of devoting themselves to the critical analysis of colonialism (in the same way as European intellectuals devoted themselves to the critical analysis of the monarchy, the despotism, and the church that preceded and surrounded them), the Creole elites of the newly independent and emerging countries devoted themselves to *emulating* European intellectuals and imagining that their local histories could be redressed by following the example of France and England and hiding colonialism – in which France and England were becoming more and more implicated – under the carpet. Republican and liberal ideas and ideals took the place of what did not happen: the critique of colonialism and the building of a decolonial project that would be neither republican nor liberal. This failure lasted almost one hundred and fifty years and shaped the socio-economic as well as intellectual history of "Latin" America, until dissenting social movements, particularly those led by Indigenous and Afro descendants – not impregnated with the republican, liberal, and socialist traditions – began to find the way that Creoles and then Latin Americans did not find after independence.

The second reason to tell this story is to dispel an illusion that you find today everywhere, among scholars and intellectuals based in Spanish- and Portuguese-speaking countries, in South America, and in the Caribbean, as well as among area studies scholars in the US and "Americanists" in Europe – the assumption that "Latin America" is a geographical entity where all these things "happened." My point here is, on the contrary, that the "idea of Latin" America twisted the past, on the one hand, and made it possible to frame the imperial/colonial period as proto-national histories, and, on the other, made it possible to "make" into "Latin America" historical events that occurred after the idea was invented and adapted. In this way, the Creole elite responsible for building nation-states according to the new dictates of the European idea of modernity needed to refashion their identity. As I have said, I am not writing here "about" Latin America in an "area studies" framework, but on how Latin America came about. As a result, the debates among republicans and liberals (the parties took many names, such as federalists and unitarians, federalists and centralists, conservatives and liberals) worked together with the search for a subcontinental identity. The "idea of Latin" America allowed the Creole elites to detach themselves from their Spanish and Portuguese past, embrace the ideology of France, and forget the legacies of their own critical consciousness. As a consequence, "Latin" American Creoles turned their backs on Indians and Blacks and their faces to France and England.

As is always the case, there were dissidents among Creole Latin Americans. Among these was the Chilean Francisco Bilbao. Dissidents like Bilbao were restricted by the need to work within the secular political framework defined by republicans and liberals. Karl Marx was unknown, and the ideas that Saint-Simon, the founder of French socialism, advanced at the beginning of the nineteenth century were not widely known. Bilbao, like the rest of his contemporaries, did not necessarily want to imitate France or England in his actions, but, rather, in his ways of thinking. Therein lies the underlying cause of one of the most radical mistakes made by post-colonial scholars and intellectuals – the attention given to the "thinking" rather than the "doing" and consequently to the local historical connection between doing and thinking. This is one of the main differences between the attitudes of Anglo Creoles in the US and Latin Creoles in the South. Latin Creoles set themselves in dependent relations (political, economic, and intellectual) with France, England, and Germany. Instead, early on in the US Thomas Jefferson concocted the idea of "the Western Hemisphere," precisely to establish the American difference with Europe. Creoles and Latin Americans could not or did not want to cut their subjective dependency on Europe; they needed Europe as Indians needed their past and Blacks needed Africa and the memories of suffering under slavery. For that reason, in defining their own terms and identities, Indians, Afro descendents in South America and the Caribbean, and Latinos/as in the US are doing what Creoles of European descent should have done two hundred years ago.

Bilbao was pointing in that direction, and he did succeed in bringing about a new epistemic perspective and making visible the geo-politics of knowledge grounded in local histories. He argued that colonial legacies in the New World needed analysis and solutions different from monarchic and despotic legacies in Europe. Of course, the local histories – that of the ex-colonies and that of post-Enlightenment Europe – were not independent of each other. They were linked by a clear structure of power, and the "idea" of Latin America was a consequence precisely of this imperial/colonial structure, which did not vanish after new nation-states came in sight. Independence, in all the Americas including the US, ended external colonialism and replaced it with internal colonialism. The Creole elite, in America and also in Haiti, sat in the driving seat from which Spaniards, Portuguese, French, and British were removed. "Dependency" did not vanish; it was simply restructured. This explains the distinction between "colonialism" and "coloniality." Colonialism has different historical and geographical locations. Coloniality is the underlying matrix of colonial power that was maintained, in the US and in South America and the Caribbean, after independence. The colonial matrix of power remained in place; it only changed hands.

The idea of "Latin" America belongs to a sphere of the colonial matrix of power that touches the question of knowledge and subjectivity – *knowledge* in the sense that a new world map was being drawn, and *subjectivity* because a new identity was emerging. At the crossroads of a dissenting new subjectivity and the remapping of the world order, Bilbao was critical of European, US, and Russian imperial ambitions and particularly focused on French advances in Mexico and France's efforts to control "Latin" America, since Spain was already out of the picture and England was concentrating on Asia and Africa. In 1856, in his *Iniciativa de la América*, Bilbao states:

Today we are witnessing empires that are trying to renew the old idea of global domination. The Russian Empire and the US are both entities located at geographic extremes, just as they are located at the political fringe. One aims at expanding Russian serfdom under the mask of pan-Slavism, and the other – the US – at expanding its dominion under the banner of Yankee individualism. Russia draws in its claws, waiting in ambush, but the US extends them more every day in that hunt that it has initiated against the South. We are already witnessing fragments of America falling into the Saxon jaws of the magnetizing boa constrictor that is unrolling its tortuous coils. Yesterday it was Texas, then the north of Mexico, and then the Pacific that offered their submission to a new master.[10]

Interestingly enough, in 1856 Bilbao felt that a second independence was needed – this time by "la raza latinoamericana" ("the Latin American race"), or by South America as a unit. In *La América en Peligro*, published in 1863, Bilbao confronted the imperial and global designs of the French civilizing mission, as well as its local version being trumpeted by "natives" such as the Argentinian Domingo Faustino Sarmiento. Bilbao understood, by then, that the civilizing ideals and the idea of progress as a march toward civilization were really sophisms hiding the fact that, in its triumphal march, civilization eliminated people from the surface of the earth and pushed backward the "dignity, prosperity and fraternity of independent nations." He underscored the civilizational fallacy behind France's invasion of Mexico, and he denounced its promoters in South America, like Sarmiento and the Argentinian jurist and politician Juan Bautista Alberdi. Bilbao already understood something that is still at work today: "Conservatives call themselves progressives . . . and make civilized calls for the extermination of the indigenous people."[11]

Bilbao was necessarily working and thinking within the liberal ideology that engendered the civilizing mission as a way to justify colonial expansion. But he was located at the receiving end and not at the giving end of the equation. Modern liberalism, in France and in Europe, emerged as a solution to the problems of Europe's own history, which was not, of course, a history of decolonization. As a critical liberal from the margins, Bilbao had to come up with his critique of the legacies of Spanish colonialism and the imperial moves of France and the US from the very same liberal ideology as was implemented by France and the US in their global designs. In his struggle, he revealed a discontinuity in the emerging colonial-liberal political philosophy, a disruption that came from the sheer fact that he had no choice but to engage in a version of liberalism without grounding, a liberalism out of place. Bilbao's discontinuity opens up a critical perspective with the potential to uncover the pervasive rearticulation of the coloniality of power in the nineteenth century through "Latinidad."

Reading Bilbao today reminds us that, for nineteenth-century intellectuals, statesmen, and politicians, "modernity" was cast in terms of civilization and progress. Some saw civilization and progress as the final destination for nation-builders who had liberated themselves from the Spanish and Portuguese Empires and whose literate culture was still cast in the Spanish and Portuguese languages. In the eighteenth century, Spanish and Portuguese were falling behind in the triumphal march of Western European civilization led by the French, German, and English languages. A major obstacle to reaching that goal was that civilization and progress radiated from the countries whose official languages were not Spanish and Portuguese. Decolonization in the US was indeed a continuation of what England had already began, and the English language was a support rather than an encumbrance. In Haiti, the language issue resulted in the adoption of Creole as the national language. Spanish and Portuguese were degraded from imperial hegemonic languages to subaltern imperial languages and superseded by French, German, and English. No one knew that the racialization of languages and knowledges was at stake (racialization, as we know, operates at many levels and not just in the color of your skin). Languages, and the instantiation of the hierarchy among them, were never outside the project of the civilizing mission and the idea of progress. As a matter of fact, languages were at the center of Christianization, the civilizing mission, and technology and development. Kichua/Kechua and Aymara speakers in South America, for example, would be twice removed and erased in the hierarchy of knowledge conceived in the Enlightenment. Language would be a constant barrier to "Latin" American intellectuals confronting the dilemma of wanting to be modern and, at the same time, realizing that they were consigned to the fringes of modernity, as the Mexican philosopher of history Leopoldo Zea clearly analyzed it in his classic book *The Role of America in History*.[12]

Bilbao, observing these changes in capitalist and liberal history from the margins of its margins, denounced not only French and US imperial designs, but the absolutism of Orthodox Russia as well. In other words, he was denouncing the imperial differences in global designs (France, US, Russia) while inhabiting the colonial difference: the historical location of South American countries gaining independence from Spain at the moment in which Spain was falling out of "modernity" and South America was experiencing the consequences. Bilbao also made visible what would be described in the late 1960s as "internal colonialism"[13] when he denounced Sarmiento as a defender of the civilizing mission and called the civilizing mission a new instrument of imperial expansion. He could already see the destructive complicity of the native elites (in this case Creoles of Spanish descent) in promoting imperial expansion and, thereby, enacting self-colonization.

The Fifth Side of the Ethno-Racial Pentagon: "Latins" in Southern Europe and in South America and the Caribbean

In South America and the Caribbean, "Latinidad" was a transnational identity uniting ex-Spanish and ex-Portuguese colonies that considered themselves the heirs of France. The French Caribbean was always marginal to "Latin" America, for several and different reasons. In Europe, "Latinidad" was a transnational identity uniting Southern countries that considered themselves the direct heirs of the Roman Empire, with a "Latin" ethos embedded in the Latin language and its vernacular offspring (French, Italian, Spanish, Portuguese). But in South America, "Latinidad" became curiously enough the fifth side of the global ethno-racial pentagon, far removed – indeed – from the Roman Empire. "Latin" America was certainly closer to a Roman colony than to Rome itself – "Latins" in the Americas were far removed from the Roman legacy that "Latins" in Europe rightly claimed for themselves. However, "Latins" in America bought into the illusion that Rome was their legacy and overlooked the three hundred years of colonialism that they were reproducing by doing so. It was not clear at that point that "Latinidad" in South America and the Caribbean would become the fifth side of the global ethno-racial pentagon, which Kant set up by linking people to continents and attributing to each continent a given color of its people. Kant suggested, in his anthropological views of human races, that Yellow people were in Asia, Black in Africa, Red in America, and White in Europe; and of course he attributed to Europeans – mainly French, English, and Germans – the superiority of reason, and the sense of the beautiful and the sublime.[14]

"Latins" in South America came in several colors and, for that reason, did not fit the racial mold of the nineteenth century. That legacy was carried over to the US when "Latinos/as" entered into its national ethno-racial pentagon (which I will address in chapter

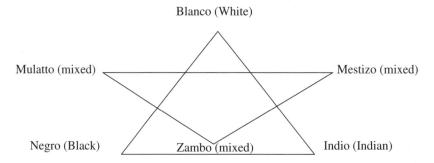

Although the racial classification by blood-mixture in seventeenth-century South America reached a numerical level that defied common sense, the basic categories are contained in this diagram. "Whites" in South America were Roman Catholics and spoke Latin (or Romance) languages; this classification was already being superseded by a "Whiteness" based on Protestantism and Anglo-Saxon languages. In the US the diagram was much simpler, reduced to White and Black. (adapted from Norman E. Whitten, Jr, and Diego Quiroga, "Ecuador," in Minority Rights Group, ed., *No Longer Invisible: Afro-Latin Americans Today*. London: Minority Rights Publications, 1995, 287–318)

3). "Latin" America, all of a sudden, became a new "racial" category defined not by blood or skin color but by marginal status (determined by a myriad of markers such as geographical location and language) in relation to Southern Europeans, and in the shadow of the fifth side of the ethno-racial pentagon. Being White "Latin" American (instead of Latin French, for instance) was not being White enough, as is made clear today when "White" Latin Americans migrate to the US. "Latinidad" associated with Whiteness, in South America, slightly remapped the colonial racial landscape. Whitten and Quiroga[15] draw a useful diagram (reproduced below) of the emergent racial spectrum in Ecuador that, mutatis mutandis, is valid at least for all the Spanish colonies.

In the nineteenth century, Whites were mainly Creoles, and so "Latins" of European descent. Racial formation in the viceroyalty of Nueva Granada, for example, between 1750 and 1810, had maintained the principles of "purity of blood" and introduced the color distinction instead of the strong religious configurations of Jews and Moors in Spain.[16] The key issue here was that while Jews and Moors

73

had the wrong religion, in the prevalent Christian conception, Indians (and Africans) had no religion.[17] Furthermore, peninsular Spanish and Creoles were both considered White but ranked according to their imperial or colonial belonging. Thus, mixture of blood was translated from belief to skin color. When Kant distributed people by color and continents, he was deriving the principle not from pure reason but well and truly from the Spanish colonial experience in the New World. While the Inquisition in Spain had "purity of blood" as a legal principle to control and separate Christians from Moors and Jews, and in the New World pursued the same goals, the local Creole elite translated the principle into a de facto social differentiation between Spanish Creoles on top, Mestizos/as and Mulattos/as in the next social group down, and Indios, Zambos, and Negroes at the bottom of the pyramid. *The colonial wound* is precisely the consequence of racial discourse. Frantz Fanon expressed the experience as "suffocation" and Gloria Anzaldúa called it an "open wound" ("la frontera es una herida abierta" – I will return to these issues in chapter 3).[18] The colonial wound in both appeared as a new location of knowledge, the shift toward the geo-politics and body politics of knowledge. (Latin) America has not yet healed the colonial wound and has not yet freed itself from "internal colonialism" and "imperial dependency."

The division of America into North and South also mirrored similar divisions within Europe, and France's articulation of "Latinidad" should be understood through its assumed position with regard to those divisions. Up to the time of Hegel's philosophy of history, Europe was basically the land of the "two races" (instead of "three religions," as it became known after the French Revolution): the "race" of the Gallo-Romans and the "race" of the Franks. More simply put, the tension was between Roman and Germanic cultures. But it was France that took the lead, to its own advantage, of course, in bridging the gap caused by "racial tension" between the Roman and the German "races" of Europe. In 1831, the French historian Jules Michelet stated that "Rome included in itself the opposing rights of two strange races, that is, the Etruscan and the Latin. France has been in its ancient legislation Germanic up to La Loire and Roman toward the South of this river. The French Revolution married together both elements in our Civil Society."[19]

74

Of course, we (you and I, dear reader) know that this is not necessarily a view most French intellectuals would promote today. But I would like to stay a little bit longer with this topic and see how remnants of the distinctions survive in discourses around European identity. Rémi Brague recently published a successful book that put forth a direct, and sometimes indirect, attempt to justify and solidify the place of France in the European Union.[20] Brague argues and defends the thesis that Europe is essentially Roman and that the borders (*alterités*) by which Europe defines itself can be summarized around the very concept of "Latinitée." Brague's thesis is the following: "Europe is not Greek only, and not only Hebrew, and not even Greco-Hebrew, but it is above all Roman. 'Athens and Jerusalem,' true, but also Rome . . . Three ingredients are necessary to come up with Europe: Rome, Greece, and Christianity."[21] Brague goes so far as to claim that there is indeed a "general Roman attitude" (remember what I was saying about the meaning of the "Baroque ethos" for Creoles claiming their own identity) that defines Europe's borders. Pursuing this argument, he attempts to show that Europe's connections with the Old Testament are a "Roman" link; that is, Christian and "Latin." By the same token, Europe can distinguish itself from the Muslim world. Brague makes a huge effort to convince his reader that Europe in its link with ancient Greece is also Roman/Latin and, therefore, different not only from Islam but also from the Byzantine world.

There is a temporal dimension to the Europe defined as "Romanité/Latinité," and it is what Brague calls the "Roman attitude." He believes that what Europe received from the Greeks and the Romans is the Greek and Roman attitude of improving upon what they took from the barbarians. He states:

The same dynamic nourishes European history. And this is what I define as the "Roman attitude" . . . The European colonial adventure, after the age of great discovery in Africa, for example, has been felt as a repetition of Roman colonization. There is a rich French historiography that draws a parallel between the colonization of the Maghrib by the ancient Romans and the more recent, French colonization . . . Colonization and European humanism after the Italian Renaissance:

will they not be linked as compensation for the sense of inferiority vis-à-vis the Greeks and the Jews? One could risk the following hypothesis. The European impulse toward conquest and colonization, since the Renaissance, perhaps has its strong motivation in the desire and the need to compensate, through the domination of people considered inferior, for [modern Europeans'] own inferiority complex in relation to antiquity, whicht humanists in the Renaissance were eager to rehearse . . . And, at the other end of the spectrum, the ending of the dominant role enjoyed by classical studies after World War II was simultaneous with the planetary movements of decolonization.[22]

While thinking about the meaning of the "Roman attitude," we should keep in mind the "colonial wound" among Indians and African slaves, among Latinos/as in the US, and among Creoles under Spanish colonial rule, as well as among leading "independent" nations under the intellectual and economic management of France and England. We have here a blueprint, a cognitive map, of Europe as Roman and Latin from the Renaissance to the end of World War II. Yet we can find an earlier version of the very same map as Brague uses in place and activated by the Creole elite who worked with the French to assert "Latinidad" in the Americas. In 1852, Juan Bautista Alberdi began his classic treatise *Bases y puntos de partida para la organización nacional* with the following statement:

> America has been discovered, conquered and populated by the civilized European races, who were carried forward by the same law as moved Egyptian people from their primitive land to bring them to Greece; later on, the same law moved the inhabitants of Greece to civilize the Italian peninsula; and finally the same law motivated the Greeks to civilize the barbarous inhabitants of Germany who were changed by the remains of the Roman world, the virility of its blood illuminated by Christianity.[23]

Alberdi, an intellectual leader of the Argentinian history of post-colonial nation-building, offers here a clear example of the reproduction – in the ex-colonies – of a genealogy of thought and subject formation that was "natural" to European history. European history and subject formation should not be confused with Eurocentrism, in the same way as race, in the sense of ethnicity, should not be confused with racism. Eurocentrism only arises when the particular history of Europe (and, in the second half of the twentieth century, of the US) and its concomitant subject formation are promoted and enforced as a universal model, and are accepted and promoted by colonial subjects embracing a model of being what they are not. The coloniality of being operates by conversion (to the ideals of Christianity, to civilization and progress, to modernization and development, to Western democracy and the market) or by adaptation and assimilation (the willingness of the native elites in the colonies to embrace imperial designs and values leading to colonial subject formation). That is, it means accepting dwelling in the coloniality of being by narcotizing the colonial wound, ignoring it with all sorts of painkillers. Let's suspend this scenario for a moment, and go back to the first half of the nineteenth century when such an idea of "Latin" America became thinkable.

It was, in fact, a little-known French intellectual, Michel Chevalier, a follower of Michelet, who contributed to the imprinting of "Latinidad" on the Spanish Americas. Chevalier, who was born in Limoges in 1806, went to the US in 1833 and remained there until 1835. He ended his trip by visiting Mexico and Cuba. In 1836, Chevalier published two volumes of letters he had written during his period in the US, titled *Lettres sur l'Amérique du Nord*. There is a lot to be said about how Chevalier foretells the future, one or two centuries after his own day; but I will limit myself to his observations and prognostications about the Americas. For Chevalier, as for Michelet, "our Europe" had a double origin as Latin (Roman) Europe and Teutonic (German) Europe, with the former being comprised of the countries and people of the Midi and the second made up of the continental countries and people of the North, including England. Latin Europe is Catholic, Teutonic Europe is Protestant. In mapping that distinction onto America, Chevalier stated: "The two branches, Latin and German, reproduced themselves in the New World. South America is, like Meridian Europe, Catholic and Latin. North America belongs to a population that is

Protestant and Anglo-Saxon."[24] It's not surprising that Chevalier talks about Anglo Americans and Spanish Americans, given that both Bolívar's vision of a "Confederation of Spanish American Nations" and Jefferson's idea of a Western Hemisphere had been advanced by that time. But Chevalier's vision for Spanish America is not very encouraging:

> The republican principle has produced the US, although the same principle has generated also those miserable republics of Spanish America. . . . Apparently the Anglo Americans will be appointed to continue, directly and without foreign intervention, the progress that the civilization to which we belong has accomplished since it [the civilization] abandoned the Orient, its cradle. . . . meanwhile, the Spanish American seems to be nothing other than an impotent race without future, unless it receives a wave of rich and new blood coming from the North, or from the East.[25]

There is a very interesting geo-political imaginary unfolding here, since "East" in the last line does not refer to the Orient. Let's follow up a little bit further. Chevalier was one of the ideologues of the ascending bourgeoisie and the new European political economy. He taught an introductory course on political economy at the Collège de France between 1842 and 1850. His geo-political concerns were not romantic imaginations of the New World order. The Roman and German division of Europe was no longer a question. The problem he saw in front of him, instead, was how the nineteenth century would be marked by the confrontation between the two greatest civilizations in history, the Orient and the Occident. And in that confrontation, he was particularly concerned with the role that France and countries of "Latin seed" would play. He was also aware of the emergence of the "Slav Race" as a third group that was beginning to encroach on "our Europe," meaning the Europe of Latin and Anglo-Saxon peoples. He knew the Anglo-Saxon and Slavic countries were dealing with the Orient, with Asia, and he worried that Latin countries were losing that contest. Chevalier foresaw, then, that the bridge between the East and the West would be America. He said:

Mexico and South America are filled with new branches growing up from the roots of Western civilization on both sides, the side that looks toward Asia and the side that looks toward ourselves. The US will soon extend itself from one ocean to the other . . . Thus it is clear from this point of view that America is located between the two civilizations and therefore it has a privileged destiny.[26]

France's articulation of "Latinidad" and cultural imperialism takes on the clear function of maintaining a presence in this area of "privileged destiny." Chevalier made this clear when he wrote: "France is the trustee of the destinies of all of the Latin nations on the two continents. It alone can prevent the swallowing of this entire family of peoples by the twin encroachment of the Germans or Saxons or by the Slavs."[27]

If France was responsible for "Latinidad" on both continents it was because Spain had been completely marginalized. As Leopoldo Zea observed,[28] after the eighteenth century Spain and Russia came to occupy, for different reasons, positions at the margins of the West, geographically and geo-politically. Spain (and the Iberian peninsula) was the territory of Catholic Christians, and Russia was Orthodox, while Protestant Christians were in the process of taking leadership in this particular stage of global coloniality.

It has been recently argued[29] that at the "origin" of the idea of "Latinidad" was the result of another, related historical event in South America: the incidents, tensions, and conflicts surrounding Panama in 1850. Rather than a frontier dispute, the problem was about controlling the place of encounter and crossing between the Atlantic and the Pacific, as an advance announcement of the 1898 Spanish–American War. The incidents and conflicts in Panama illuminated tensions between two opposing forces that, in the terminology of the time, were named "the Anglo-Saxon race" and the "Latin race." The Colombian writer and diplomat José María Torres Caicedo, living in Paris, was not alien to the Panama incidents and made his voice heard on several occasions. This crucial moment, the continental conflicts around 1850, was the moment in which Bolívar's dream of the "Confederation of Spanish American Nations" began to be translated into "Latin America" in the sense of the domain of the "Latin race." Aims McGuinness revisits the reproduction, in the Americas, of the division in Europe between the North and the South, and states:

> Torres Caicedo's articulation of the antagonism between "America del Norte" and "America del Sud" also reliedon the opposition between the "Saxon race" and the "Latin race" that owed more to theories of race circulating in the 1850's than to Bolivar and included notions of pan-Latin racial unity similar to those advanced in France by Saint-Simonians such as Michel Chevalier. By the mid-1850s . . . Chevalier had developed a vision of pan-Latin diplomacy that pitted the Latin nations of Europe (including Belgium, Spain and Portugal, and led of course by France) against the Germanic or Anglo-Saxon peoples of northern Europe and the Slavic nations of Eastern Europe. A similar opposition between the Latin and Anglo-Saxon "races" found its expression in Torres Caicedo's 1856 poem "Las dos Américas" . . .

> > The race of Latin America
> > finds itself confronted by the Saxon Race
> > Mortal enemy who now threatens
> > To destroy its liberty and its banner[30]

McGuinness's conclusion allows for a summary of my argument on the reorganization of the logic of coloniality and the redistribution of the world among changes of imperial leadership. The distinctions between the North and South of Europe and the North and South of America were not simply "cultural" differences. They masked the colonial power differential that was translated from its construction in Europe and imposed on the Americas. It is precisely the differential of power that permits us to see that what are more generally understood as "cultural differences" are indeed "imperial" and "colonial" differences that have been dictated by leading imperial designers. It was in France, Germany, and England that the distinction between the South and North of Europe was imagined (imperial difference). And it was in Spain and Portugal, first, and in England, France, and Germany, later, that the differences between

80

Europe and the two Americas were defined, described, and implemented (colonial difference). Imperial and colonial differences work
under the same logic: the devaluation of the human conditions of
those targeted to be dominated, exploited, controlled – the *objects
of the differences*. On the other hand, the differences are established
by the *subject of the differences* – the authority of the imperial voice
over lesser imperial voices and, above all, over colonial voices.

The differentiation between Europe and the Americas, on the
one hand, and between North and South America, on the other,
was not only spatial but temporal as well. The French Enlightenment
promoted the idea of a young and immature New World that would
have been totally alien to Spanish missionaries and men of letters
in the sixteenth and seventeenth centuries. The "barbarians" who in
the sixteenth century were located in space became the "primitives"
in time. From here to the idea of Latin America as an underdeveloped subcontinent, there is just one step and a change of global
designs: from British civilizing to the US developing and marketing
mission. Hegel is, once again, behind such assumptions. He had a
tantalizing capacity to convert what borders on nonsense into a
serious proposition:

> The World is divided into Old and New; the name of New
> having originated in the fact that America and Australia have
> only lately become known to us. But these parts of the world
> are not only relatively new, but intrinsically so in respect of
> their entire physical and psychical constitution . . . I will not
> deny the New World the honor of having emerged from the
> sea at the world's formation contemporaneously with the old:
> yet the Archipelago between South America and Asia shows *a
> physical immaturity* . . . New Holland shows a not less immature
> geographical character; for in penetrating from the settlements
> of the English farther into the country, we discover immense
> streams, which have not yet developed themselves to such a
> degree as to dig a channel for themselves; but lose themselves
> in marshes.[31]

I have the impression that if one speaks from the perspective of
the empire, even to criticize it, one can demonstrate that nature in

certain parts of the world is younger than others or that there are weapons of mass destruction even if one cannot find them. The changes in the idea of "nature" paralleled the changes in the ideas of continental divides and world order. When development replaced the civilizing mission as a project of the developed countries, the Third World was (and still is) equated with "nature"; that is, not with the "industries" and "sciences" of progress that put the First World ahead in the temporal imagination. If, in the sixteenth century, "nature" was conceived in terms of lands and territories to be mapped or as the spectacle of the world through which its Maker could be known, from the beginning of the nineteenth century "nature" became the fuel, the raw material, for the Industrial Revolution and the forward-moving engine of progress and capital accumulation. This transformation put a premium on the already-existing continental division, and "nature" became increasingly associated with South America, Africa, and Asia. Thus, the idea of "Latin" America was coetaneous with the increasing value of South America as "nature" and the increasing value of Europe's new imperial countries as the sources of "culture" (the university, the state, philosophy, science, industry, and technology).

Colonialism, The Missing Ideology of Modernity, and "Latin" America: The Reconfiguring of the Logic of Coloniality

To understand the intricate web in which differences are transformed into values, and the colonial matrix of power naturalized and disguised under the triumphal project of modernity, let's look more closely at the rhetoric of modernity and its darker side. Sociologist Immanuel Wallerstein has suggested that the "modern world system" did not have its own imaginary (i.e., a series of ideas giving it conceptual coherence) until after the French Revolution. He describes that imaginary as relying on the emergent configuration of three competing, and at the same time complementary, ideologies: conservatism, liberalism, and socialism. Looking from the empire to the colonies, or from the march of modernity toward the rest of the word, the three ideologies seem adequate.[32] Looking from the colonies to the empire, or at the invasive march of modernity into the rest of the world, it is clear that the full story cannot be rendered within these three Enlightened European ideologies alone. There is one important ideology missing that is crucial for an understanding of the "idea" of Latin America and that dates back to the sixteenth century: colonialism. The display of the four ideologies of the modern/colonial world together makes visible the rift between the former three and the latter, which is important to an understanding of how they function in the geo-politics (modernity/coloniality) of knowledge, rather than simply in the internal history of Western political theory and its underlying epistemology.

From the internal history of Western political theory and epistemology, colonialism is a mere derivative, an unpleasant process that leads to a better world. Colonialism is, precisely, what remained hidden and unnamed, covered by the three acceptable ideologies and the visible face of the empire, which itself hid the colonies and made them marginal in time and space. Colonialism as the fourth ideology is a vital distinction to make if we are to comprehend European imperialism since the sixteenth century and US imperialism after World War II. Colonialism (and I am referring here to the particular forms that emerged in the modern/colonial world and not, for instance, in previous Roman or Inca "colonies") refers to the result of imperial actions that have capitalism as the principle and foundation of "modes of social life and organization." That is, imperialism/colonialism are one and the same, like modernity/coloniality, insofar as they are linked with mercantilism, free trade, and the industrial economy. Imperialism/colonialism characterizes specific moments in history (like the Spanish, the British, or the Russian imperial/colonial empires), while modernity/coloniality points toward a set of principles and beliefs in which certain imperial/colonial empires are framed.[33] Colonialism is the historically concrete complement of imperialism in its diverse geo-historical manifestations, just as coloniality is the logical complement of modernity in its general principles. Colonialism as ideology is implemented by *coloniality* as the logic of domination.

"Colonialism" as the hidden ideology has two aspects that distinguish it from the three visible ones. First, it is an ideology that nobody wants to promote and everyone claims to want to end.

83

Colonialism is the shameful member of the family – it's always there, people know about it, but they prefer not to mention it, like talking about money with an aristocratic family. As such, colonialism is not a project of which imperial leaders and global designers could be proud – and they openly declared themselves against it. The explicit projects are described in positive terms, like civilization, development, or democracy, but not as colonization, even if colonization is the necessary step to "bring" Good to deserving and wanting people. "Civilization," "development," "modernization," and "socialism," for instance, are all projects that conservatives, liberals, and Marxists are eager to promote and carry to distant places – but not colonialism! (Recent situations such as the post-9/11 period, when even good liberals accepted colonialism as a necessity of US foreign policy, may be exceptions to that observation.) Colonization, in that view, is something that cannot be avoided if you want to "bring" prosperity, democracy, and freedom to the world. Eurocentrism could be defined precisely in those terms – a view of history in which modernity is there to supersede traditions and colonialism is a means to a better end.

Second, in that forward movement of modernity, colonialism works to cover up its own ideological trail by erasing and displacing that which differs from the ideal or opposes the march of modernity. Thus, modernity can be defined and conceived, in terms of "reason, progress, political democracy, science, commodity production, new conceptions of time and space and rapid changes,"[34] without acknowledging the erasure of both what preceded a given moment within the logic of modernity (that is, the colonization of time – Middle Ages, early modern period, modern period, postmodern period, etc.) and what differed from a given moment outside the logic of modernity. Fanon in the 1960s said it very clearly in a way that is still valid today for the new form of neo-liberal colonialism:

> *colonialism* is not simply content to impose its rule upon the present and the future of a dominated country. *Colonialism* is not satisfied merely with holding a people in its grip and emptying the native's brain of all form and content. By *a kind of perverse logic*, it turns to the past of the oppressed people, and distorts, disfigures and destroys it.[35]

The Aztec and Inca Empires, before the Indias Occidentales and co-existing with them for a short period, came under the erasure of the imperial, noble mission. Colonialism – the hidden ideology of Christianity in the sixteenth and seventeenth centuries, and the fourth secular ideology – allows us to conceive of modernity in terms of its irrationality, its disruption and fractures of other forms of life (e.g., look at the current situation in sub-Saharan Africa and in Latin America), and its totalitarian tendencies based on the myth of rationality and on the time/space/nature configuration that modernity dismembered and destroyed (and continues to destroy) in the name of industrialism and technology. Of course, Indians in the Americas, slaves from Africa, and later on people in Africa and Asia met the "arrival" of modernity with a wide spectrum of reactions that went all the way from the opportunity to jump on the bandwagon of modernization to the painful process of decolonization. For either of those perspectives, "modernization" was something "coming from" elsewhere and not something that "was" in their own past. The simple difference was how global designs were received – not conceived – by people imbued with other histories and speaking different languages.

It was to colonialism as ideology and practice and to the underlying logic of coloniality that the first wave of decolonization in the Americas responded. All the "revolutions" of this wave were in the paradigm of co-existence rather than in the paradigm of newness (as I explained in the preface). US independence (called the American Revolution) in 1776, the rebellions in what was then part of Peru (now in Bolivia) led by Tomas Katari and Túpac Amaru (1780–1), the Haitian Revolution in 1804, and the first set of Hispano and Luso American independences between 1810 and 1830 were all responses to "colonialism," as the imperial ideology projected toward the colonies. Decolonization at this point, as well as in the second wave post-World War II, meant political and, in a less clear way, economic decolonization – but not epistemic. The theological and secular frames of mind in which political theory and political economy had been historically grounded were never questioned. This is precisely the crucial difference between older forms of decolonization and the struggles since Césaire and Fanon and more explicitly since the 1990s. Now decolonization of knowledge and subjectivity, through the imagination of alternatives to capitalism and alternatives to the modern state and its reliance on military power, and through the creation of new ideologies other than the four mentioned, is taking place. Yet all the "successful" movements of decolonization in the Americas were in the hands of Creoles of Spanish, Portuguese, English, and African descent, and it was not on their horizon to imagine ways of thinking beyond what the European tradition offered them. Colonialism should have been the key ideology targeted by decolonial projects. However, in the first wave of so-called decolonization, colonialism as ideology was not dismantled, as the goal was to gain ostensible independence from the empire. There was a change of hands as Creoles became the state and economic elite, but *the logic of coloniality* remained in place.

The only social movement initiated by the natives (the Indians) "failed" in terms of pushing the colonizer out of the territory. As a matter of fact, Indians in the viceroyalty of Peru had a double force to fight against: the Creoles and the Spanish imperial administration, which, although decadent, was still in place. In the hypothetical case that Túpac Amaru had come to power, most likely there wouldn't be a "Latin" America today. The Haitian Revolution offered also the possibility of an epistemic delinking but instead was reduced to silence, as Michel Rolph-Trouillot has convincingly argued.[36] When Chevalier was writing that France was responsible for all the nations of the Latin group in both continents, Haiti was not in his mind. Haiti belonged to "Africanidad," not to "Latinidad"! Strangely (or not), Haiti never clearly counted as part of "Latin" America. "Latins" were supposed to be not Black but White Creoles or, at most, Mestizos/as or perhaps Mulattos/as in blood but Europeans in mind.

To conceive of themselves as a "Latin" race (as Torres Caicedo put it), Creoles in "Latin" America had to rearticulate the colonial difference in a new format: to become the internal colonizers vis-à-vis the Indians and Blacks while living an illusion of independence from the logic of coloniality. Internal colonialism was indeed a trademark of the Americas after independence and was directly linked to nation-state building. Nation-states in the colonies were not a manifestation of modernity leaving colonialism behind. The roads of (and not toward) modernity/coloniality in the Americas, followed in one instance by US independence and in another by the former Spanish/Portuguese colonies, differ both among themselves and also, considerably, from the road of modernity/coloniality that brought about the Haitian Revolution. In all three cases, however, coloniality was reinscribed almost immediately in the internal colonialism enacted by nation-states emerging from decolonization. While US independence also led to internal colonialism, the novelty here is that the US became at once a postcolonial country, a country with imperial ambitions, and a country anchored in internal colonialism. The imperial ambitions, inherited from the mother country, mark one specific difference between the US and South America and the Caribbean in the subsequent reorganization of the global order during the nineteenth century.

In Europe, racial differences did not function as internal colonialism. Modern nation-states in Europe, after all, did not arise with imperial independence and political decolonization as a goal. Their point of origin was, instead, a struggle for the emancipation of a new social class, the bourgeoisie, and not a colonial second-class population. In Europe, internal colonialism could be used as a metaphor for class exploitation linked to the Industrial Revolution, but the historical conditions of inequality were quite distinct from the ones in the Americas: the European bourgeoisie did not decolonize itself by its emancipation from monarchic and despotic regimes, similar to the decolonizing struggles by Blacks in Haiti. The rise of the bourgeoisie paralleled the broadening reach of the Industrial Revolution and the constitution and control of the state. The control of the economy and the state by a new social class had generated a new oppressed stratum of the population (the proletariat); but racism was not part of the problem. Class differences, not racial ones, shaped the European political scene. The proletariat as the identity of a social class was defined by conditions of labor and capital rather than by racial classification, which came into its full force as a consequence of the transformation of the exploitation of labor in the colonies. There is no doubt that a class distinction is embedded in racial classification and internal colonialism in the Americas, but the principle of classification is not based on a social class formed out of a group of workers employed in the industries emerging from the Industrial Revolution. It hinges, instead, on a social stratification that emerged from colonialism. Of course, the social classification was not "naturally embedded" in the group of differentiated people; it was – rather – an epistemic classification foundational for the establishment of the modern/colonial world.[37] This is precisely how the colonial matrix of power is "glued" together by racism, by the discourse that demonizes entire populations by portraying them as inferior human beings, if human at all.

Jamaican philosopher Lewis Gordon summarized the divergence between the historical logic of modernity/coloniality as experienced in Europe and that of modernity/coloniality in the Americas. For Gordon, class is so *indigenous* to Europe that it emerges even in European efforts toward socialism. One can "feel" class in Europe as the air that one breathes, observes Gordon, looking at Europe from his subjective understanding and personal location in a Caribbean history rooted in slavery, racism, and European colonialism. In the Americas, Gordon continues, race became an endemic motif of New World consciousness, and that is why one can "feel" race here in the same way as in Europe one can "feel" class.[38] However, the issue is not to dwell on that distinction, but to be attentive to the consequences of it. These are crucial to understanding that, today, the "idea" of Latin America is being refurbished against the very backdrop of the modern/colonial world. Gordon observes that:

> The agony experienced globally, then, is not simply one of intensified class division but also one of an asserted New World consciousness on those not indigenous to it . . .
>
> Something new is being formed. Just as a new oppressive relation emerged when Europe expanded westward (and subsequently, eastward), so, too, are new oppressive relations emerging as the New West goes global. Is it racism? Classism? Sexism? In my view, it is none of these uniquely, but instead *a pervasive ethos against humanistic solutions* to any of them. In short, it is the ethos of counter-revolution and anti-utopia.[39]

The quotation encapsulates the predominant ethos of the modern/colonial world, from the sixteenth to the twenty-first centuries. The "idea" of Latin America, in the nineteenth century, was forged in the movement of imperial institutions for the control of meaning and of money, supported by a Creole elite eager to cut the umbilical cord to Spain and Portugal, and join the club of emerging empires. However, while class division was shaping the life and institutions of Europeans, racism continued to shape the life and institutions in the colonies – and not only the new colonies of France and England but also the new, apparently independent nations in the process of identifying themselves as "Latin" American nation-states.

The Many Faces of "Latinidad"

In summary, "Latinidad" is the consequence of imperial and colonial conflicts in the nineteenth century and the way in which the imperial and colonial differences have been constructed. While in Europe "Latinidad" allowed French politicians and intellectuals to establish the imperial difference with the competing forces of the Anglo-Saxon world in Europe (England and Germany), in South America the idea of "Latinidad" was useful to Spanish Creole intellectuals and politicians defining themselves in confrontation with the competing force of the Anglo-Saxon world in the Americas – the US. However, "Latin" America came into the new world order as a subaltern historico-political and cultural configuration. In other words, the colonial difference that ideologues of the Spanish Empire constructed to justify the colonization of America (e.g., the inferiority of the Indians and the non-humanity of the African slaves) was maintained and intensified by the ideologues of the new, independent republics. Thus, the colonial difference was reproduced, after the independent republics' formation, in the "internal" colonial difference. "Latinidad" contributed to disguise the internal colonial difference under a historical and cultural identity that apparently included all while, in reality, producing an effect of totality that silenced the excluded. "Latinidad" produced a new type of invisibility for Indians and for people of African descent in "Latin" America.

"Latinidad" worked to define the identity of a community of Creole/Mestizo/a elites and, later on, the people descended from the European immigrants who began to arrive in South America in the second half of the nineteenth century. The ethos of

"Latinidad" encouraged European immigration. It was one of the measures to promote progress and civilization and, indirectly, Whiten the nation-states. New economies developed in the South as the need for crops and meat complemented the exploitation of the tropical plantations that, no longer in the hands of Dutch, British, or French colonizers, were now in the hands of a Creole elite, who transformed "colonial exploitation" into "modern exportation." Since the second half of the nineteenth century, "Latin" American countries have continued a consistent descent in the world economy in relation to Europe and the United States.

The last decade of the nineteenth century was a turning point for world history even though the events of this decade took place in the "periphery" (Spain, Latin America, the US, and Japan), and remain still on the margins of the triumphal history of modernity from the French to the Russian Revolutions and to the different manifestations of totalitarianism in Europe. During that decade, Spain lost its last colonies in the Caribbean and the Pacific (the Philippines) and the US started its imperial march after the defeat of Spain in the Spanish-American War of 1898, while Japan also initiated imperial control of China in 1895. "Latin" America slid down one more step, in relation to the world order around 1900, not only economically but in the North Atlantic imaginary. That is, "Latin" America became darker and darker in relation to the increasing discourse of White supremacy that was implemented during the last decade of the nineteenth century in the US by the ideologues of the Spanish-American War. In parallel fashion to the way Spaniards were seen by Northern Europeans (as darker skinned and mixed with Moorish blood), "Latin" America began to be perceived more and more as "Mestizo/a"; that is, darker skinned. And although "Latin" American Creoles and elite Mestizos/as considered themselves White, particularly in relation to the Indian and Afro population as well as to the Mulattos/as and Cholos/as (Mestizos/as perceived, by ethnicity or class, as closer to the Indians), from the perspective of Northern Europe and the US, to be "Latin" American was still to be not White enough. This was the waiting room for the next step, to come after World War II: "Latin" America became part of the Third World, and the Indian and the Afro population remained invisible.

However, also in the last decade of the nineteenth century, José Martí, a Cuban writer, activist, and ideologue who lived a significant portion of his life in New York, launched a new and more open version of "Latinidad" with his famous political proclamation "Nuestra América." Martí's program turned its back on Caicedo's and Alberdi's project and on France and Greece as the emblems of European historical foundation, and turned toward Mesoamerican civilizations (Maya, Inca, Aztec) as the emblems of "Nuestra América"'s historical foundations. After Martí, and after the Peruvian intellectual and political leader José Carlos Mariátegui in the 1920s, the idea of Latin America underwent a radical change in the 1960s through both the philosophy of liberation and dependency theory as elaborated by philosopher Enrique Dussel. Also in the 1960s, Fanon's description of colonialism, quoted above, changed the terms of the conversations in which French imperial designs had shaped the idea of "Latinidad." The idea of "Latin" America that emerged during the Cold War and from the historical perspective of coloniality radically unlinked itself from the French idea of "Latinidad."

Today, "Latin America is in effervescence," as *Manière de voir/Le Monde diplomatique* proudly announced in Paris in the summer of 2003. And indeed it is. In the last decade, major transformations have taken place. Aymara activist and intellectual Victor Hugo Cárdenas was appointed vice-president of Bolivia in August 1993. Though they do not completely share Cárdenas's politics, Felipe Quispe Huanca and Evo Morales, as intellectuals and leaders of Indigenous social movements, have climbed through the institutional aperture that the vice-presidency opened. "All of them Aymaras, but so different" is the title of Xavier Albó's political analysis of the parts played by Cárdenas, Morales, and Quispe Huanca in the transformation of the Bolivian state and society in recent decades. The leading role and the perspective on the future that we see in the Indian social movements in Bolivia is mirrored in Ecuador. The intellectual and activist leadership of Nina Pacari (currently the minister of foreign relations) and Luis Alberto Macas (recently reappointed president of the Confederación de Nacionalidades Indígenas del Ecuador, and ex-minister of agriculture and president of the newly formed Amawtay Wasi, or Universidad Intercultural de las Nacionalidades y Pueblos Indígenas), plus the significant number of Indian members in the

Congress and the presence of Indian administrations in more than thirty cities in Ecuador, all clearly show that although formal government is in the hands of pro-neo-liberals, the state is no longer the indisputable domain of the "White/Mestizo/a" elite.

No less significant have been the emergence of Afro social movements, and their presence is giving new meaning to something that we (in Latin America, the US, or Europe) always knew was part of Latin America. From the Andes to Mexico, and from Argentina to the Caribbean, Afro rhythms have always been beating and continue to beat (and they have come to be known all over the world as 'Latin American music'). We (the same as above) also always knew that from the north of Brazil and the northeast of Colombia and in all the Caribbean Islands, "exotic" religious practices (Candomblé, Santería, Voodoo, Rastafarianism) were practiced and disrupted the application of Christianity. Afro religious practices that "absorbed" Christianity and turned it into something that Christians could not recognize, and often reject or fear, have not, like music, been subsumed under "Latinidad" since, as we have seen, Christianity and "Latinidad" are two sides of the same coin. How then could one (in "Latin" America or Europe or the US) not take seriously the fact that Afro religious practices are key elements both for resistance to oppression and for creative survival? Not every Christian speaks Latin, but the foundation of Christianity in the modern world is "Latin." As Derrida reminded us, "We all speak Latin," and he claimed a "global Latinization." While many in Europe and in South America will look at such a claim with enthusiasm, I suspect that it will awaken less enthusiasm among Indigenous, Afro-Andean, and Afro-Caribbean critical consciousnesses. After all, it was global Latinization from the sixteenth century on that repressed the contribution that Indians and Afros were making to the globalization of the Atlantic economy. Felipe Quispe Huanca, Rigoberta Menchú, and Bob Marley – to give some examples – may not agree with Jacques Derrida on this point.

As if the examples in the previous paragraphs were not enough to show the *point of no return*, epistemic as well as political, being enacted by the Indians and Afros, the democratic victory of Ignacio Lula da Silva in Brazil adds to the radical scope of current transformations. He is leading the way and showing the possibility of a new path toward the future conduct of the state. And this case is indeed quite important in the history of "Latin" America, since Brazil has been, since the time of Simón Bolívar and the wars of independence, a stepchild in a "Latin" America whose image was more "Spanish" than "Portuguese." Furthermore, Lula da Silva is not only showing his "Spanish" American partners the possible paths toward the future; he is doing the same with the European and Latin American "Marxists" who have enormous difficulties articulating race and class in the history of ex-colonial countries. He is on his way to making obsolete any postmodern debate, in Europe, about making Lenin useful again for the future of the humanity. Nestor Kirchner in Argentina has also taken a significant dissenting step forward to show, with Lula da Silva, that there are avenues of social organization and politics that are not necessarily those dictated by the IMF, the World Bank, or the European states of the G8 that claim the rights of their imperial pasts. Lula de Silva seems to be thinking from the very colonial history of Brazil and of the Americas, rather than from manuals based on the modern history of Europe and the Industrial Revolution. As the Indian and Afro intellectuals and leaders have shown, it makes more sense to think from the fractures of colonial history and the colonial differential of power than from the history that sociological and economic manuals telling the "truth" about the world promote. And if Lula da Silva is not enough supporting "data" for a radical transformation, the World Social Forum, whose past three meetings took place in Porto Alegre (a city controlled by the PT, Lula's Working Party), has contributed to seeing "Latin" America not by reflecting on its underbelly and its position as the victim under Uncle's Tom cabin, but as the location of a shared world leadership working "toward an-other globalization."[40] Lula da Silva's preliminary conversations about constituting a G3 economic bloc (Brazil, South Africa, and India) will move these countries toward a proactive role in "an-other globalization" instead of the subaltern role that about a hundred and ninety countries in the world seem ready to accept.

While "Latin" America remains a comfortable name that functions at the level of the control of land, of labor, and of authority, in the spheres of the colonial matrix of power, at the level of subjectivity and knowledge, the legacies of European colonialism in

South America are being challenged and displaced by Indian and Afro legacies disputing languages, knowledges, religions, memories. In the US, the parallel struggle is being delivered by Latinos/as in both theoretical and artistic production. While at the level of the state – in South America and the Caribbean – economic and political control remain in the hands of Creoles, the possibility of transforming the state by an open dialogue with the sectors of society that have been marginalized because of race, gender, and sexuality is today opening up in new ways. Ecuador is a case in point. Other changes, however, are also revealing that "Latin" political projects (liberal, neo-liberal, and socialist) are not in a one-to-one relationship with the ontology of the subcontinent, as we will see in the next chapter. When the relation between the name and the subcontinent is called into question, the political projects that brought "Latin" America into being have to co-exist with political projects originating among the silenced population, who do not see themselves as they have been constructed and do not care to belong to the "Latin" ethos.

3

After "Latin" America: The Colonial Wound and the Epistemic Geo-/Body-Political Shift

The U.S.–Mexican border *es una herida abierta* where the Third World grates against the first and bleeds.

Gloria Anzaldúa, *Borderlands/La Frontera*, 1987

How to articulate "interculturalidad" within the limits of epistemology and of the production of knowledge? How to contribute to the adventure for human knowledge from new sources? ...

Runa Yachaikuna: Cycle of Indigenous Sciences. This cycle has as objective the socialization of indigenous knowledge, so students can re-affirm their identities and strengthen their self-confidence; that is, for learning to be.

Luis Macas, Amawtay Wasi (Universidad Intercultural de las Nacionalidades y Pueblos Indígenas), *Boletin ICCC-RIMAI*, 2/19, 2000

Accounts of the present state of radical political thought are still embedded in a Western episteme that revolves around two historical events, the 1789 French Revolution and the 1917 French Revolution. Even those who proclaim the death of

Eurocentrism still survey radical thought within these two historical exemplars.

Anthony Bogues, *Black Heretics, Black Prophets: Radical Political Intellectuals*, 2003

"Latin" America from Above: A Convenience Store

The global idea of "Latin" America being deployed by imperial states today (the US and the imperial countries of the European Union) is of a vast territory and a resource of cheap labor, full natural resources, exotic tourism, and fantastic Caribbean beaches waiting to be visited, invested in, and exploited. These images developed during the Cold War when "Latin" America became part of the Third World and a top destination for neo-liberal projects, beginning in Chile under General Augusto Pinochet (1973) and followed up by Juan Carlos Menem in Argentina (1989) and Sánchez Gonzálo de Losada (1993) in Bolivia. Thus, for example, today many of the major technological corporations are shifting production to Argentina (post-crash) where they can hire technicians for around ten thousand dollars a year while the US salary plus benefits, for the same type of job, could be as high as fifty or sixty thousand dollars a year.

The section on "Latin America" in the CIA's report *Global Trends 2015* relies on the same "idea of Latin" America, which originated in the imperial designs of nineteenth-century French ideologues in complicity with Creole elites. The CIA forecasts that:

by 2015, many Latin American countries will enjoy greater prosperity as a result of expanding hemispheric and global economic links, the information revolution, and lowered birthrates. Progress in building democratic institutions will reinforce reforms and promote prosperity by enhancing investing confidence. Brazil and Mexico will be increasingly confident and capable actors that will seek a greater voice in hemispheric affairs. But the region will remain vulnerable to financial crises because of its dependence on external finance and the continuing role of single commodities in most economies. The weakest countries in the region, especially in the Andean region, will fall further behind. Reversals of democracy in some countries will be spurred by a failure to deal effectively with popular demands, crime, corruption, drug trafficking, and insurgencies. Latin America – especially Venezuela, Mexico and Brazil – will become an increasingly important oil producer by 2015 and an important component of the emerging Atlantic Basin energy system. Its proven oil reserves are second only to those located in the Middle East.[1]

However, from the perspective of many who are being looked at and spoken at (not to), things look a little bit different. The CIA's report cites many experts *on* Latin America but not one person *in* Latin America who is critical of the neo-liberal invasion to the South. For instance, the articles published by Alai-Amlatina, written in Spanish in the independent news media, do not "exist" for a world in which what exists is written in English. That is part of the "reality" of the "idea" of Latin America. The story is never fully told because "developments" projected from above are apparently sufficient to pave the way toward the future. "Expertise" and the experience of being trained as an "expert" overrule the "living experience" and the "needs" of communities that might subsume technology to their ways of life, and not transform those ways of life to accord with capitalist requirements, using technology as a new colonizing tool. The blindness of the CIA's experts, and their reluctance to work with people instead of strolling over expecting everyone to act according to their script, have led a myriad of social movements to respond – a blatant example of the double-sided double-density of modernity/coloniality. It is increasingly difficult for the CIA and other institutions controlling and managing knowledge and information to silence them. The key issue here is the emergence of a new kind of knowledge that responds to the needs of the *damnés* (the wretched of the earth, in the expression of Frantz Fanon). They are the subjects who are formed by today's colonial wound, the dominant conception of life in which a growing sector of humanity become commodities (like slaves in the sixteenth and seventeenth centuries) or, in the worst possible conditions, expendable lives. The pain, humiliation, and anger of the continuous reproduction of the colonial wound generate radical political projects, new types of knowledge, and social movements.

During the Cold War, "Latin" America projected the image of a subcontinent in danger of being taken over by communism (e.g., the Cuban Revolution in 1959, Salvador Allende elected president of Chile in 1970). Consequently, it became a destination for US development projects, which held that modernization was a way of saving the world from the communist menace (e.g., Puerto Rico in the 1960s). The dreams of modernization in Latin America crumbled as the welfare state economy ended in the 1970s. Instead, dictatorial regimes took hold (Pinochet in Chile, Jorge Rafael Videla in Argentina, Hugo Banzer in Bolivia) and inaugurated the new political-economic model of "neo-liberalism": a political theory combined with political economy that makes the market the main principle of the organization of society. Thus, the collapse of the welfare state at the end of the 1970s led to privatization and market-driven state regulation.

What remains unsaid in the official reports prepared by international agencies, like the CIA or the World Bank, is hundreds of situations like the following: a farmer in Mexico has to spend $800 to cultivate two acres of corn. When he sells it, he only gets between $400 and $600. Sophisticated technology and state subsidies in the US and Canada allow these two countries to pour cheap corn into Mexico's markets. Two consequences of this deal are massive farmer protests to the Mexican government and massive profits for farmers and traders in Canada and the US, who make corn into a profitable commodity at the cost of increasing the poverty and worsening the living conditions of Mexican farmers. Mexican farmers petition their government to change the conditions of NAFTA (North American Free Trade Agreement) in order to have a more equitable exchange. President Vicente Fox listens both to the farmers and to the US government, which is reluctant to change the agreement because NAFTA is the first stage of a larger plan to open similar (profitable) free trade routes throughout the Americas, in the Free Trade Agreement of the Americas (FTAA).

Among the stated goals of the FTAA is the liberalization of trade to generate economic growth and improve the quality of life.

Nothing is said about equity in distribution. All the goals emphasize growth and increases (like the increase of the levels of trade in good and services). Nothing is said about the fact that the "increase" means capital accumulation, not the improvement of quality of life for the totality of the population. The agreement states that one of its goals is to enhance competition among its parties. Yet, again, nothing is said about the fact that the goal of competition is capital accumulation for the strongest, since actors in the economic games are ruled by the principle of individuality and disregard (or exploit to personal gain) the community of people. The goals also purport to eliminate barriers among the parties. But those parties do not begin with equal conditions; so the elimination of barriers favors the centers of industrial and technological production and financial accumulation. No mention is made of the fact that the elimination of "barriers" in economic trades is parallel to the enforcement of the "frontiers" to keep immigrants from entering from the South. Each goal only tells half of the story. Either those who are in the position of formulating and implementing global designs are blind, and truly believe their own rhetoric of development as the improvement of people around the world, or they are using that rhetoric to cover a lie. Whoever pays attention to the history of the world in the past thirty or so years will understand the implications of each of these goals and know that they imply the increasing marginalization of the majority of the world's population, and the decrease in their quality of life and decent living conditions.

The principles of the FTAA are no less illusory or misleading than its goals. The first principle states that the participants are committed to advancing toward economic prosperity, strengthening ties of friendship and co-operation, and protecting fundamental human rights. This principle is contradicted daily by the facts. Economic prosperity means the increasing concentration of wealth in fewer hands. Friendship translates into persecution through the lobbying and enforcing principles that favor the landowners, shareholders, and bankers over the people of a given participant country. Each goal and principle clearly shows that the missionaries of the sixteenth century have changed their habits and now count the number of acres of land and stocks acquired rather than the number of converted souls. What we see in the FTAA is, simply, a particular recent example of the rhetoric of modernity charging forward while hiding its insidious twin, coloniality.

Today, some thirty years after its instantiation, neo-liberalism not only faces the opposition to the FTAA that is coming from different sectors of the population in different countries, but also confronts a new logic, a new way of reasoning, and a delinking from the basic premises upon which the IMF or the World Bank or the White House built their rhetoric. The "new logic" is coming from at least two different directions – the state and the grassroots. Suppose, for example, that the "Latin" American states of the Atlantic (Venezuela, Brazil, Argentina, Uruguay) turn away from the IMF and, instead, begin to negotiate with China, whose international projects are not in line with the IMF's agenda of increasing the foreign debts of countries receiving their "help." The new logic is also coming from the vocal reasoning and activism of those who are not supposed to have reason. Changes in the "idea of Latin" America are now being enacted by and in political society – that is, by the active sector of society that does not have access to the state or the markets (and that is constantly repressed and marginalized by them). It does have, however, the power to disrupt the set of beliefs in which modern science, philosophy, political economic and political theory, ethics, and aesthetics are "founded," as if those principles of belief were "natural" to the world. That potential, the epistemic potential,[2] is being actively pursued by sectors of the population who think from principles other than those of Aristotle, Plato, or the Bible and, for that reason, have been dismissed, racialized (translated as "inferior"), and colonized (subjected to a set of the values of the superior beings that were intended to improve the inferior values of people not quite human, like Indians, Blacks, women, homosexuals, etc.).

The most radical struggles in the twenty-first century will take place on the battlefield of knowledge and reasoning. The difference between socialist/communist movements during the Cold War and the Indigenous movements of today is that the latter are no longer thinking and operating within the logic of the system; they are attempting to change its logic and not just its content. The marginalization of Fidel Castro and the defeat of Salvador Allende are only two examples of how the global designs of an expanding capitalism operate against any possibility that might inhibit its expansion, even those alternative possibilities, like socialism or communism (which just change the content of the system, not the system itself), that come from *within modernity itself.* The various movements today (in their enormous complexity) are introducing a fracture in the rhetoric through which democracy, freedom, and development have been marketed and justified by those in power, even though democracy is sold through the violent imposition of autocracy.

Let's turn now toward the transformations of knowledge and subjectivity occurring across the Americas, and suspend for a while the narrative of the appropriation of Amazonian and Pacific lands, exploitation of labor, militarization, and other strategies deployed for the control of authority being enacted by the US and the European Union. Beyond the spheres of the inter-state system and the transnational financial flows, the struggle for life is becoming a struggle for knowledge and the liberation (or decolonization) of subjectivities that had been controlled by the state and the market (and, of course, the church). Certain social movements are calling into serious question the epistemology of colonial difference that sustains the uneven distribution of power. While liberation theology, as it was articulated from the perspective of dissenting "Latin" theologians, contributed to raising consciousness in the twentieth century, critical consciousness and liberation (decolonization) today will come from the actors that have been left out of the Eurocentric idea of "Latinidad." Delinking from that concept and building an "after-(Latin)" America is one of the steps being taken by Indians, Afros, women of color, gays, and lesbians. Leadership is coming from the energy of each locality and from the history of the colonization of knowledge and of being. Leadership can no longer come only from Eurocentric projects of liberation, whether they are within the theology of liberation or socialist Marxism. "Truth" must be elsewhere.

Afro-Andeans and Afro-Caribbeans are Not Necessarily "Latins"

We are entering uncharted terrain here, although the conversation there has already begun. It is about the surfacing of new self-identifications: Afro-Latinidad, which opens up the question of

101

Indo-Latinidad. That is, it opens up the question of power relations and, in a way, of their inversion, insofar as people of Afro descent claim "Latinidad" for themselves and therefore put in question the "Latinidad" that identified the Creole and Mestizo/a population in contradistinction from the Afro and Indian. Furthermore, Afro-Latinidad opens up uncharted territory and invisible histories in continental Latin America, and more specifically in the Andes, where an estimated population today of fifteen million people of Afro descent had been literally non-existent until recently. Afro-Latinidad, then, is a category that identifies people of Afro descent in the ex-Spanish and Portuguese colonies. Referring to Afros in the French ex-colonies (Guadaloupe, Martinique, Haiti), the term sounds like a pleonasm, in the sense that "Latinidad," as we have seen in the second chapter, was an identity label invented by the French government and its organic intellectuals. However, the emergence of Afro-Latinity in South America and in the Spanish-speaking Caribbean opens up the question of a similar possibility vis-à-vis the Afro population in the French-speaking Caribbean. Indo-Latinidad is not yet a label used by Indigenous people themselves, although "Indo-America" was proposed by Creole intellectuals at the beginning of the twentieth century. "Indigenismo" was a category necessary for a manifestation of national ideology in the hands and the minds of the Creoles, in which the Indians themselves did not have any role to play or anything to say.

New labels are also being proposed by non-African and non-Indigenous intellectuals to refer to the Afro population in particular regions (e.g., Afro-Andeans) or to particular nations (e.g., Afro-Colombian, Afro-Ecuadorians, Afro-Brazilians). The equivalent label is not necessary for Indians. To speak about Andean–Indians sound redundant because the Andes was always recognized as the regional habitation of Indigenous people, but not of the Afro population. Afro-Caribbean instead is an identification that today is being shared by intellectuals of African descent as well as by non–Afro scholars, intellectuals, and journalists. Although the Caribbean (both the insular and the extended continental Caribbean, from Salvador de Bahia in Brazil to Charlestown in South Carolina and New Orleans in Louisiana) has been the most common dwelling place of people of African descent in the Americas, the economy and the state have been generally in the hands of Euro-Caribbeans. Last but not least, the emergence of a population of about forty million Latinos/as in the US further complicates the picture. "Latinso/as" are a population no longer of European but of "Latin" American descent. However, a small part of that population is composed of Afro-Latinos/as and Indo-Latinos/as.

With these caveats in mind, let's move on to the reconfiguration being provoked by the emergence of social actors that the very idea of "Latin" America made invisible in the nineteenth and the twentieth centuries.

In October of 2004, hundreds of scholars from or working on the Pacific region of Andean countries, particularly Colombia, sent a letter to President Alvaro Uribe Vélez in protest at the Proyecto de Ley 16, 2003, from the National Senate. The project approved new "Normas Organicas de Ordenamiento Territorial" and revoked the cultural and territorial rights of Afro-Colombians that had been recognized by a previous Proyecto de Ley (70, 1993). The taking away of collective territories as well as (Afro-Colombian) Consejos Communitarios – legal institutional entities that govern and administer those territories – not only contravened the specifics of the previously approved Proyecto de Ley but, more seriously, challenged a series of related projects in which the equality of all Colombian citizens had been recognized. The outcry against the Proyecto de Ley 16 is just one recent example among many of an important shift taking place today that threatens the continued persistence of the colonial matrix of power (e.g., the forced appropriation of labor, the exploitation of natural resources, the exploitation of human labor, increased militarization, the control of gender and sexuality, and the control of knowledge and subjectivity): *those who have been silenced are calling into serious question the epistemology of colonial difference that sustains the uneven distribution of power.*

As we have seen, the "idea" of "Latinity," in its complicity with European imperial designs, worked to erase the colonial memory of the Americas, which consisted of the simple fact that the colonial matrix of power was built around Indians, Europeans, and Africans in the New World by Europeans fighting among themselves for the control of the economy and of authority over the New World. Sylvia Wynter, an intellectual and scholar from Jamaica, has revisited the "celebration" of the "discovery" of America through the destiny of Black folk connected to that event. Wynter's contribution in her radical "1492: A New World View"[3] is twofold. First, she reinscribes the silenced and forgotten presence of Africans in the making of the New World and the Americas beyond Latin and Anglo. Africans and Indians provided the labor force that built America, but Indians, who provided the land, have been the primary focus of critiques. Thus, by breaking away from the dichotomy between Europeans and Indians and inserting the dense histories and memories of Africans, Wynter shifts the geography of knowledge in an unprecedented way.

Confronting that imperial/colonial project through the perspective articulated by people of African descent in the Americas grounds us in the history of slavery, and in the Afro population in the Americas as the third component of the ethno-racial triad: Indians, Europeans, and Africans. The point of reference can no longer be "Latin" and "Anglo" America (or America in the restricted sense of the US), but changes to focus on the Atlantic economy, as shaped by the needs and desires of Western Christians. The Portuguese led the way, during the fifteenth century, crossing back and forth between the Mediterranean and the Western coast of Africa as they sailed around the Cape of Good Hope to the Indian Ocean. The Spaniards (through Columbus's obsession) then opened up the Atlantic to a New World where Indians, Europeans (Latins and Anglos), and Africans carried over from West Africa would form the basic demographic and ethno-racial triad. But the triad was not evenly distributed in power relations. If, on the one hand, the "discovery of America" has been variously interpreted from the single perspective of the "paradigm of newness," the "invention" of America, as argued not only by Creoles of European descent but also by Indians and Africans in the Americas, creates a coherent diversity that opens the "paradigm of co-existence."

Wynter's second, and more important, contribution is her thesis on the formation of the *frame of mind* that became the hegemonic macro-narrative (accommodating various perspectives and offspring within the same frame) of the advent of modernity and, consequently, of coloniality. That second contribution helps us to understand the enormous significance of the shift from the paradigm of newness to the paradigm of co-existence. She goes back to the fifteenth century to understand the shift in the geography of knowledge that took place therein and that made it possible for European interpretations of the "unprecedented" event to prevail over the perspectives of Indians, Africans, and White Creoles. We should be able to understand her thesis better if we remember the T-in-O map from the first chapter. In the T-in-O map, Jerusalem is the center, but the map is a Christian, not a Jewish, one. Wynter remarks on the complementary character of Jewish and Christian world views until the second half of the fifteenth century, when Jews became a problem for the unifying march of Christianity in Spain under Isabella and Ferdinand; more precisely, at the same time Columbus was persuading the queen and king of Spain to fund his westward trip to Cipango (China). The confluence of "discovering" a new continent, on the one hand, and expelling Jews and Moors from the Iberian peninsula, on the other, gave Western Christians the opportunity to translate their local view into the universal perspective that shows up in their world maps (like Mercator's and Ortelius' that I referred to in the first chapter). Colombian philosopher Santiago Cástro-Gómez described this moment in terms of the emergence of the "hubris of the zero-point."[4] That is, an insidious confidence emerged from the belief that Europeans occupied a universal locus of observation and of enunciation from which the world and its people could be classified. The radical shift in the geography of knowledge at that moment consisted in the subsuming under the Christian perspective of all other loci of observation.

This is, precisely, what the theological politics of knowledge was all about. The very idea of "modernity" cannot be separated from this shift, made possible by the simultaneous triumph of Christianity over the other religions of the Book, the emergence of a new continent, the navigation as well as physical and conceptual appropriation of the globe, and the subsuming of all other forms of knowledge. Wynter's thesis is based, on the one hand, on the recognition of how that transformation of the modern/colonial geography of knowledge in the sixteenth century sustained the imperial constitution of Europe and its relentless colonial expansion; and on the other hand, it also arises from the decolonial shift that is taking place in our time. The linear history of Europe itself (i.e., from Renaissance modernity to Enlightenment modernity, and from that to post-modernity) – that is, the paradigm of newness – is being displaced by the emergence of the paradigm of co-existence.

Changing the geography of knowledge requires an understanding of how knowledge and subjectivity are intertwined with modernity/coloniality. The imperial and colonial differential of languages shapes the modes in which knowledge is produced and circulated. As such, knowledge and subjectivity are two sides of the same coin. Political theory and political economy, for example, were thought out and written down by men who did not have a conflict between the language they spoke and the civilization carried in that language. Not just knowledge is carried in language. Social order, organization, and ranking values are as well. Political theory, political economy, ethics, and knowledge we call "scientific" are all determined in the conceptual fabric of a given language. There is a continuum, so to speak, between the English language and experience and Adam Smith's political economy in *The Wealth of Nations* and *Theory of Moral Sentiments*, or between the French subjectivity of Marie Jean Antoine Nicolas de Caritat, marquis de Condorcet, and his mapping of the human spirit in his *Esquisse d'un tableau historique des progrès de l'esprit humain*. For an Afro-Caribbean, then, the perspective from which the wealth of nations, moral sentiments, or the progress of the human spirit can be articulated will be from the experiences of the colonial wound rather than from the sensibility of imperial victories. As I have been insisting throughout our discussion, these are not merely different perspectives within the same paradigm. They are perspectives from two radically different paradigms, intertwined and articulated by the colonial matrix of power; articulated also in the unfolding of heterogeneous structural histories of language and knowledge. The paradigm of the *damnés* is formed by the diversity of heterogeneous structural histories of those who have lived in the condition of having to deal with imperial languages and the weight of the imperial civilization that those languages carry; that is, the paradigm of all those who have to deal with the colonial wound in all its manifestations.

Fanon, an Afro-Martinican himself, expressed the difference in the opening pages of *Black Skin, White Masks* (1952) when he wrote that "to speak (and we could add, to write) means to be in a position to use a certain syntax, to grasp the morphology of this or that language, but it means above all to assume a culture, to support the weight of a civilization."[5] Fanon explains that the problem, more precisely, is that:

> The Negro of the Antilles will be proportionately whiter – that is, he will come closer to being a real human being – in direct relation to his mastery of the French language ... Every colonized people – in other words, every people in whose soul an inferiority complex has been created by the death and burial of its local cultural originality – finds itself face to face with the language of the civilizing nation.[6]

Focusing on knowledges and subjectivities in the sphere of language takes us beyond the question of bi- or pluri-lingualism or multi-culturalism. It is more, much more. Language, epistemic, and subjective borders are the foundations of new ways of thinking, of an-other thinking, an-other logic, an-other language, as I have elaborated elsewhere.[7] Confronting Fanon's predicament of colonial language and subjectivity amounts to provincializing the totalizing effect of "Latin" and "Anglo" (and the consequent power differential between both) in America, as one way to understand the shift introduced by rewriting the "discovery" from the history of African slavery and of the problem of the "Negro and language," as Fanon puts it. It is the opening of an epistemology of the borders built on the colonial difference, on the subjectivity of the colonial wound. It is taking us from the paradigm of newness to the decolonial paradigm of co-existence.

The rule applies not only to the colonial epistemic difference, the example I just gave, but to the imperial difference as well: *thinking in Spanish from the colonial history of South America is also a necessary practice in shifting the geography of knowledge.* For Creoles of Spanish and Portuguese descent, the problem of their own history and language was not as acute as for Afro and Indigenous people. A sentiment of autonomy and creativity, rather than dependence, was developed. Jorge Luis Borges's famous indictment of Spanish philosopher and historian Américo Castro could be taken as a contrasting example of Fanon's predicament. In his well-known article

"The Alarms of Dr. Américo Castro," Borges mocked Castro's concerns about the corruption of Spanish in South American lands. The colonial wound, so pronounced in Indigenous and Afro sensibilities, was, for "Latin" Americans, a source either of confrontational pride, as in Borges, or of concern about the secondary global role of Spanish and Portuguese in relation to English, French, and German. Those three languages set global standards of knowledge and subjectivities across the globe for all those who do not have English, French, or German as their "native" language. In that sense, Spanish and Luso America is, in this respect, at a disadvantage vis-à-vis ex-colonies of the British Empire, such as India, Australia, New Zealand, and South Africa, because of the simple fact that English, and not Spanish or Portuguese, is the global language of scholarship, trade, and the media. However, we are talking here about languages of imperial difference. Instead, Fanon's description of "the Negro and language" set the problem in the domain of the colonial difference. Thus, on the one hand, his observation applies simultaneously to the diversity of borders between imperial languages, knowledges, and subjectivities and colonial subalternity, the condition of the *damnés* – the wounded of the imperial/colonial world order. It also serves as a theory from which to understand the problems of language and subalternity at the imperial level (e.g., the subaltern position of Spanish vis-à-vis English).

In Spanish- and Luso-speaking America, dependency theory and theology/philosophy of liberation shifted the geography of knowledge within the local history of "Latins" proper; that is, among the population of Spanish and Portuguese descent. In that regard, dependency theory and theology/philosophy of liberation were the equivalent of Fanon's epistemological shift, and all of them took place in the same time span (in the 1960s). Before then, and within the local history of Africa and the African diaspora in the Caribbean, however, the radical philosophy of "Negritude," "Antillaneité," "Creolité" started another shift in the geography of knowledge. At the beginning of the Cold War, intellectuals and activists from Africa and the Caribbean gathered around *Présence Africaine* in Paris. Alioune Diop (its creator), Leopold Sedar Senghor, and Aimé Césaire were among them. They gained the ear of Jean-Paul Sartre, who was concerned with the Jewish question. Even if Sartre couldn't have thought of it as such then, unconsciously perhaps there was a feeling that something was changing, that a seismic shift in knowledge and understanding was taking place. The basic idea of *Présence Africaine* was to question the imperial ambitions of Western civilization, as V. Y. Mudimbe has explained: "It wishes to bring to the very center of the French power and culture what was being negated in colonies, that is, the dignity of otherness."[8]

Given our discussion of the limits of epistemology encoded in the categories and histories of particular languages, the reader may ask what Afro-Caribbean *philosophy* would be if not trapped in the practice that originated in Greece, was articulated in Latin, and was redefined as a discipline in European universities from the time of the Renaissance. To answer the question, we have to question the question. The standard procedure for answering would be to look for several definitions of philosophy in, say, Greece and in eighteenth-century Europe and, then, look around and see whether the philosophy of Afro-Caribbeans matches that standard. Instead, maybe we should ask first what kind of human activity it was that Greeks named philosophy and which was taken to be the only way to think. Just because Greek thinkers named what they were doing and the way they were doing it philosophy, does anyone who ventures to "think" have to request permission from Greek sources or their Western gate-keepers in Germany, France, or England? One could argue that Greek thinkers "discovered" philosophy. Or, one could argue that Greek thinkers just gave a name to a common activity in which all human beings engage and, perhaps in spite of themselves, it became institutionalized and universalized. Consequently, once philosophy was constituted as a feature of Western civilization, the regional definition of a global human activity, it became not only the standard by which to measure "thinking" but also *the* model for the *thinking* of civilized human beings. What calls for thinking in the domains of the *damnés* is precisely the colonial wound. The generalized "idea" of Latin America is of a place where "things happen" (democracy or lack of it; corruption and cartels; Indians and opportunities for business). The further down a people, a country, a language, or a subcontinent slides in the scale of humanity, the lower the possibilities of and the call for "thinking." This is one of the major challenges that Indigenous people and Afros in South

America and the Caribbean are facing: to bring a new perspective, to delink from the categorical frame of Western modernity.

The reader immersed in the Western tradition of thought, philosophy, and science may wonder if there can really be any other (an-other) mode of thinking beyond it. For instance, can you really think in Mandarin, and its long-lasting memory, after it has interacted with Western categories of thought since the nineteenth century? Do the Chinese think in German or Russian, after Mao's revolution? Are they thinking in English now because an economy based on *capital* is transforming the country? The same kind of questions could be asked about Arabic-Muslim countries, even though the path they are following significantly differs from that of China. In fact, the questions I am asking apply to every local history articulated in the borders between the expansion of Western histories and Western modes of life and the rich diversity of local histories and local ways of life around the globe. "Latin" America is one of those local histories, sharing with the rest of the world the experiences of the imperial/colonial borders and the colonial difference. If we turn back to Afro-Caribbean philosophers, we can see that they are, indeed, writing in English and French. But are they "thinking in English or French"? To answer that question, it is necessary to question the question itself, which necessarily changes the geopolitics of knowledge. Otherwise, it will be impossible to pop the bubble, the totalizing effect of a regional way of knowing encoded in Greek and Latin, and in the six modern/colonial and European languages. Of course, I am not saying that one has to write in Swahili or Aymara, but that you could *write in English* and be *thinking in Aymara and from Aymara* (or any other language disqualified as a tool for thinking). Imperial/colonial local histories are the conditions of border thinking. Imperial local histories alone are the conditions for monotopic and territorial, partial thinking.

Once again, I needed this excursus to convey the radical shift in the geography and geo-politics of knowledge confronting the hegemony of theological and egological politics of knowledge. To return to Afro-Caribbean philosophy, then, let us look to Padget Henry. Note again, he is not a "Latin" philosopher but an "Anglo" one, as he belongs to the history of Afros and the British colonies in the Caribbean. This history nourishes his thought. He *sees* that history and *thinks* from it (is that "Caribbean studies"?) in confrontational dialogue with the European history of philosophy. The intellectual and political legacy of *Présence Africaine* and its consequences are – for Henry – the grounding of a genealogy of thought as much as the Greeks and Kant were for Martin Heidegger, or as much as Kant and Heidegger are for "Latin" philosophers in South America. As you can imagine, Henry is far removed from Greece and Germany, as far removed as Heidegger is from Africa and *Présence Africaine*. Heidegger, however, belongs to the paradigm of newness while Henry belongs to the paradigm of co-existence.

Henry published a comprehensive introduction to Afro-Caribbean philosophy.[9] For him, Afro-Caribbean philosophy is, like any other philosophy, a "unified set of problems," a set of embedded discourse around a common and evolving problematic. One of the particularities of Afro-Caribbean philosophy, however, is that "its formation and current structure reflect the *imperial history* of the cultural system that has housed the larger discursive field of Caribbean society."[10] Henry adds that this larger problem set of Caribbean philosophy emerged as a "series of extended debates over projects of colonial domination between four major social groups: Euro-Caribbeans, Amerindians, Indo-Caribbeans and Afro-Caribbeans."[11] When Afro-Caribbean philosophy was born from an unequal imperial/colonial discursive field, it produced a "seismic shift in the orientation of Caribbean philosophy."[12] The orientation of Afro-Caribbean philosophy is made still more explicit by the title of the first meeting of the Caribbean Philosophical Association (Barbados, May 2004): "Shifting the Geography of Reason."

The "seismic shift" that Afro-Caribbean philosophy introduces shakes the calm ideology that would have an entity called "Latin" America and another called America and conceived as the "land of the Anglos."[13] The unthinkable aberration of Haiti has always been discreetly absent from that geography because Haiti took its own route and was the first "deviant" example. "Haiti" is an idea that is neither Latin nor Anglo. The island's original name was "Ayiti," which means "mountainous land" in the language of the Indigenous inhabitants of the island. The Afro Haitian revolutionaries appropriated that name as a tribute to the victims of the genocide at the beginning of the "conquest," displacing the Spanish and French names that the island had borne. It was named Santo Domingo by the Spaniards and became Saint Domingue when the French took possession of it. Thus, Haiti was "Latin" from day one, since both Spanish and French are Latin languages. In spite of the strong presence of Spanish colonialism in Haiti, Haiti is still peripheral, if not absent, from the "idea of Latin" America.[14] The name *Ayiti* (normalized as Haiti) marks the historical and epistemic shift that the revolution introduced, and it breaks away from both the slavery period and French imperial domination. Language and the power of naming, as these movements show, contain radical potential for "epistemic revolution." Paradoxically, "Haiti" did not fit the pattern of "Latin" America because "Latin(s)" were supposed to be of European descent (and if they were Mestizos/as they were supposed to embrace European cosmology and not Indigenous) and not of African descent! Haiti was seen in terms of "Africanidad" rather than "Latinidad" by the engineers of the White subaltern identity of South America and the Caribbean. Today, the "idea" of Latin America is undergoing the consequences of still another "seismic alteration" introduced by the growing influence of Afro-Andeans. Because Afro-Caribbeans were equated with French and English, "Latins" speaking Spanish and Portuguese had an excuse to turn their back, with few exceptions, on Afros in the Caribbean. Now, Afro descendants in the Andes, invisible until recently, are claiming their right to knowledge, to philosophy, to epistemology, which undermines the premises on which the very idea of a "Latin" America was constructed and sustained.

Afro-Andeans − those who speak Spanish rather than French Creole − are in the process of reactivating their own principles of knowledge and memory.[15] By creating a series of theoretical concepts that allow them to conceptualize themselves, such as "ancestry" and "lo propio" ("what belongs to us," "our own"), they enter into critical dialogue with the unavoidable Western categories of thought that were implanted in their souls by the Spanish language they had to learn. Here we see the practice of engaging in a non-imperial and decolonial geo-politics and body politics of knowledge. That is, Afro-Andeans are thinking from the personal and historical experience of the colonial wound in the same way as Descartes or Heidegger (for example) thought from the personal and historical experience and tensions of imperial conflicts. For Afro-Andeans, reformulating the concept of "ancestry," for instance, avoids the trap of "History," a discipline which includes the control of memories around the world through one conceptual package and, in creating people without history, reactivates the traces of slavery, oppression, racism, marginalization, lack of recognition, and dehumanization ignored in the translation of memories and experiences into "History" through the European tradition. Likewise, the term "lo propio" does not refer to a museum of "essentials," an ontology of "things that belong to us," as a Eurocentric interpretation might have it. Afro-Andean intellectuals conceive "lo propio" as a frame for "appropriating" concepts or ideas and redefining them through the colonial wound. Instead of "alienating" themselves by thinking from conceptual frameworks that do not belong to their own experience, owning "lo propio" allows them to define ideas and experiences for themselves. It is an energy and a conceptual matrix of "appropriation," enrichment, and empowerment that liberates by decolonizing and works toward a possible future that will no longer be dictated by the church, the capitalist states, or the private sector (and neither, of course, by honest liberal, Marxist, or Christian intellectuals and activists with prescriptions for the good of everyone). The reappropriation and redefinition of terms is an actual way in which the disfiguring and distorting grasp of history and language that Fanon described is being undone from the perspective of those who have undergone its perverse logic.[16] That is, again, we see the practice of shifting the geo-politics and body politics of knowledge.

We have seen that, from the Black memories and histories of oppression and exploitation, a number of philosophical, political, and ethical projects have been emerging in the Caribbean as well as in the Andean region. A question that is raised time and again, when I make this or similar statements on occasions when there can be a reaction from the audience (lectures, workshop, undergraduate and graduate seminars, or personal conversations) is this: isn't that pure and simple essentialism? The question, coming from self-defined progressive people, arises because progressive minds, like others stuck in the paradigm of modernity, have difficulty thinking beyond the parameters of modern principles of knowledge and understanding.

Beneath such questions lie various assumptions. First, many presuppose that if a project comes from, say, Afro-Caribbean or Afro-Andean actors it should "represent" all Blacks in the Caribbean and/or in the Andes. The modern myth of "representation" further assumes that such projects can only be for, in this case, Blacks. The limits of modern and Western principles of knowledge (that is, of the ingrained and totalizing myth of modernity) deprive my interlocutors of the understanding that a project that emerges from the Black experience of slavery in the modern/colonial world does not necessarily (or even desirably) (1) represent *all* Blacks or (2) restrict itself to Blacks. I am endorsing, joining, promoting, and supporting the project of the Caribbean Philosophical Association or the Afro-Ecuadorian social movement not because I am Black but because I see it as a project of liberation and epistemic decolonization. Scholarly and political projects that emerged from the experience and needs of White populations are not restricted to the Whites. The only condition is that you assume it as a political project – you do not have to be Indian or Latino/a to endorse a politics that contributes to decolonizing knowledge and fighting against oppression. The same is true in the case of Blacks – you do not have to be Black to join an intellectual or political project created to liberate Black people and decolonize knowledges and subjectivities that reproduce oppression and exploitation. *There is no safe place, racial, ideological or religious.* It is not enough to be Christian, or Liberal or Marxist; Jewish, Christian or Muslim; Black, Yellow, Brown, or White; heterosexual or queer to join imperial or decolonial projects. The question, in the last analysis, is ethical and cannot be justified in and by the right color, the right religion, or the right ideology. You cannot envision alternatives *to modernity* if the principles of knowledge you hold, and the structure of reasoning you follow, are molded by the hegemonic rhetoric of modernity and the hidden logic of coloniality working through it. Diversity within modern epistemology (diversity in political theory, diversity of opinion in political economy, different philosophical school) is not an-other thinking. An-other thinking requires a change in the terms, content and questions. To understand this difference better, let's look at the Indigenous contribution to shifting the geo-politics of knowledge.

Indigenous People are Not Necessarily "Latin" and Perhaps Not Entirely "Americans" Either

The *Global Trends 2015* report released on December 18, 2000, by the National Intelligence Council noted the potential challenges coming from Indigenous people in the Andean region, Chile, Central America, and southern Mexico as one of the major global trends on the horizon of 2015. Indeed, the continued presence and new "trends" in social, economic, and life organization of the Zapatista uprising (starting in 1994 in Mexico: see below) mark a crucial turning point in five hundred years of Indigenous struggle against exploitation, domination, and colonization – above all against the totalizing mirage of modern epistemology. The Zapatistas have made a radical move toward shifting the geo-politics and the body politics of knowledge.[17] In Bolivia and Ecuador, mainly, the Indigenous movements have also given substantial proof that they are around to stay. The most important challenge has not come from blocked roads or forced presidential resignations (as have happened in both countries). As with the Afro-Caribbean and Afro-Andean movements, knowledge is increasingly the key site of struggle. True, the struggle for knowledge has been going on since the colonization of Tawantinsuyu and Anáhuac, the territories of the Incas and the Aztecs. Latin America has seen many insurgencies and uprisings, from Túpac Amaru in colonial Peru to the Zapatistas in neo-liberal Mexico. The opening lines of the Zapatista Declaration of the Lacandon Struggle, in fact, underline five hundred years of struggle for liberation and decolonization of knowledge.

Less visible, however, is the accumulation of *decolonial critical theory* (complementary to that of the Frankfurt School, but at the same time across the colonial epistemic difference) in the struggle for the control of knowledge that is center stage today. Anti-colonial resistance but, above all, decolonial projects and utopianism have been there since the early period of the Spanish presence in Mexico and the Andes. Knowledge is not only *accumulated* in Europe and the US and, from there, spread all over the world. Knowledge is produced, accumulated, and critically used everywhere. However, it is more difficult for societies deprived of money and, with it, the technology (books, library, printed press, internet, CD-R) that contributes to maintaining the power of imperial knowledge over all other kind of knowledges. The awareness, however, that what is dominant is not necessarily hegemonic is awakening; and hegemony, like the stock market, is becoming diversified. Insofar as these struggles remain invisible, though, the idea of "Latin" America will continue to succeed in repressing and silencing Indigenous knowledge in the same way it did with Afro-Andeans and Afro-Caribbeans; and institutions like the World Bank will continue "representing" the interests of Indians and Blacks in South America, the Caribbean, Africa, Australia, and New Zealand. But let's move toward the search of lost and silenced sources, to build genealogies of thought similar to the one built by imperial knowledge.

In colonial Peru, after the double colonial revolution (e.g., conquest and *Pachakuti*, the revolution in reverse from the perspective of Andean people), Waman Puma de Ayala was to critical decolonizing thinking what Karl Marx was, in Europe, to critical emancipatory thinking after the Industrial Revolution. Once again, the former introduced the paradigm of co-existence while the latter transformed the paradigm of newness. That both Waman Puma and Marx were off the mark with their proposed solutions (Waman Puma proposing a social organization that would return power to Indians and Marx envisioning a global dictatorship of the proletarian class) matters less than the fact that they were right on the mark in unveiling the logic of colonial domination (the first) and the logic of industrial capital exploitation (the latter). Their miscalculation of the outcome does not diminish their *initiations* of critical analysis of the excesses of *the two* historical foundations of capitalism: *the colonial and the Industrial Revolutions.* Unlike Marx, who grew up with German Jews and was reared on the principles of the Enlightenment, Waman Puma, born around 1540 of presumably Indigenous or, perhaps, mixed Indigenous/Spanish parentage, lived through the first eighty years of the conquest of Tawantinsuyu (1532) and the creation of the viceroyalty of Peru. The experience of *Pachakuti* was foundational for Waman Puma. He dwelled in a situation in which the knowledge that had been accumulated in Aymara and Kechua over centuries was discounted. His life's work, a manuscript in more than eight hundred folios addressed to Philip III and entitled *Nueva*

116

Corónica y Buen Gobierno ("New Chronicle and Good Government,"
finished around 1615), presents an alternative project for government in the Andes as envisioned by someone who knew both the
Indigenous society and Spain's projects to organize the government
of the viceroyalty of Peru, which dismembered the previous structure and organization of the Inca Empire.

Waman Puma inaugurated a practice of "double critique" – of
simultaneous critical theory and epistemic decolonization. He critiqued both the Spaniards and the Incas.[18] Today, when Indigenous
social movements in the ex-Spanish colonies of the Americas claim
epistemic rights (that is, rights to the principles of the politics of
knowledge), we should look to Waman Puma as men of the European
Renaissance looked to Aristotle, or as contemporary European
thought looks to Kant. Indigenous leaders have learned the futility
of claiming land rights under the principles of Western political
economy (as laid down by the legal theologian Francisco Vitoria in
the sixteenth century, the political economist Adam Smith in the
eighteenth, and onward), or linguistic rights under the principles
and assumptions of Western concepts of literacy, or cultural rights
under the Western practice of putting the state in control of multiculturalism. The difference is that an Indigenous intellectual still has
to know Kant alongside Waman Puma to be conversant, while a
German or French intellectual can dispense with Waman Puma and
solve the problem of rights for all and for ever with Kant and Hegel.
Therein lies the colonial epistemic difference: Indigenous scholars
and intellectuals who do not want to submit to the Western standards of knowledge must delink from a concept of knowledge that
is taken for granted as the only way in which world history can be
told and known. Delinking means, among other things, that thinking other-wise is possible (and necessary) and that the best solutions
are not necessarily found in the actual order of things under neo-
liberal globalization, and it also means *knowing* that thinking otherwise is not only possible but very necessary.

The notion of "interculturalidad" was introduced (in the early
1990s) by Indigenous intellectuals and leaders of social movements,
and it was linked to the projects of bilingual education that were
associated with the Confederación de Nacionalidades Indígenas del
Ecuador (CONAIE). Bilingual education is a concern of long

duration among Indigenous populations. Once you are involved in it from the Indigenous perspective, you become aware that (1) only Indians are expected to be bilingual, not the Creole/Mestizo/a (White by Latin American standards) population, and (2) because of that, there is a disparity (a colonial differential) between bilingual projects designed and sponsored by the state and those imagined and planned by the Indigenous leaders of social movements.[19] The state is interested in introducing small changes so things remain the same. Indigenous people are interested in decolonizing knowledge/ being by participating in the decision making of the state to implement projects that return their dignity and humanity to the Indians and unveil the imperial ethics of state management. Bilingual education is not reduced to language, but encompasses political theory and economy as well. "Interculturalidad" doesn't mean speaking the same logic in two different languages, but putting into collaborative conversation two different logics for the good of all. For the state, "interculturalidad" thus understood is not convenient. Therefore, the state promotes an idea of a "multicultural" society (albeit some times the state uses the word "intercultural," which still means "multicultural," indeed).

What is the difference? "Multicultural" means that the hegemonic principles of knowledge, education, the concept of the state and government, political economy, morality, etc., are controlled by the state, and below the control of the state people have "freedom" to go with their "cultures" as far as they do not challenge "the epistemic principles" grounding politics, economy, and ethics as managed by the state. "Interculturalidad," instead, as used in Indigenous political projects, means that there are two distinct cosmologies at work, Western and Indigenous. There are differences between defenders of the Western cosmology in Ecuador, as you can see from all the official political parties and the church. There are also differences between Indigenous people from the Ecuadorian Amazon and from the Andes, from the South and from the North. However, in each case, the diversity also has a common ground: if you think in Kichua, you do not think in Spanish in the same way as a native speaker does, even after five hundred years of interaction with Spanish. "Interculturalidad," in its broader sense, is the radical claim, by Indigenous people, of their "epistemic rights," which are quite different from "cultural rights."[20] "Cultural rights" are celebrated by the state, in Ecuador and in the US. "Epistemic rights," however, provoke, at most, a nervous smile from both the right and the left. Now, I am not talking here about Anthony Giddens's idea of moving "beyond left and right," since Giddens's was a "beyond" that was still "within the framework" of left and right. I am thinking of a "beyond" that is inter-epistemic, following the teaching of Afro-Caribbean and Indigenous philosophers and thinkers. Waman Puma is a canonical and key figure for epistemic and decolonial delinking. In this respect, he is to intercultural delinking what Machiavelli is to republican ideas or Adam Smith is to free-market liberalism. Waman Puma was claiming, openly, his epistemic right to tell the king of Spain what the real history of people from Tawantinsuyu was and what he, the king, had to do in order to have a peaceful government. Although the connection has not been yet explicitly established (to my knowledge) between Indigenous intellectuals today and Waman Puma, the specific concept of "interculturalidad," holds within it the type of experiences that led Waman Puma to compose his *Nueva Corónica*.

In their efforts to decolonize knowledge and being from the concept of knowledge and being that places them in an inferior position, Indigenous intellectuals had to first change the geography of reason, since any attempt to claim rights within the official concept of knowledge and being without doing so would have been moot. Vine Deloria, Jr, a self-identified Sioux Indian, lawyer, and activist, provides a good way to think about the problem: "One of the foremost differences separating Whites and Indians was simply one of *origin*. Whites derived predominantly from western Europe ... Conversely, Indians had always been in the Western hemisphere."[21] His dictum, however, helps in understanding the colonial conditions of all Indigenous people in the Americas, New Zealand, and Australia. "Origin" here is not to be understood as a pure essence, either for Indians or for Europeans. It should be understood, in Wynter's felicitous expression, as "subjective understanding" – subjective understanding for both, Europeans and Indians. What characterizes Indians (and Blacks, and Creoles, and Indians from India since the arrival of the British, and north Africans, etc.) is that their subjective understanding is built, as is that of colonized people in general, on the colonial wound. Conversely, European subjective understanding is more based on imperial leadership than on the colonial wound. Thinking critically from the subjective understanding of the colonial wound takes you into decolonial paradigms of co-existence, while thinking critically from the subjective understanding of imperial leadership keeps you in the paradigm of newness.

"Interculturalidad," then, is a claim made from the perspective of Kichua, in Ecuador, and not from that of Spanish. Even if the claims are "pronounced also in Spanish," Spanish is only a tool to translate Kichua and, in the process of translation, to take away the memory imbedded in Spanish (or any language) in order to reinscribe the Kichua memory that the imposition of Spanish contributed to making invisible. No doubt, Spanish is in the soul of every Indian and every Black in Spanish America; although in a different manner than the language is in the soul of Creoles of European descent. That does not mean, however, that Indians and Blacks are cultural Spaniards; or that they want to be. Santería is a far cry from canonical Spanish beliefs, just as Andean rituals and celebrations do not fit with the traditions of the Christian church. Spanish is the language of the state, the official language, while Kichua is the language of one of the branches of the Inca Empire (which is today Ecuador and southern Colombia). Through "interculturalidad" (which is also inter-epistemology), the claim is made for the right of Indigenous people to co-participate in the making of the state and in education. It is not a claim for simple recognition (like "multiculturalism" in the US) that begs for acceptance into a nation in which they, Kichua as a civilization and a language, do not have a place because their position on the margins, precisely, defines the limits of the modern nation. Instead, "interculturalidad" would lead to a pluri-cultural state with more than one valid cosmology. And "pluri-culturalidad," at the level of knowledge, of political theory and economy, of ethics and aesthetics, is the utopian goal toward which to build, a new society constructed over the cracks and the erosions of the liberal and republican state.

The creation of Amawtay Wasi (the Universidad Intercultural de las Nacionalidades y Pueblos Indígenas) is a natural consequence of a claim for epistemic rights.[22] There is no space for Indigenous people attending a state (or private) university to address their own needs. The entire philosophy of education remains in the hands of the state or private capital. Above all, it is determined within the framework of knowledge that was put in place with the Renaissance university, changed with the Enlightenment university, and has now developed into the corporate university modeled in today's US and applied around the world. That is, the university itself remains within the march of progress and newness. Amawtay Wasi doesn't fit into that history.[23] Amawtay Wasi has been conceived in the paradigm of co-existence. It represents a spatial shift in the geography of knowledge rather than a temporal break in the linearity of Western thought. When the idea of "Latin" America came into existence, as we saw in chapter 2, the colonial universities (in Mexico, Peru, Argentina, and the Dominican Republic) became state universities in the service of building new nations, and no longer universities serving the church and the king. "Latin" America was born under the sign of the so-called Kantian-Humboldtian university, the university of the Enlightenment in which philosophy supplanted theology and culture and disseminated the idea of "national" cultures. It was a state-oriented university, although it also contributed to the formation of intercontinental identities, such as "Europe" and "Latin" America. A similar process can be traced in the US. (The University of Mexico was founded in 1552, Harvard in 1636.) Philosophy and science reigned over theology. That was part of the transformation of theology into egology. Kant put philosophy above theology, medicine, and law and attributed to it – and to a transcendental Subject – the task of vigilance in the production of knowledge. The Enlightenment university has egology (philosophy and science, and the sovereignty of the individual) as its master framework. After World War II, another transformation took place in the linear series of Western thought, and the corporate university (the US contribution to this story) emerged with "organology" (the knowledge of organization and the organization of knowledge, where the sovereign subject vanishes) as its master framework.[24]

The relevance of the individual recedes as organization takes its place. The corporate university is marked not only by a different philosophy, but also by the marketing of particular values: expertise and efficiency are the desired goals, rather than the humanist ones of the Renaissance university or the critical, philosophical, and scientific ones of the Enlightenment university. Organization of knowledge and knowledge of organization lead to expertise and efficiency. The institution of the Enlightenment university, in which "Latin" America was born as an idea, is now being dismantled and replaced by the corporate one. Similarly, in the US, the humanities are becoming a commodity bought by wealthy families, who give money to universities to teach Western civilization. The benefactors purchase education that will not be critical but promotional.

Amawtay Wasi (the Universidad Intercultural) breaks away from these events in the paradigm of newness. The fact that it is still called a university does not mean that it surrenders to the demands of the state and imperial institution. It only means that the paradigm of co-existence works at the crossroads between Indigenous and Western forms of knowledge. However, the frame of mind and the goals are no longer inscribed within the existing principles, values, and functions of knowledge. Rather than being another university led by Indigenous leaders, it is an-other university led by Indigenous needs and principles of knowledges and values. It should be called instead a "pluri-versity," since its curriculum integrates the "subjective understanding" of Indigenous civilization into the contributions of Western civilization. Knowing that and still calling it a "university" is a sign of how "interculturalidad" works – not by rejection and negation but by integration into the paradigm of co-existence. "Interculturalidad" doesn't reject or suppress non-Indigenous knowledge, as the agents under Western universities from the Renaissance to today did. To do so would be to act *under the same Western logic and to change only the content and not the terms in which knowledge is produced.* To maintain the name of the institution, and at the same time to radically change the principles and the philosophy of knowledge and, therefore the curriculum, is indeed a signal move in the shifting geography of reason. This is not the place to go into a detailed presentation of the institution's structure, and to differentiate it from the Western university. Suffice it to say that Amawtay Wasi is constructed on the basis of an-other "origin," as Deloria put it, an "origin" that at some point in time became entangled with and overruled by the languages and ways of thinking of European universities. When the first documents of Amawtay Wasi were written, the location was referred to as "America Andina," not as

"Latin America."[25] Today it would be called Abya-Yala. Amawtay Wasi is also constructing an institutional genealogy with the historical Yachahuasic (a site of training for future functionaries of the government) and Aclla Huasi, which had a similar function but included women. The institutional genealogy is complemented by the genealogy of thoughts and the curricula in learning institutions during the Inca Empire.

The raison d'être of the university is founded in Kichua's theoretical presuppositions, and it is engaged with the situation of Indigenous communities. However, the university is not restricted to Indigenous people but open to the entire population of Ecuador. For that reason, the philosophical principle is to imagine a plurinational uni-versity. Thus, Amawtay Wasi includes in its curriculum also knowledge that it is not based on Kichua's philosophical and theoretical principles, although Kichua's cosmic vision remains as the overall frame of reference. Kichua, as a language and knowledge, was broken up and supplanted by Spanish in the business of the state, in administration, and in education. Amawtay Wasi has both a historical and an epistemic repair to make. And the way to do it, the way it is planned, is to "include" Western knowledge in a curriculum "framed" by Kichua language and categories of knowledge. For example, the curriculum is organized in three cycles: "runa yachaikuna" (learning to be), "shukitak yachaikuna" (knowing to be), and "yachaikuna pura" (knowing to do). If we make a quick comparison with the Greek principles of knowledge inherited by the West, such as *knowing how*, *knowing what*, and *knowing that*, we see that the principles of Amawtay Wasi are not the *direct opposite or contrary* (the false construction of West vs. non-West) but just simply *different*! They cannot be reduced or compared one to the other. The most radical difference is the first one, "runa yachaikuna." "Learning to be" is a basic claim made from the "epistemic wound" of the colonization of knowledge and of being, since it is a project of higher education oriented toward the decolonization of knowledge and of being, instead of orienting itself to training experts at the service of the state and the corporations, reproducing coloniality of knowledge and of being. Think about a project like that being implemented by Harvard University and you will understand the scope (as well as the difficulties and the risk) of what Amawtay Wasi is trying to achieve. Difficult to do, no doubt. But the project is already in place and has reached a point of no return.

Amawtay Wasi and the extensive and radical work by Afro-Caribbean philosophers, as well as the process unfolding among Afro-Andeans, are realities that are here to stay. These scenarios were unthinkable in the nineteenth century, when "Latinidad" was the only talk in town. You could say that Amawtay Wasi and Afro-Caribbean and Afro-Andean philosophies are changing the face of "Latin" America. If you are a conservative and for some reason need to preserve "Latinidad" as the distinctive feature of the Spanish- and Portuguese-speaking subcontinent, you can also acknowledge that there are millions of people in that subcontinent for whom "Latin" America means a dwelling place that it is not theirs; a house that does not belong to them; a space where they have to ask permission to enter. Inclusion granted by generous "Latin" Americans (in the state, the church, or civil society) will not do. *The question is not inclusion but inter-culturality, a shared project based on different "origins" confronting the colonial wound and overcoming the imperial/national pride and interests.* In the words of another Indigenous movement, the Zapatista uprising in Chiapas, Mexico, it means dwelling in a "world where many worlds co-exist."

The Zapatistas' theoretical revolution,[26] since 1994, has not stopped its quiet but radical march toward that world. In 2001, after President Vicente Fox took power, the Zapatistas marched on foot to Mexico City in the hope of initiating collaborative work with the new government. The San Andres Accords signed at the time of that opportunity failed because the government did not fulfill its promises. The response of the Zapatistas was not to complain but just to turn their backs on the government and to begin their own work of creating alternatives. They put in place autonomous socio-economic organizations called "Los Caracoles." What are "Los Caracoles" and what is their significance for my argument?

Let's say, to begin with, and to give the reader an overall picture in a familiar language, that "Los Caracoles" are Indigenous community assemblies that are connected with one another and work collaboratively with each other to "invent" (and I will come back to the quotation marks on "invent") their own forms of social, political, and legal organization. Their economic structures are based on reciprocity rather than on a competitive market. Their subjectivities are formed through collaborative practices rather than through competition. And, finally, they are creating a new subject tangentially related to the national subject promoted and controlled by the state in Mexico, while at the same time detached from the canonicity of national subject formation. It is a subjectivity of the border, as it were, in which national subjectivity is only a residual part. The individual assemblies within "Los Caracoles" are called "juntas de buen gobierno." It is obvious to everyone familiar with the cultural history of Abya-Yala that "buen gobierno" refers to Waman Puma's *Nueva Corónica y Buen Gobierno* and not, for example, to the canon for every "Latin" American intellectual and nation-builder in the ninteeneth century: Plato, Machiavelli, Hobbes, and Montesquieu. "Los Caracoles" are, in the south of Mexico, a project for socio-economic and political organization parallel to the project of Amawtay Wasi in Ecuadorian higher education, insofar as both shift the geography of reason, increasing the visible presence of the paradigm of co-existence, and building the possibility of different worlds beyond the ideals of modern imperial designs and their colonial consequences.

Imagine, now, what Waman Puma was confronting when composing his recommendations to Philip III on how to interpret Andean history before the arrival of the Spaniards, and Andean history over eighty years of colonial invasion. And doing so on the spot, so to speak, since he did not have the five hundred years of historical perspective that Indigenous movements have today. He was already in his thirties when Spaniards managed, after three decades of war, to control Indian resistance and to implant a Spanish viceroyalty, the viceroyalty of Peru. On the basis of his "nueva corónica," Waman Puma also recommended how to organize a "good government" on the ruins of the structure of Tawantinsuyu. His proposal suggested a convenient arrangement that included aspects of both Inca and Spanish forms of political and socio-economic organization. As far as the variety of Spanish and of Andean (Kechua and Aymara) concepts of life and of government co-existed, "buen gobierno" could have been neither exclusively Andean nor exclusively Spanish. If there were two "origins" co-existing, why would one of them rule over the other? Spaniards were acting on the belief supported by the paradigm of "newness" (and that is one of the reasons why "New World" was a name that came to the mind of European men of letters). Waman Puma was not in a position to rule but neither was he disposed to give up. He understood that a particular way of social organization in the "Indias del Peru," the name he gave the structure built over a dismantled Tawantinsuyu, would have to harmonize local ways of life and Spanish ways of life. He drew a map in which both Spaniards and the Indians of Peru have their place.[27] He suggested his son as ruler of the new form of government; you could interpret this as self-interest and nepotism, or more generously and creatively see the implications of having a ruler with Indian rather than Spanish origins. Waman Puma's solution in the "Indias del Peru" co-existed, in his view, with the Spanish form of government in Castille, but was not subservient to it. Thus, Waman Puma initiated the paradigm of co-existence, from the perspective of Indian "origins" (in Deloria's word) while the Spaniards, deaf to it, overruled it with the paradigm of newness.

To reduce both worlds to dogmatic binary opposition would be really to miss the point that Deloria was driving at and that I am trying to make here. First, the differential of power and origins is not just twofold – Spanish and Indian – but threefold – Spanish, Indian, and African – as Sylvia Wynter strongly reminded us. Second, as time went on, Dutch, British, and French colonizers joined the Spanish and Portuguese. And third, the internal diversity among Indians, Europeans, and Africans also makes them multiple. Racism ingrained in the paradigm of newness was enough reason to disregard any attempt coming from a paradigm of co-existence. Ways of understanding human interaction also kept the colonizers from opening up to the model of co-existence. The Spanish forms of governance were based on a tree model with the monarch on top, while the Incan structure could be described as a horizontal series of interconnected and reciprocal nodes or cells – named *ayllu* in the Andes and *altepetl* in Anáhuac. The two forms of social organization were founded in different philosophical principles. There would be nothing wrong with that, except that at a certain point in history, the people dwelling in the ethos of the *ayllu* and the *altepetl* had to fit into the ethos of *pueblos*, *municipios*, *alcaldias*, and an overall superstructure, the Spanish viceroyalties, that reproduced the social organization of the empire. Waman Puma's *Nueva Corónica y Buen Gobierno* offered a history that Spaniards had difficulty understanding, and, based on that history, a form of governance with which the Spanish were not ready to come to terms.

At this point, one can see that the Zapatista description of "Los Caracoles" as "juntas de buen gobierno" sends us back not only to Waman Puma but also to the historical "origin" of many ways of social organization that were disrupted by the Spaniards' "original" forms of social organization (hence the quotation marks on "invent" above). If there was disruption and *Pachakuti*, resulting in a colonial wound, it is because the existing forms of government in Abya-Yala were different. If they were not different, power would have changed hands easily within the same paradigm, as happened when the Creole leaders managed to expel the Spaniards and continued to rule society with few changes. It was not like that between Iberian conquerors and Indians. How these two models of social organization interacted over five centuries is, of course, more than I can handle in this book. Suffice it to say that both Indigenous and foreign (Spanish) forms of governance went through constant processes of transformation of different intensity. By the end of the sixteenth century, Inca and Aztec social organizations were no longer what they were before the arrival of the Spaniards. By the end of the sixteenth century, Spanish institutions set up in the lands of the Inca and the Aztecs were no longer what they were in the Iberian peninsula. The difference was that, in this interaction and mutual transformation, Spaniards controlled the power. The colonial matrix of power came forward out of that interaction, and Waman Puma's was one of the first contestations of it. "Los Caracoles" are a continuation – through many Indigenous uprisings through the centuries – of that history and also a reactivation of previous forms of social organization in an attempt to reconstitute the power imbalance and the structure of domination. "Los Caracoles" reinscribe in contemporary society the interconnected nodes or cellular model of Indigenous organization that has survived until today, in spite of the power differential during the colonial period as well as the national period.

The structure of the Zapatistas' "juntas de buen gobierno"[28] inhabits the structure of the *altepetl* and the *ayllu*, resembles the social organization of the Greek *oikos*. Distinguished Nahuatl scholar

127

James Lockhart offers a succinct and useful description of this form of governance as it is being reinscribed today by Indigenous social movements – not only by the Zapatistas but also in Ecuador, Bolivia, Colombia, and Guatemala:

> A very widely diffused type of organization employed by indigenous peoples in pre–Columbian times, not only in Mesoamerica but in the Andes and elsewhere, could be called cellular, as opposed to a more hierarchical or linear mode. It was characteristic of pre-conquest Nahua cosmography, land allocation, rhetorical and poetic speech, artistic expression and even grammar ... [this cellular matrix was] the sociopolitical entity that contained Nahua life in the same way that the polis contained the life of the Ancient Greeks.[29]

It has taken a long time for scholars to come to terms with the fact that there is an *Indigenous ethos* (repressed by the Spanish one and, later on by the *Baroque* and *Latin (Creole) ethos*) that has never vanished, although it was transformed, since colonial times. The *Indigenous ethos*, contrary to the *Creole ethos* (in its colonial and postcolonial versions), was founded on a logic other than the one in which the Spaniards and Portuguese were formed and programmed to think. "Los Caracoles," as well as Amawtay Wasi, are vivid and existing manifestations of an ethos that never went away and that, today more than ever, is resurging to intervene in the *ethos* of Eurocentric modernity inhabited by neo-liberal global designs.[30] It is obvious today, all over the globe (and particularly in Iraq), that "memory" is what imperial/colonial domination always failed to conquer. The multiplicity of memories, languages, knowledges, ways of life, and wounded human dignities resound in a cry like the Zapatista "Basta!" ("Enough!") or the "Nunca mas!" ("Nevermore!") of the Argentine Truth Commission which investigated the crimes of Videla's dictatorship.

Latin America, a Phantom "Civilization"?

For institutions like the World Bank or the CIA, there is no reason to question the "idea" of Latin America. For those who, based in

Spanish- and Luso-speaking countries in South America, found themselves identified with the Creole and the "Latin" American ethos, there is no reason either, albeit their "idea" of Latin America certainly may not coincide with that of the World Bank and the CIA.[31] For these institutions as well as for progressive and conservative citizens of European descent, Latin America is an ontological, geo-political entity in the world order as-is. Yet the CIA, Samuel Huntington, the World Bank, the Inter-American Development Bank, and Latin American studies programs in the United States all coincide in an "idea" of "Latin" America that is not necessarily the idea that Blacks, Latinos/as, or Indigenous people have of it, or the "idea" that those working in the modernity/coloniality paradigm have.[32] Why should these groups share the same idea, if "Latin" America is not an objective entity but a political project formed by Europeans of Latin descent, in which Indians and Afros (with the exceptions of those from Haiti and Martinique) did not have any participation? My argument, here, comes precisely out of the modernity/coloniality project that, although derived from the very foundation of "Latinidad" in South America, questions the reproduction of coloniality by the Creole elite. In this regard, the modernity/coloniality project joins forces with Indigenous, Afro, and Latino/a projects, at the same time as it critically reveals the colonial underpinning of the idea of "Latinidad" and its limitation for the future of "Latin" America.

Today, "Latin" America (as an idea) occupies an ambiguous position in the imaginary of the modern/colonial world. It serves as an imaginary that is defended, from different loci of enunciation, by state officers, journalists, and intellectuals who see themselves as "Latin Americans," meaning, for them, a distinctive identification in the Western triangulation of Western and Southern Europe and the US. For dissenting Creoles, Mestizos/as, and immigrants of European descent, the "idea" of Latin America is believed to provide a unified front to confront the growing military, economic, and technological invasion coming from the US. The problem is that, at the same time, Black and Indigenous communities are fighting for the same cause (particularly the growing Indigenous forces around the struggle against Free Trade of the Americas); but they are not doing it in the name of "Latin" America, since "Latin" Americans have also been their exploiters. Indigenous groups struggle in the same area under the name of Abya-Yala, and Blacks look for other, less territorial identifications, like the clear memory of slavery and their construction as "less than human" by Europeans, Creoles, and immigrants alike. Shifting the geography and the biography of reason is a dangerous move for the hegemonic order of things; it means the co-existence of the "subjective understanding," again in Wynter's words, of social and economic organization, which is not good for those anchored in hegemonic ways of life. Political insurrections could be totally or partially controlled by a powerful army. Ideas that threaten the rationality of military interventions, justified crime, and the paradigm of newness (spreading democracy, freedom, markets) are more difficult to control. They can be slowed down, but not killed.

In the "world order" submitted by Samuel Huntington, opposing civilizations teeter on the brink of a "clash" and "Latin" America has been generating, as of late, much of what can be slowed down but not stopped. What Huntington doesn't see, or doesn't want to see, is that the "challenge" is not just that of the Hispanic crowd invading the Anglo yard. Likewise, in the case of Islam, the challenge is not just from terrorism that threatens "American" lives. The real challenge is that, beyond the Hispanic crowd and terrorist bombs, there are Muslims and Latinos/as changing the geo-politics of knowledge. You can justify the killing of terrorists, but it is more difficult to justify or enact the paralysis of the thinking of Latino/a and Islamic thinkers, working toward a paradigm of co-existence and shifting the geo-graphies of knowledge and of social organization. Huntington's conception of Latin America, and his inference about Hispanics, is unabashedly based on an ontological idea of "Latin" America and of "Hispanics." He writes:

> Latin America, however, has a distinct identity which differentiates it from the West. [Remember Deloria?] Although an offspring of European civilization, Latin America has evolved along a very different path from Europe and North America. It has had a *corporatist*, authoritarian culture, which Europe had to a much lesser degree and North America not at all [*sic!*]. Europe and North America both felt the effects of the

130

Reformation and have combined Catholic and Protestant cultures. Historically, although this may be changing, Latin America has been only Catholic. Latin American civilization *incorporates* indigenous cultures, which did not exist in Europe, [and] were *effectively wiped out* in North America ... Latin America could be considered either a sub-civilization within Western civilization or a separate civilization closely affiliated with the West and divided as to whether it belongs in the West. *For an analysis focused on the international political implications of civilizations, including the relations between Latin America, on the one hand, and North America and Europe, on the other, the latter is the more appropriate and useful designation.*[33]

If, instead of reading what Huntington says on that page, the reader were to look at his map of "World of Civilizations Post-1990," she would see "Western" Europe and the US, of course, but also Australia, New Zealand, and ... the Falkland Islands! Is it possible that a scholar from Harvard would make the mistake of mentioning Latin America as a separate civilization key to, if not part of, Western civilization on one page and then forget it completely on a different page of the same book? I do not think it is a mistake. For Huntington, "Latin" America seems to be an eroded section of Western civilization that fell off the First World map and can now be replaced by Australia, New Zealand, and, maybe eventually, South Africa. Since, after providing this image of Latin America in *The Clash of Civilizations*, he went on to write about the "Hispanic Challenge" in *Who Are We?*,[34] one can surmise that Australia, New Zealand, and South Africa (all members of the British Commonwealth) are more reassuring, for Huntington, than Latin America, where English is only spoken in a few Caribbean islands and the majority are Spanish and Portuguese speakers, with several million speakers of Indigenous languages also.

Why is it that "Latin" America is not in the West and Australia and New Zealand are? In what frame of mind can "Latin" America be considered a civilization if, indeed, South America and the Caribbean make up a geo-historical space where for five hundred years at least three kinds of civilizations – people of Indian descent, of European descent, and of African descent – have been cohabiting? Latin America can be disqualified as part of the West (even after recognizing its involvement) because, Huntington argues, Western civilization actually dates further back, "to AD 700 or 800." Huntington's omissions are often illustrative; they are indeed the productions of silence. Take, for example, the fact that he does not mention that the centuries in which he sees the "emergence of Western civilization" are also the dates that mark the foundation and expansion of the Islamic Empire, to which the West was in a subaltern "civilizational" position. Islamic expansion into Western Christendom began in the seventh century and continued until the forces of the Habsburg Empire pushed the Ottomans back in 1683. This constant movement into Europe brought an excitability along with it, which pushed the Europeans to guard themselves from Islam. The Islamic expansions took Christian lands. Muslim influence covered Spain, Portugal, southern Italy, and parts of France. This influence on Western European soil lasted eight hundred years, until the fall of Granada in 1492. Thus the emergence of Western civilization is not due to the inner wisdom and exceptionality of Western Man, as Huntington would like, but has as one of its motivations the Christian resistance to a powerful and expansive Islamic Empire. Is it a coincidence that today we have a Christian and capitalist empire pounding, after the Cold War and the end of communism, into Islamic countries that beyond being religious are also part of the capitalist world and are seated over vast amounts of oil?

I do not intend to dispute Huntington's decision to leave Latin America outside of the West and replace it, as he does, with New Zealand and Australia. But I do want to underline Huntington's logic of (1) placing Latin America outside the West, (2) locating the Muslim world as a threat to the West, and (3) identifying Hispanics as a challenge to Anglo American identity. Huntington's move is interesting enough in itself to prevent me from debating whether he is right or wrong and whether Latin America is or is not part of the West. I would, however, like to remark that the official imperial language of both New Zealand and Australia is English (that is, Anglo), while in Latin America, the official imperial languages are Spanish and Portuguese, which are not Huntington's "mother tongue." Suffice it to say that Latin America happens to be a region where English is not the official language, as it is in the US, the United Kingdom, New Zealand, and Australia; and, for Huntington, the West is basically the English-speaking part of the planet that can be traced back to the British Empire – identity politics at its most blatant. Recent political events may prove him right, since France and Germany, although part of Western Europe, have been at odds with US and British international politics as implemented by George W. Bush and team. Of course, English is a necessary but insufficient condition for being included in the West. The West, after all, was originally *Latin* in terms of cosmopolitan languages. Furthermore, South Africa and India are not included in his own scheme by Huntington, although their official language is English and they gained independence from Britain. Something else is at work.

Yes, Kant's ethno-racial tetragon is still creeping up in the hegemonic imaginary. Why are "Latin" Americans not White in the global ethno-racial pentagon if the governing elites (with the exception perhaps of Venezuela, Ecuador, and the very problematic case of Peru) consider themselves White? Are they not White because they are "Latin" Americans, or are they "Latin" Americans because they are not White? "Latin" Americans have been downgraded in the racialization of the languages and of continental divides (e.g., Third World countries, emerging, underdeveloped). Of course, Afros and Indians do not have that problem; they know straightforwardly that they are not-Whites. Latin America is a region where Indigenous people have not been "effectively wiped out," as is clear today in the Andes, in Guatemala, and in Mexico. Latin America, for that reason, is a set of countries where "mestizaje" ("blending") has been celebrated – curiously enough – as the most important feature in homogenizing the nation, while in the US, mestizaje was never even a valid project. The US "melting pot" did not celebrate mestizaje but, rather, the coexistence of different homogeneous groups of European descent. When immigration from the Third World began in force, in the 1970s, the "melting pot" of people of European descent was exchanged for a "multicultural society" in which people of various colors co-existed in the same territory with White people. In "multiculturalism," mestizaje may take place, but it is never celebrated or emphasized either in the official discourse of the state or in the discourse of identification put forward by diverse ethnic groups. Recently, however, Latinos/as in the US have begun to question that stance and embrace mestizaje critically as a way to show the racism underneath "multiculturalism." The possibility of such a shift terrifies Huntington, who fears that the "American melting pot" of the beginning of the twentieth century (when immigration was mainly from Europe and assimilation was not a problem) will be transformed into a multicultural salad bowl in which "Hispanics" are not ready or willing to melt.[35]

The Mexican-American war, during the first half of the nineteenth century, left vast numbers of Mexican people and areas of land (from Colorado to Texas and from Texas through Arizona and California) "inside" the United States. Mexicans became immigrants in the territory of their own ancestors. From 1920 until the Nixon administration, the Bracero program brought Mexicans in as cheap labor to fill the jobs created by the two wars and by rising standards of living among US citizens. From 1970, immigrants from Puerto Rico and the rest of South America and the Caribbean also began to come in search of jobs or to escape dictatorship. By 2004, the estimated numbers of "Hispanics" in the US approached 40 million, a number larger than the population of either Colombia or Argentina, each of which counts around 35 million inhabitants. In fact, 40 million represents not much less than the combined populations of Chile (16 million), Bolivia (7 million), and Peru (22 million). With the exception of Mexico and Brazil, the "Hispanic" population in the US outnumbers the population of any individual country in South America. Thus, we have reached a moment in time when the distinction between an Anglo North and a Latin South that Thomas Jefferson and Simón Bolívar once embodied no longer applies. The idea of "Latin" America is being detached from fixed territorial contours.

But Latinos/as are not simply a group of people who dance salsa in US discotheques, who eat nachos, and of whom the majority are brown skinned, Catholic, and Spanish-speaking (although there are those Latinos/as who also speak Portuguese and sometimes French as well). Huntington's fears come not only from a brown population of service workers who refuse to assimilate; the deeper "Hispanic challenge" is to his own epistemology, and comes from knowledges that move in a different direction from the canonical disciplinary norms of the social science that he uses to argue his case. The next section will be devoted to Latino/a/Hispanic contributions to shifting geo- and bio-graphy and to incrementing the paradigm of co-existence. I suspect that Huntington's fear is unconscious, as he may have difficulties in recognizing that we Hispanics/Latinos/as also, like Anglos and Europeans, very much think and theorize. The dramatic challenge is that Latinos/as are part of a paradigm of knowledge that co-exists with Huntington's, and that even Harvard can no longer stop or delegitimize.

Between Bolívar and Jefferson: Are Chicanos/as and Latinos/as "Latin" Americans?

Like the diverse knowledge claims that we have seen coming from Indigenous and Afro-American communities and histories in the Caribbean and Latin America, the theoretical production by Chicanos/as and Latinos/as in the United States contests not only the content but the very principles of knowledge production that shape academic trends, disciplinary foundations, and entire social fabric. For, if Latinos/as (as any other subaltern community) cannot think on their own, they will be dependent on the supremacy of disciplinary formation and institutional regimes. It was thus for a while in the colonial histories of Western empires, but it is no longer the case. One of the most radical contributions is Gloria Anzaldúa's *Borderlands/La Frontera*, which is comparable in its ability to radically shift the geo-graphy and bio-graphy of knowledge to René Descartes's *Le Discours de la méthode* (1637). Descartes was able to shift from a theologically based concept of knowledge to an ego-logically based one with the statement "I think, therefore I am," which put the ego in the center and displaced God. Likewise, Gloria Anzaldúa's *new Mestiza* consciousness has decentered the Cartesian ego to replace it with a geo-graphically and bio-graphically centered way of thinking.

During the twentieth century, mestizaje functioned alongside the idea of "Latin" America as a way of constructing national identities after post-independence decolonization. "Mestizos/as" began to claim their right to the space appropriated by the Creole elites after

135

independence. Mestizaje became, curiously enough, an ideal for homogenizing national identities. Yet mestizaje was always a mirage, since the mixture of blood never accompanied a mixture of cosmologies (or epistemologies if you like). "Latins" in America, Creoles or Mestizos/as, always subscribed to the paradigm of newness and preserved their ties to remote European "origins." Mestizos/as never claimed Indian or (in the case of Mulattos/as) Afro origins.[36]

When the idea of Latin America emerged and flourished in the nineteenth century, it did not include Indian cosmology (epistemology) and always turned toward the European. Mestizos/as were mixed in blood, but pure in mind.[37] Mestizaje, as we can see in José Vasconcelos's *La raza cósmica*,[38] became a philosophical category that embodied the spirit of "Latinidad." The "cosmic race" for Vasconcelos emerges in South America with the meeting of the four existing races, White, Red, Black, and Yellow. Unconciously, Vasconcelos was accepting Kant's ethno-racial tetragon. According to him, the Spanish and Portuguese, unlike the English in the North, mixed from the very beginning with Indians and Blacks. Mestizaje, then, is taken in a much larger sense than the usual conception of two-way mixing between Spanish–White and Indian–Red. Yet the key for us is that, while Vasconcelos celebrated and encouraged all kinds of mestizaje, the "cosmic race" remained Ibero-American:

> One could say [states Vasconcelos at the closing of his essays] that it is Christianity that is going to be consummated, now not only in the souls, but at the root of beings. As an instrument for this transcendental transformation, a race has been developing in the Iberian continent; a race full of vices and defects, but gifted with malleability, rapid comprehension, and easy emotion, fruitful elements of the seminal plasma of the future species.[39]

The Hispanic race, in general, still saw itself as having ahead of it the mission of discovering and conquering new regions of the spirit, since all lands had already been explored. Vasconcelos conflates biological mestizaje and epistemic purity – people mix biologically but a rigid structure of thought, Christianity in its Ibero-American version, remains in place. Basic principles of thought, knowledge, and aesthetics do not mix but maintain a firm grounding in the Western tradition. Also, by setting Ibero-America as the exceptional location in the triangulation of European Iberians, Anglo Europeans/Americans, and Latin Mestizos/as, Vasconcelos perpetuates the idea of Hispanics as a fifth race, the fifth corner of the ethno-racial pentagon that will later work as a category for marginalization. It is precisely at this junction that Latinos/as disrupt the Latin American version of Western cosmology.[40]

As a Chicana and lesbian intellectual and activist, Gloria Anzaldúa enters into a conflictive dialogue with Vasconcelos in the most crucial chapter of her book ("La conciencia de la mestiza/Toward a New Consciousness"). From the very beginning, the chapter announces and enacts an aggressive and radical delinking from Vasconcelos (and, more broadly, from the masculine version of "Latinidad" and "Hispanidad"). Anzaldúa translates and modifies one of Vasconcelos's dictums ("Por mi raza hablará el espíritu," "Through my race, my spirit speaks") in the epigraph of this chapter: "Por la mujer de mi raza, hablará el espíritu/Through the woman of my race, the spirit speaks." Anzaldúa then moves from Vasconcelos's celebration of biological mixture in the fifth race of Hispanics to announce the emergence of a "new consciousness" (instead of a new Spirit à la Hegel), a Mestiza (not Mestizo) female consciousness of the between, a consciousness of the Borderlands.[41] While Vasconcelos remapped a unified and homogeneous "Spanish Spirit" under his "cosmic race" of biological Mestizos/as, Anzaldúa fractures the very idea of homogeneous unity. The idea of Latin America perpetuated in the masculine, Spanish/Portuguese, and later French/Mestizo elite colonial traditions is not only broken up by the massive migration of people from the South to the North but also by the critical consciousness that develops in that movement, the epistemology of the borderlands and the Mestiza consciousness. Thus, the Latino/a experience in the US parallels the emergent critical consciousnesses of Afro-Andean, Afro-Brazilian, Afro-Caribbean, and Indigenous people throughout the Americas. The idea of Latin America as put forward by Creole/Mestizo men is not, of course, erased. It is simply downsized, reduced to proportion.

The radical move made by Anzaldúa (as well as by Indigenous and Afro people in continental South America and the Caribbean) is no longer one of "resistance" but one of conceptual (epistemic) "delinking;" a radical shift in the geo-politics and body politics of knowledge. However, in order to delink and move forward, you need a new pair of shoes. If you do not invent a new pair of shoes, you remain kicking around in the old ones, the same ill-fitting system, begging for recognition and celebrating "multiculturalism" while never reaching the crucial moment of "interculturalidad" (which is "inter-epistemology," as I explained above). Anzaldúa uses the concept of "counterstance" to name that moment of delinking and moving forward. Compare the following paragraph with the previous one by Vasconcelos:

> In a constant state of mental nepantilism, an Aztec word meaning torn between ways, *la mestiza* is a product of the transfer of the cultural and spiritual values of one group to another. Being tricultural, monolingual, bilingual, or multilingual, speaking a patois, and in a state of perpetual transition, the *mestiza* faces the dilemma of the mixed breed: which collectivity does the daughter of a dark-skinned mother listen to?[42]

Anzaldúa uncouples the "homogeneous mestizaje" prototype of Latin/Ibero America by revealing the masculine heterosexual perspective operating beneath it, and by opening a hole through which to escape from that asphyxiating opposition between Latin and Anglo America upon which the very "idea of Latin" America was founded and maintained.

The "critical consciousness" emerging from the consciousness of being Mestiza works toward a double decolonization, both of knowledge and of being. It is a decolonization of *knowledge* because the philosophical foundation of modernity was built on the knowing subject that was constructed from the prototype of White, heterosexual, and European men. There is nothing wrong in principle with that epistemology, since you cannot be what you are not. But when you assume, for example, as a contemporary politician does, that whatever is good for you is good for Texas, whatever is good for Texas is good for the US, and whatever is good for the US is good for the world, then you have excluded the knowledges and experiences of all those who are not like you. The "Mestiza critical consciousness" shows the limits of the hegemonic concept of knowledge. It is a decolonization of *being* because, precisely, the imperial assumption of the validity of only one concept of knowledge, with its Eurocentricness, provides the justification for assuming the inferiority of all other knowing subjects who are not White, heterosexual, male, and European (or of European descent). The "Mestiza critical consciousness" opens many doors that have been discreetly left closed.

A *counterstance*, affirms Anzaldúa, is not enough, because it locks one "into a duel of oppressor and oppressed; locked in mortal combat, like the cop and the criminal, both are reduced to a common denominator of violence."[43] She links *counterstance* with liberation, and liberation with action based on delinking and disengagement from the hegemonic system of beliefs in which the formation of subjectivity is based. For example, the "ideas" of "Latin" or "Anglo" America are cages for subjectivity that someone like Samuel Huntington can use to defend an "Anglo" American identity challenged by Hispanics/Latinos/as. The *counterstance* confronts both Anglo and Latin assumptions and modes of subject formation (and simultaneously patriarchal and Eurocentric epistemology), but it cannot remain simply in opposition. So Anzaldúa argues:

> The counterstance refutes the dominant culture's views and beliefs and, for this, is proudly defiant. All reaction is limited by, and dependent on, what it is reacting against. Because the counterstance stems from a problem with authority – outer as well as inner – it's a step towards liberation from cultural domination. But it is not a way of life. *At some point, on our way to a new consciousness, we will have to leave the opposite bank*, the split between the two mortal combatants somehow healed so that we are on both shores at once and, at once, see through serpent and eagle eyes. Or perhaps we will decide to disengage from the dominant culture, write it off altogether as a lost cause, and cross the border into a wholly new and separate territory. Or we might go another route. *The possibilities are numerous once we decide to act and not react.*[44]

And, clearly, it is more than an oppositional or resisting consciousness. It is a practice of disengaging and looking toward a future in which "other worlds are possible," as the World Social Forum has it, or "toward a world in which many worlds can co-exist" as the

Zapatistas have taught us to think (all of us, that is, who believe in delinking and in disengaging from the monoculture of the mind to build a new world composed of many worlds).

Next to the military and economic power that rules the world, today, Anzaldúa's manifesto may seem idealistic and evoke the response of "oh, well this is nice but ..." Civil and political society is definitely limited by the web of transnational corporations, military secrecy, and G8 highly confidential negotiations. However, the transformation of the geography of knowledge happens at the level of decolonization of being and of knowledge, through which other possible worlds can be construed beyond the dominant systems. There is no way out for the *damnés* (who, under neo-liberalism, are increasing and including White Europeans and White US citizens who are also losing their privileges and moving toward the expendable part of society) through the paradigms in place. They must engage in paradigms of co-existence, in practice and in thought. What is left to civil and political society is such massive manifestations (multitudes of them, perhaps) as we saw in the loud outcry against the war in Iraq. But, more than the multitude of protests, what we have been witnessing is the emergence of previously invisible social actors with a myriad of concrete political projects and new ethical paradigms. The multitude only dissents within the paradigm of modernity. It is from the *damnés*, from the colonial wound, that the radical change is taking place, because it leaves the paradigm of modernity and newness for another one. That is what comes after "Latin" America. What is left to those who cannot live in this world is the active decolonization of knowledge and of being – the production and valorization of knowledge that does not underhandedly legitimate what Anzaldúa calls the "dominant culture," which always need to devalue the humanity of all those who do not conform to its values in order to maintain its position. The Zapatistas' theoretical revolution, Indigenous and Afro-Caribbean and Andean intellectuals, as well as Latinos/as in the US are building toward a future, toward an ideal of society not controlled by totalizing Western principles of knowledge and sovereignty of being. And there are more places where those working from the geo-politics and body politics of knowledge are generating *alternatives to the modern/colonial world*. The idea of "Latin" America is being superseded by the emergence of

140

new social actors claiming their epistemic rights and the trust that "an-other world is possible," beyond the one that has been naturalized under the control and management of the G8.[45]

We have seen that Huntington reflects Anglos' fear of losing their grip on their identity as the country is being claimed by many others – like Latinos/as. Yet the facts that in 2004, 44 percent of Latinos/as voted for George W. Bush, and that in 2005 Alberto Gonzáles replaced Attorney General John Ashcroft, both affirm that just as not every Christian is a theologian of liberation, and not every liberal or Marxist is necessarily progressive, so not all Latinos/as do or should think like Anzaldúa. At the same time, many non-Latinos/as are joining her political project and ethical stance. Thus, when I talk here about Afro, Indigenous, and Latino/a, *I am not talking about the totality of people identified as such but, on the contrary, about the political projects and ethical conduct that emerge from and assume histories of oppression and a share of the colonial wound.* Not every Black person will join the political project advanced by the Philosophical Caribbean Association; and at the same time, nothing prevents a White person from doing so if he or she shares the principles on which the project was founded and advanced. In other words, one doesn't have to be Greek and male to endorse some of Aristotle's ideas; and one doesn't have to be Black or Lesbian/Chicana to endorse and think from the platform advanced by Fanon or Anzaldúa! The point is not that an Indigenous, Latino/a, or Afro political and epistemic project should "represent" all people of the same color; and the same goes for the Whites. If you are Latino/a and would like to be with the political projects of White Republicans, it is a question of ethics, of choice, and not of skin color. Totalizing identity politics belongs to the paradigm that uses identities to hierarchize and exclude.

Global Americas: The Zapatistas, the World Social Forum, the Indigenous Summit, and the Social Forum of the Americas

In this new imaginary of the global order, the idea of America can be a terrain for the reorganization of conflicts. If the Indigenous social movements and the emergent visibility of the Afro population in Latin America have been gaining ground recently and providing the outlines of a new vision (beyond neo-liberal and neo-Marxist ideals), it is the emergence of the World Social Forum (WSF) that provides them with a new platform for new ways of making politics that is indirectly changing the idea both of "Latin" America and of America in general.[46]

We should understand the WSF and one of its outgrowths, the Social Forum of the Americas (inaugurated in Quito, Ecuador, in July of 2004), as another element of the social turn being enacted by the diverse groups of social actors we have discussed thus far, the Indigenous people from Chile through Canada, the Afro Andeans and Afro Caribbeans, and the Latinos/as in the United States. Yet the objection can be made that the WSF was founded and managed by the "Latin" components of the Americas. In other words, Indians, Afros, and Anglos were not players in its organization. This is a simple matter of fact (not criticism) that gives the WSF a particular profile. The fact that the WSF works to disrupt and transcend the legacy and the ideological frame of the "idea of Latin America" that had previously been promoted by the predecessors of these same Latin components should, however, indicate a clear change. "Latin" America is an idea that is still at work; but it is no longer the only valid idea/identity, it sustains one project among many which are finding new ways of relating, and one no longer negates the others. The litmus test of the WSF should not be the ethnicities of its organizers but the ethics of its founding principles.

As is well known, the WSF was created in response to the World Economic Forum (WEF). The logo of the WEF is "Committed to improving the state of the world." The WSF goes in another direction with its slogan, "Another world is possible." The WSF is working not only to reveal the fact that the world cannot be improved if it continues to rely on the hidden logic of coloniality expressed by the WEF, the World Bank, the IMF, and the Interamerican Development Bank, but also to build a world on principles other than those that have been naturalized in the past five hundred years of "diverse" (but Western, from Aristotle and Plato to Hobbes and Locke, to Smith and Marx, to Galileo and Max Planck, etc.) political theories, political economies, scientific discoveries, and technological "advances." The WSF recognizes that promoting progress in all these areas has meant and will increasingly mean a growing culture of death (not only by economically motivated war but by the worsening of minimal living conditions for more and more people). Thus, the WSF is a place for the enactment of the counterstance to neoliberalism and the crushing role of the US. If the WSF is bringing the Americas into the global imaginary as something other than a dependent, postcolonial subcontinent, the Social Forum of the Americas (SFA) cuts across the transnational in a different way. Rather than an Anglo American or Latin American transnational identity built on imperial legacies, the SFA stresses a truly American transnational identity – transnational, not trans-state. That is to say, the American transnational also includes emerging projects that move beyond the (modern) nation-state, like the Indigenous, Afro Continental and Afro Caribbean, and Latino/a social movements and epistemic/political projects (as exemplified, for example, in the legacies of Frantz Fanon, Waman Puma, and Gloria Anzaldúa).

I have suggested above that a similar project was announced by the Zapatistas in the early 1990s, before the WSF. Their motto is "A world in which many worlds would co-exist." The Zapatistas operate on an-other philosophy and an ethics that is not based on Christian, liberal, or Marxist principles but does not reject them either. What both the WSF and the Zapatistas reject is the totalitarianism of the three ideologies of modernity: Christianity/conservativism, liberalism, and Marxism. They reject entirely the fourth ideology, colonialism, as it necessarily institutes hierarchy. What they do not reject are the humanitarian and liberating ideas in Christianity's theology of liberation, the liberal ideas of democracy and emancipation, or the Marxist critique of capitalism and its call for a more equal world. No element, however, has the final word in the construction of the future. That is precisely one of the radical contributions of the WSF that was already implicit in the Zapatista dictum. "A world in which many worlds can co-exist" is the general formula for "Another world is possible." It cannot be reduced to the good intentions, wills, and ideas of the three Western macro-narratives, and it cannot be exchanged for a non-Western one like Islamic fundamentalism, which replicates with different content the fundamentalist tendencies in Western Christianity, neo-liberalism, or state controlled

143

socialism. The Zapatistas and the WSF/SFA demonstrate, in action, *the end of abstract universals competing for their superiority over others.* These ideas are not daily debated on CNN or the BBC, or by *Le Monde* (or even by *Le Monde diplomatique*, although their enthusiasm for and support of the Zapatistas, WSF, and SFA is remarkable). The fact that these ideas are not yet recognized or taken seriously in hegemonic discourse does not mean that they do not exist and do not move people in directions unseen by the overwhelming noise of the media.

Translation has a fundamental function in working toward a world where many worlds can co-exist. Translation in the rhetoric of modernity that hides the logic of coloniality was always unidirectional and served the needs of imperial designs.[47] The various colonial moves we have discussed earlier, the invention of America and the articulation of "Latinidad," are examples of the kind of modern/colonial translation that captures and transforms people, cultures, and meanings into what is legible and controllable for those in power. Latin America, as we have seen, was translated as a second-class set of nation-states in the global order, and its citizens were translated as second-class as well. A different kind of translation would be based on mutual respect and acknowledgement for both what can be seen through one's own lens and what exists outside of it because of the limitations of experience and geo-historical location. Instead of translating rich, diverse histories and knowledges into abstract universals, the kind of translation called for in the world of many worlds would allow each its own dignity without reduction, and maintain the autonomy of local, non-dependent histories. To recognize the limits of modern translations of identities such as "Latin" American and Indian does not necessarily mean we must eradicate them. We open them to the different identities, possibilities, and contradictions both inside and outside them. Thus the current division between "Latin" America and Abya-Yala is a moment of trust and of hope for entry into that world where both co-exist and neither assumes supremacy. Creoles/Mestizos/as can inhabit Latin America and share space with Indigenous groups inhabiting Abya-Yala without either staking a claim for priority.

The Zapatistas do not only theorize about a world where many worlds co-exist; they create it and live within it. "Los Caracoles" are not happening in "Latin" America but perhaps in Abya-Yala, or in a not-yet-imagined, coming community. They are happening "after Latin" America. The imperial-cum-national complicities in the "Latin" American project, as thought out and implemented from the nineteenth century against the US, have been exhausted. You do not have to be "Latin" to counter the devastating influences and actions of US imperialism. You (Latins, Afros, Indians, women and men of color and White too) need to enact the conceptual delinking. "Los Caracoles," Amawtay Wasi , the WSF and the SFA, the emerging Afro-Andean movements, and radical thinking in the French and British Caribbean are all part of that march, moving "after Latin" America toward a world in which many worlds will co-exist.

If "Latin" America emerged in the nineteenth century as the imaginary in which the identity of Creoles of Spanish descent was grounded, the "colonial wound" surfaced in the late decades of the twentieth century, bringing to the forefront the hidden side of "Latinidad" in South America. Curiously enough, "Latinidad" in the US emerged from a "colonial wound" that places "Latinos/as" closer to the ethical and political projects of Black and Indigenous people in South America and the Caribbean than to Creoles of "Latin" descent. The "idea" of Latin America is no longer apt to refer to the radical transformation in South America and the Caribbean. The future is open to the varied numbers of social movements and the transformations of the state.

Postscript

The manuscript for this book was already finished when the first summit toward a "South American Union" (or "South American Community of Nation-States") took place in Cuzco, Peru, in December of 2004. The meeting, promoted by Argentine ex-president Eduardo Duhalde, took place without the presence of the current Argentine president, Nestor Kirchner. The participants in the summits were all South American countries, including Guyana and Suriname; not exactly "Latin" countries but without doubt South American, sharing the same imperial/colonial history in the modern/colonial world. Caribbean countries and Mexico were excluded. Mexico, of course, belongs to the "North American" union of a sort. Argentinian writer Abel Posse published an article in the well- known Argentinian newspaper *La Nación,* and titled the article "Unión Sudamericana: ser o no ser" ("South American Union: to be or not to be"). Posse enthusiastically endorsed the idea and, with the European Union in mind, celebrated the need for such a union. He went further, and suggested: "In the face of some exercises in easy geo-politics, we should ensure that this South American (*or eventually Latin American*) Union doesn't emerge against the US or the FTAA, in the same way as the European Union was not born out of a confrontation, but to consolidate their cultures in new political and civilizing projects."[48]

Not all endorsements of the Unión Sudamericana come from intellectuals and writers once in the opposition and now turned right-wing. But it should be noted how difficult it is for intellectuals of Creole descent (like Posse or Mario Vargas Llosa) to "let it go": Posse cannot see (or does not want to see) the shift that the Unión Sudamericana is enacting, and for that reason he needs to *translate it back* to "eventually Latin American," for, if "Latin" America is reduced to a sector of the population of South America, the Creole subaltern hegemony is in danger. On the other hand, the history of Spanish and Portuguese colonialism – topped after the nineteenth century by British and then US control of the economy, in parallel with French intellectual influence since the nineteenth century and with US technological and corporate values (complemented of course by military bases and a CIA information network) – makes clear that the dream of a Unión Sudamericana that will consolidate a "Latin" American culture is a vision totally out of history. "Latin" America carries – in the name – the weight of imperial ideology (Spanish, Portuguese, and French) as much as "British" India carries the scar of the British Empire. Afros in South America, the Indigenous population from Chile to Canada, and the 40 million Latinos/as in the US have already given themselves a shake and begun to brush the imperial memories out of their/our bodies. What to do at the level of the state is one of the next steps.

Political analyst Isaac Biggio is more realistic and more aware of historical forces. Rather than having the historical idealism of Simón

Bolívar and José de San Martín, Biggio recognizes that the Unión Sudamericana cannot be equated with the US, and even less with the EU. As he points out, the reason why the idealistic dreams cannot materialize is basically the dependent nature of the economies and the political structures of all South American countries in the international arena.[49] The attempt to move toward a "Unión Sudamericana" shows, within the framework of my argument, that "Latin" America is no longer a viable project, even for the "Latin" population. It shows too that if a "Unión Sudamericana" is viable, it would have to emerge as an "oppositional" project to the two major Western blocks, the United States and the European Union. Projects like this one in the sphere of the state, controlled by peripheral Creoles of European descent both in blood and in mind, confront the imperial bent of the US and are moving toward delinking (although not according to the Marxist vision, as Samir Amin suggested in the mid-1980s[50]). The problem for the future would be to what extent such projects are not yet prepared to make alliances with the oppositional projects coming from Indigenous and Afro epistemologies, political theories, and political economies that I have described briefly described in this chapter.

Whatever the future of the "Unión Sudamericana" may be, it is now a signal statement that the cycle of "Latin" American ideology is over. Creoles controlling the state are regrouping and remapping "Latin" as "South" America (including Guyana and Suriname). The consequences of the move are quite significant, since it displaces Eurocentric "Latin" epistemology (and its consequences in political theory and political economy) with an "epistemology of the South," as Portuguese sociologist Boaventura de Sousa Santos has been claiming since the mid-1990s. Furthermore, an "epistemology of the South" relocates also the order of Europe, since the South is to Northern Europe what the South of America is to Northern America.

An "epistemology of the South," then, which is already imbedded in the philosophy of the WSF, opens up new avenues along which to work out alliances with claims made by the Indigenous movements about their dwelling place: they are no longer living in "Latin" America, as I explained above, but in "Abya-Yala." Parallel to the Indigenous claims, Afro-Andean remapping of their

147

territoriality in terms of "la gran co-marca" (see chapter 2) contributes to a trilogy that dismembers the one-to-one relation between the name and the territory, and thus breaks away from the control of meaning (of that name) by those who control epistemic (and not only political and economic) power. Last but not least, "la Frontera" as a key category of Chicano/Latino/a thought – equivalent to "the territory" for ideologues of nation-state categories of thought – further dismantles the Latin and Anglo ideological camps of Simón Bolívar and Thomas Jefferson. Briefly, the old "Latin" America is being remapped as South America, Abya-Yala, La Gran Commarca, and La Frontera.

Postface: After "America"

At the conclusion of this study, I want the world to recognize, with me, the open door of every consciousness.
Frantz Fanon, *Black Skin, White Masks*, 1952

"Latin" Americans have historically complained about and resented the US for appropriating the name "America" to refer to itself as a country. Painter Joaquin Torres-García (1874–1949) of Uruguay made a lasting contribution by inverting the content and denaturalizing the image of the Americas,[1] but the silence of missing Indigenous and Afro cartographies remains. Inverting the naturalized view of the Americas, with the South on top, is indeed one important step, but far from being sufficient. It changes the content, not the terms of the conversation. The image of the world upside down was also expressed by Waman Puma de Ayala, but he did not invert the map. Rather, he redraw it from the Andean perspective and with Tawantinsuyu, the fourth part of the world, twice reproduced in the same image (see next page).

His "Pontifical Mundo" ("Pontifical World," rather than "Orbis Universalis Terrarum" – "Universal World" – as Ortelius has it) expresses the imperial/colonial co-existence of the Indies, above, and Castille, below, as Castille is rendered in the same spatial matrix as Tawantinsuyu. In other words, Waman Puma's "world upside down" points toward an-other logic rather than toward an inverted content, as is the case with Torres-García's work.

PONTIFICAL

MVИDO

las yñs del piru
ento alto deespaña

cuzco

castilla enlo avayo
delas yñs –

castilla

encste

The "Pontifical Mundo" is one of the two "maps" that Waman Puma included in his *Nueva Corónica y Buen Gobierno*. In both of them, Waman Puma followed the spatial logic of Aymara and Kechua thinking and incorporated into it the information provided by the Spanish invaders. In the second "map" Waman Puma redraw Ortelius' "Orbis Universalis Terrarum" and imposed upon it the spatial logic of Tawantinsuyu. In both cases we have a radical displacement of the complicity between geography and epistemology in both the T-in-O and Ortelius' world map. Waman Puma established here a different complicity between spatial conceptualization and epistemology: a clear example of border thinking, the unavoidable condition of colonial subaltern subjects and the potential for decolonial epistemic and political projects. (Courtesy of the Royal Library of Copenhagen.)

Why should everybody have their own cartography, you may ask? Why not just accept America for what it is now? Certainly, that is one kind of argument that has been made. This Manifesto intends, precisely, to illuminate how history has produced silences and absences. But there are other arguments, like my own argument here, that are trying to change the terms and not only the content of the conversation. Just as the original naming of the "American" continent occluded all previous territorial designations, so "America" taken as a referent to the US as a country subsumed other countries and realities into an imagined totality. The objection made by "Latin" Americans that "America" is a name that belongs to everyone and not the US alone is justified. The reason, however, for the appropriation of the name by the US is seldom addressed. Why did the hegemonic voices in the US choose to claim "America" as the name of their own country? And what "idea" of America materialized as a consequence of that decision?

What allowed the US to appropriate the name, and thereby to subsume the name of the entire continent under that of only one country, was the same logic as led Christians in the sixteenth century to imagine the "Indias Occidentales" as the fourth continent, redrawing the T-in-O map onto the "Orbis Universalis Terrarum." The same logic, subsequently, also allowed secular Northern Europeans from the eighteenth century onward to name that totality "America" despite the fact that it had not existed as such in the consciousnesses of its original inhabitants, and even less in the consciousness of African slaves and their descendants. As we have discussed, America, as the fourth continent appended to the Christian cosmology of three, was not an "objective reality." Rather, it was a semantic construction with enormous political, economic, epistemic, and ethical consequences arising from the occlusion of Indigenous conceptualizations of Anáhuac, Tawantinsuyu, Abya-Yala, and other ideas of space. Thus, it is important to underline that it is a name imposed by European Christians, not Aymaras or Muslims. Europeans, at a time when Europe was not just one of four continents but *the* central and privileged one, had the power to name that others did not have. The "idea" of America is not only a reference to a place; above all, it operates on the assumed power and privilege of enunciation that makes it possible to transform an invented idea into "reality." This fact has been overlooked as if the continent already had its name inscribed naturally on the face of the earth. "America" did not name itself as such, despite the invisibility of the power relations behind its nomenclature. At work here is the coloniality of knowledge, which appropriates meaning just as the coloniality of power takes authority, appropriates land, and exploits labor.

In the same process, the coloniality of being shaped the subjectivity of the people involved. People, like continents and subcontinents, have been subsumed under overarching European concepts like "Human Being," which was conceived on the empirical evidence and experience of the Christian and White European Man and, from that definition, the universality of the Human is defended as the standard over all sort of differences (sex, gender, race, nationalities, languages, etc.). The racial occlusion of differences has it roots in the idea of the "Indias Occidentales" and of "America": the fourth part of the world became, in the prevalent Christian classification of the planet by continent and people attached to continents, the lowest in the scale of human beings, next to Africa. Europe, as we have seen, was for Kant the dwelling place of the White race that, as Hegel later pointed out, migrated to "America" and displaced the Red race. "Latins" in the South were, by the time of US independence, as subsumable as the Indians of Tawantinsuyu and Anáhuac were for Christian Europeans. If it had not been for the invention of "Latin" America as an entity through which European imperial powers could oppose the imperial march of the US, Creoles of Hispanic and Luso descent might not have had their own dwelling place. Indians and Afro descendents, of course, did not have the advantage of imperial help to name the territory after their own political and ethical projects. However, as discussed in chapter 3, the Haitian revolutionaries did manage to change the Spanish and French name back to an Indian name, Ayti; and Indigenous people, today, are living in Abya-Yala and not in "Latin" America. Nevertheless, imperial epistemic privileges remain in place. The universal idea of human being, the universal idea of a planet naturalized on the Christian idea of continental division (founded on the Holy Trinity and its perfunctory reproduction on the three sons of Noah: see chapter 1), and the idea that a continent can be subsumed by one country are three distinct moments and aspects of imperial knowledge formation through the logic of coloniality.

Control of money and control of meaning and being are parallel processes. Out of the top ten universities in the world, seven are in the US and three in Europe. If control of meaning and knowledge is concentrated in the ten top universities that produce the leaders of tomorrow's world, control of money is concentrated in the same geo-historical location. Almost 48 percent of major corporations and banks are located in the US and Europe. Ten percent are in Japan and the remaining 40 percent are scattered all over the world. If the geo-politics of economy is concentrated in three locales, with Japan having significantly less economic power, and the control of knowledge is located in Europe and the US, then talking about "deterritorialization" and a "floating" empire only masks the fact that the geo-politics of knowledge and economy remains anchored firmly in the West. Note, I use the term "geo-politics of economy" and not "political economy" because this term can only tell part of the story, the story of Western capitalism as seen by its own agents and intellectuals. Alongside the economic and epistemic hegemony is the simultaneous control of authority, state, and army. Out of around two hundred countries in the world today, most of them weakened by globalization, those of the G8 (mainly the US and the Atlantic axis of the European imperial countries of the past five hundred years) become stronger every day.

Today, the idea of "Latin" America is that of a dependent subcontinent that is subaltern to the continental totality, America. In the 1898 war with Spain – an empire in decline – political leaders, historians, and geographers in the US – an empire on the rise – began to twist the former European imperial mechanisms and strategies to their own ends.[2] The racial discourse that justified the war against Spain relied on selling the inferiority of "Latin" Americans as White but not White enough. In the war, the US played two roles: it was not only a *rising empire* fighting a declining one but also a *consolidated nation* that could take advantage of the two remaining Spanish colonies wanting to become nation-states, Puerto Rico and Cuba. It is precisely this double role that would allow for the identification of the country of the US with the continent.

153

The end of the Cold War started a new form of imperialism (but certainly within the same logic as the previous Spanish and British ones) led by the US. Celebrated as the end of history, the collapse of the Soviet Union was, in the long run, more of a problem than a solution for the US as new imperial leader of the capitalist world (once again, like Spain and England in the past). After the Cold War, it has increasingly become more difficult to contain the proliferation of knowledges and ideologies that differ from the hegemonic. They can no longer be easily packed into one enemy (communism). The US tried to substitute Islamism for communism, but the rules of the game were no longer the same. Perhaps the ideologues of "enemy substitution" simply missed the fact that *communism is part of and operates under the same logic as Christian and liberal modernity, with a difference only in content. Islam, on the contrary, operates under a different logic.* The misunderstanding that arises from ignoring that difference is at the root of the irrational war against Iraq. While things look bleak now (after the re-election of President George W. Bush and with the mounting numbers of dead Iraqi people in a war without justification), the problems faced by the US may actually be good for the rest of the world insofar as the drive to subsume the planet under one logic is being challenged.

It is precisely in the climate of fear provoked by that possibility that Samuel Huntington's two books, *The Clash of Civilizations* (1996) and *Who Are We?* (2004), found their raison d'être. Both books document the fear experienced most intensely by right-wing, Protestant, and White political elites that they will lose the economic and epistemic privileges that they have accumulated over two hundred and forty years. In other words, Huntington's fears are not merely his personally but reflect the feelings of those who currently "own" the state (that is, the US) and have the privilege of "being" the nation. A strong sense of property (economic and political capital) entitlement supports the fear and racism that are shared today by a large portion of the country's population. The Islamic world threatens the security of "the American people" by subjecting them to the possibility of mass slaughter at some unexpected moment, but the menace is constantly resuscitated to maintain a level of fear and to justify the government's right to operate at will on the basis of that fear. The Hispanics, on the other hand, are a long-term metaphorical bomb,

according to Huntington. No, I am not saying Hispanics are terrorists. Huntington fears, rather, the subtle erosion of the Anglo, White,
and Protestant identity by the non-assimilation of "Latinos," who are
presumably Catholics and of color or not quite White. Of course, this
is a simplification. Of the 44 percent of Latinos/as that voted for
President Bush in the last election, there was a good proportion of
Evangelicals and Pentecostals, two branches of Protestantism that
have been gaining significant ground in Spanish and Luso America
(although not necessarily in the Black, Anglo, and French Caribbean).
Nevertheless, in spite of a significant number of "Hispanics" voting
Republican, Huntington's fears do not dissolve: They may vote
Republican but still they are Hispanics!

What Huntington should fear most (if he does not already) is
not that "Latinos/as" are not assimilating. Some do, some don't. The
real problem is what I would like to call "Anzaldúa's threat,"
which is epistemic. Gloria Anzaldúa's theoretical revolution, in the
US, equivalent (at different level) to the Zapatistas' theoretical
revolution in Chiapas, began to erode all the sacred scientific principles, ideological convictions, and body reactions under which
Huntington, a serious political theorist playing the game of scientific
objectivity, operates. Thus, Latinos/as puzzle Huntington for the
same reasons as Islam escapes understanding in the dominant paradigms. Yes, "Latinos/as" or "Hispanics" of Spanish and Luso descent
are all children of European colonialism and its system of education,
from school to university, from the family to the church. But we
belong to the Latin language's version of history and mode of
being and, as Anzaldúa realized, we are all related closely to the
Indigenous and Afro populations because we share in different ways
the colonial wound. Additionally, as I showed in chapter 3, Afros
and Indians in South America are not depending any more on
generous "recognition" by Latin or Anglo Whites and have begun
to carve their own epistemic paths. In sum, what was once a nice
package of communist enemies today is exploding, literally and
metaphorically, into hundreds of political projects coming from the
experience and the anger of the *damnés*, coming, that is, from the
colonial wound.

The colonial wound, like the polis for Aristotle, the city-state for
Machiavelli, or the emergent bourgeois commercial and civilized

city for Hobbes, makes visible the experiences and subjectivities that shape a way of thinking, which, in this case, leads to a pluriversality of paradigms that are no longer subsumable under the linear history of Western thought, managed as a totality from imperial institutions that control meaning and money. The proliferation of other paradigms can no longer be determined by *uni*versal liberating projects, be they the theology of liberation or Marxism. Why would Islamic progressive intellectuals wait to be liberated by Christian theologians? Why would Afros in South America and the Caribbean, and Indians from Chile to Canada, want to be liberated following a Marxist blue-print for revolution? Cannot there be salvation from neo-liberalism outside of Christianity and Marxism (or Europe, as Jacques Derrida, Slavov Žižek, and Susan George would argue)? The explosions coming out of the theoretical, political, and ethical awareness of the *colonial wound* make possible the imagination and construction of an-other world, a world in which many worlds are possible. Examples of the practical implementation of that future are coming from South America (the Zapatistas, Amawtay Wasi, the World Social Forum, the Social Forum of the Americas, the Cumbre de los Pueblos Indígenas[3]) and from Latinos/as in the US. The imperial/colonial economic, political, and military power is still in the hands of Washington. However, *decolonization of knowledge and of being* (and more generally, of politics and the economy) cannot be thought out and implemented other than from the perspective of the *damnés* (and not from those of the World Bank or from an updated Marxism or a refreshed Christianity); that is, from the perspective, provided by years of modern/colonial injustices, inequalities, exploitation, humiliation, and the humiliations and pains of the colonial wound, of an-other world where creative care for human beings and the celebration of life will take precedence over individual success and meritocracy, and accumulation of money and of meaning (e.g., personal CVs, the personal satisfaction of celebrity, and all other ways in which alienation is being reproduced and encouraged). The imperial perspective (advanced and implemented by European and US men and institutions) cannot find the solution for the problems of the world created because of imperial designs and desires. Las Casas and Marx are necessary, but far from being sufficient. They should not only be complemented by Waman Puma,

Fanon, and Anzaldúa; their very critical foundation should be displaced. The "idea of Latin" America and the "idea of America (as the US)" came into being in the process of building the modern/colonial imaginary and the colonial matrix of power organized through the colonial and the imperial (epistemic) differences. Huntington's fears are justified as he sees history taking the US toward a non-White, non-Anglo future. The silences and absences of history are speaking their presence; the rumor of the disinherited can no longer be controlled, in spite of desperate moves like Huntington's, and its remarkable marketing success.

How to imagine a world "after Latin" America and "after America as the US," and the place of a continent that lies at the foundation of the modern/colonial world? Indigenous peoples' claims for the renaming of their dwelling place implies the reinscription of Waman Puma's cartographic logic. Abya-Yala is not just an inversion of the existing maps, but a questioning of the very nature of the existing maps. In 1570, around the same time Ortelius was publishing his "Orbis Universalis Terrarum," López de Velasco (Philip II's official chronicler, in charge of mapping the "Indias Occidentales," and manager of the famous questionnaire called *Relaciones geográficas de Indias*) took it for granted that the Isthmus of Panama was the natural division between the Southern and Northern parts of the "Indias Occidentales." About two hundred and fifty years later, the name of the continent was no longer "Indias Occidentales" but "America," and Hegel – directly or indirectly – followed López de Velasco's assumption and added that the natural division corresponded to an inherent difference between the people of the two parts, in which the South provided natural resources and cheap labor while the North (according to both Hegel and Alexis de Tocqueville after him) was the land of democracy and human rights. Obviously, the division of the two Americas between Latins and Anglos was not yet in sight when López de Velasco, ignoring Indigenous territorial mapping, established a division of the continent based on his own cartographic memory.

As we also saw in chapter 2, the supposed South of "America" was correlated in the nineteenth century with the inferior South of Europe, which was "tainted" by Catholicism and the infusion of Moorish blood, thus further degrading the South of America. The bottom line is that the North has been constructed as the leader of the South and the "natural" location of economic, political, military, and epistemic power. In general, given the economic status of the United States, "America" seems to still conform to Hegel's idea of a "natural" division between North and South. Indeed, for Europe and the US, South America provides a location for investment in natural resources and cheap labor as well as a cheap and exotic place for tourism. For European and US state politics, it is a place to establish alliances in favor of the G8. And if we maintain the idea of "Latin" America as a set of homogeneous countries, a civilization as Huntington would have it, the subcontinental unity joins Africa and Central Asia as one of three regions of the world with an enormous wealth of natural resources matched by growing poverty and misery.

However, "Latin" America today is also being transformed by left-oriented states (Venezuela, Brazil, Argentina, and Uruguay, mainly) that are emerging after the Cold War, different from previous leftist governments like Fidel Castro's Cuba, to challenge the continued application of the nineteenth-century idea of the Americas. At the level of the state, the path initiated by Hugo Chávez, Ignacio Lula, Nestor Kirchner, and Tabaré Vázquez seems to indicate an alliance of Atlantic countries moving toward the left. Hugo Chávez has returned to the ideas of Simón Bolívar and of a República Bolivariana that preceded the imperial invasion of the French and differ completely from the nineteenth-century idea of "Latin" America. Likewise, the Andean countries, as I insinuated in chapter 3, are becoming less and less "Latin" American, as Indigenous and Afro-Andean social movements make their presence felt and Indigenous people take an active role in state and local politics. The idea of Afro-Latinidad has already been accepted to describe people of Afro-American descent who speak Spanish and Portuguese rather than English, and who live in continental South America rather than in the British Caribbean and North America.[4] Last but not least, if Lula da Silva's project to constitute a Southern cell of the "G3" (Brazil, South Africa, and India) prospers, there will be still another reason to believe that "Latin" America is an idea that has run its course and can no longer be sustained.

Nor will it be necessary to sustain this idea. MERCOSUR (a trading bloc consisting of Argentina, Brazil, Paraguay, and Uruguay, with Bolivia and Chile as its associate members) and NAFTA (North American Free Trade Agreement between Mexico, the US, and Canada) illustrate the two competing poles of the situation. MERCOSUR turns to the South and has Brazil as a leading force. Brazil was marginal to the idea of "Latin" America and had remained until now as the younger brother of the family, albeit a quite large and very rich little brother. MERCOSUR establishes an "American" alliance that does not depend on the North. NAFTA and the Plan Puebla-Panama,[5] on the other hand, put Mexico in a tense position in relation to the family of "Latin" American countries, insofar as it is considered "North American" and an ally of the United States in facilitating US exportation, but still remains "Latin" and marginal to North America. Mexico's tenuous relation to the US is complicated by matters of immigration and the displacement of maquiladoras (or subcontractors) as the US moves to China and East Asia looking for cheaper wages. However, the Zapatista opposition to NAFTA and state policies shows that within Mexico there is a demand to change the traditional relation of the country to its Northern neighbor. The paradox today is that Hegel's idea of the Americas is being inverted: the growing organization of Indian and Afro social movements, the increasing philosophical, theoretical, and ethical inquiries in the Caribbean and in continental South America, and the growing numbers of states turning toward the left all indicate that democracy and respect for human rights are increasing in the South, while totalitarianism, violation of human rights, the use of violence to achieve domination, and extreme conservatism are on the rise in the North. History, which has not ended yet, will let us know, perhaps sooner than anticipated, what will come "after Latin America" and "after America."

The tectonic shift in progress is being enacted by the diversity of Indigenous epistemic, political, and economic projects – from the Mapuches in Chile to the Fourth Nation in Canada, with Native Americans in between – that do not respect the division between Latin and Anglo America, and think even less of the idea of an America that encompasses all other "Americas." Likewise, the rich diversity among people across the "Americas" of African descent, who speak Spanish, Portuguese, English, French, Dutch, and Creole and practice Santería, Voodoo, Candomblé, Rastafarianism, and varieties of Christianity, is not contained by an "Anglo" or "Latin" American identity or political projects in the name of "Latinidad" or "Anglicidad." Furthermore, the Latinos/as have been making the borderland, rather than the territory of the nation-state, the location of their subjectivity. Some Latins in the South confront these struggles and are threatened while others are joining forces with Latinos/as, Afros, and Indigenous people and working in solidarity on common projects. Thus an "*intra*cultural dialogue," to use an expression learned from Afro-Colombian activist Libia Grueso, is taking place among political projects originating in diverse but parallel experiences of the colonial wound. Intracultural dialogue among subaltern projects and communities generates intercultural struggles with the state and institutions managing the spheres of the social (economics, politics, gender and sexuality, subjectivity and knowledge).

Geo-political identities, it seems, have not been the concern of women until recently. You can certainly go to Google and type "woman, writer in Latin America" and find an enormous amount of information; but it will be more difficult to find a significant number of texts by women in which the idea of "Latin" America has been called into question. It would be interesting to explore why subcontinental identity has traditionally been more of a male than a female question. Where women made interventions, since the nineteenth century, was at the level of the nation and of national culture, both in "Latin" and in "Anglo" America. That is, they were mainly women of European descent, from either Latin or Anglo countries. The situation has changed in the years since the early 1970s, when gender and ethnicity on the one hand, and patriarchy and racism on the other, have risen to new levels of concern and struggle, as we see clearly in the work of Anzaldúa. Feminist scholarly and political projects (consider those of Anzaldúa and Sylvia Wynter among many others not mentioned here) cut across the distinction between "Latin" and "Anglo" America from a different angle. If "Latin" and "Anglo" America are both patriarchal, feminist geo-political concerns today are global and transnational, rather than subcontinental, ones. Indigenous women in Ecuador, for example, will create alliances in Ecuador and the Andean countries, and also with Indigenous women in Canada or Australia. Black Caribbean women, whether with French, British, or Spanish colonial legacies, are joining forces, on the one hand, with Black men against racism and, on the other, with Indigenous and White women against patriarchy. The idea of a "Latin" and "Anglo" America is, more often than not, an impediment to decolonial movements, as both subcontinental identities connote the sphere of state and imperial power rather than decolonial struggles.

"After America" is a process and a continental movement that is eroding the ethnic (Latin/Anglo) and geographic (North/South) frontiers. I began with the T-in-O map translated into Mercator's and Ortelius' "Orbis Universalis Terrarum." Thus, I finish with the radical dislocation of the Americas and of Latin America by Waman Puma, who translated *Pachakuti* as "the world upside down." He, too, drew his own map, not by following Ortelius but by updating Andean cosmology to account for a world that was not only turned upside down by the Spaniards but had, like the one around us, become a world where different logics co-exist(ed), although linked by the colonial matrix of power differentials.

Thus, for the future continental imaginary, the Americas upside down (placing "Latin" on top of "Anglo" America) won't do any longer. A change in content without questioning the logic is necessary but far from being sufficient. An "epistemology of the South" should take a second step, blurring the memories of a planet divided into four continents, and promote a process of critical border thinking, an epistemology in which people of Afro descent in the Americas as well as the whole diversity of Indigenous people in the South, Native Americans in the US, and the Fourth Nation in Canada have much to say. We are, indeed, in the middle of a seismic shift that CNN and the BBC are not reporting (and perhaps not yet quite understanding). The diverse social movements connected by the word and web address "noalca" ("No to ALCA – Área Libre Comercio de las Américas") close each of their public statements with the expression: *Otra América es posible* ("An other América is possible"). Waman Puma's map, and his *Nueva Corónica y Buen Gobierno*, become, like Niccoló Machiavelli for the history of Europe, a point of reference for the Other América of the future and for the decolonial task of the present. They join forces with Frantz Fanon's dictum – "At the conclusion of this study, I want the world to recognize, with me, the open door of every consciousness" – and with Latina Gloria Anzaldúa's conjecture:

> *En unas pocas centurias*, the future will belong to the *mestiza*. Because the future depends on the breaking down of paradigms, it depends on the straddling of two or more cultures. By creating a new mythos – that is, a change in the way we perceive reality, the way we see ourselves, and the ways we behave – *la mestiza* creates a new consciousness.[6]

Notes

Preface: Uncoupling the Name and the Reference

1   Martin W. Lewis and Karen E. Wiggen, *The Myth of Continents: A Critique of Metageography*. Berkeley: University of California Press, 1997.

2   Arturo Escobar, "'World and Knowledges Otherwise': The Latin American Modernity/Coloniality Research Program," *Cuadernos del CEDLA*, 16 (2004), 31–67.

3   For the European reader unfamiliar with this term, "Chicanos" and "Latinos" (the canonical forms) are terms of self-identification by a population in the US of Mexican descent and Caribbean descent, respectively. "Latinos" has been generalized and includes "Chicanos," without erasing the particular history of each group (e.g., Puerto Rican, Cubans, Mexicans). Furthermore, the strong intervention of women has led to the need, because of the gender markers in the Spanish language, to speak of "Latinos/as." All these variations are, as I have said, self-identification, in contrast with the identification "Hispanics," which was imposed from above by the Anglo-government of Richard Nixon.

4   For the question of "nature" in the imperial Spanish mentality, see my "Commentaries" to José de Acosta's *Natural and Moral History of the Indies*, trans. Frances López-Morilla, ed. Jane E. Mangan. Durham, NC: Duke University Press, 2002, pp. 451–519. For a current view on the question of "nature" and "Latin," see Arturo Escobar, *El final del salvaje: Naturaleza, cultura y política en la antropología contemporánea*. Bogota: CEREC, 1989; and Gabriela Nouzeilles, ed., *La naturaleze en*

disputa: Retóricas del cuerpo y del paisaje en America Latina. Buenos Aires: Paidos, 2002.

5   Ariruma Kowii, "Barbarie, civilizaciones e interculturalidad," in Catherine Walsh, ed., *Pensamiento critico y matriz (de)colonial*. Quito: Universidad Andina and Abya-Yala, 2005, 277–96. Aymara intellectual Marcelo Fernández Osco has done extensive work on Aymara concepts of law and justice, extremely relevant to an understanding of scholarly intellectual production, that contest the mainstream "Latin" American conceptions, and show the limits of national and state narratives about education, democracy, equality, etc. See Marcelo Fernández Osco, *La ley del Ayllu*. La Paz: PIEB, 2000; see also, by the same author,"La ley del *Ayllu*:justicia de acuerdos"and"Descolonizacion jurídica," *Tinkazo: Revista boliviana de ciencias socials*, 9 (2001), 11–28 and 41–4.

6   A recent and sophisticated theorization of the concept of "interculturalidad" is Catherine Walsh, "Interculturalidad, conocimientos y (de)colonialidad," lecture delivered at the II Encuentro Multidisciplinario de Educacion Intercultural, Mexico City, October 27, 2004 (e-mail cwalsh@uasm.edu.ec). See chapter 3 for more on "interculturalidad."

7   This arguments has been advanced in the postface to the English edition of my *Local Histories/Global Designs: Coloniality, Subaltern Knowledges and Border Thinking*. Princeton, NJ: Princeton University Press, 2000; and in the "Prefacio a la edición castellana" of the same book, *Historias locales/diseños globales: Colonialidad, conocimientos subalternos y pensamiento fronterizo*. Madrid: Editorial Akal, 2003.

1   The Americas, Christian Expansion, and the Modern/Colonial Foundation of Racism

1   All translations are mine unless a translator is specified.

2   Edmundo O'Gorman, *La invención de América: El universalismo de la cultura occidental*. México: Universidad Autónoma de México, 1958.

3   The imperial character of the US surfaced after the end of the Cold War. See, for example, Neil Smith, *American Empire: Roosevelt's Geographer and the Prelude to Globalization*. Berkeley: University of California Press, 2003. Since the war in Iraq, there has been talk about "reluctant imperialism" and "light imperialism" in the pages of the *New York Times, Foreign Affairs, Harvard International Review*, etc.

4 One of the defenders of "empire light" is former socialist Michael Ignatieff. See www.wsws.org/articles/1999/nov1999/koso-n27.shtml; and www.counterpunch.org/neumann12082003.html. Another is Sebastian Mallaby: see his article published in *Foreign Affairs*, March–April (2003), www.foreignaffairs.org/20020301facomment7967/sebastian-mallaby/the-reluctant-imperialist-terrorism-failed-states-and-the-case-for-american-empire.html;2.

5 I explore these issues in detail in "Delinking: The Rhetoric of Modernity, the Logic of Colonialty and the Grammar of De-coloniality," in Ramón Grosfoguel, Nelson Maldonado-Torres, and Ramón Saldívar, eds., *Coloniality, Transmodernity and Border Thinking*. Durham, NC: Duke University Press, forthcoming.

6 Waman Puma de Ayala, analyzing the colonial viceroyalty of Peru in the late sixteenth and early seventeenth centuries, is one of the earliest cases. See chapter 3.

7 *Pachakuti* is a complex Aymara word. *Pacha* could be interpreted as the energetic confluence of space and time, and therefore the radiation of life. *Kuti* could be interpreted as a violent turnaround, a "revolution" in Western terms. Andean people described as *Pachakuti* what happened to them and their way of life with the arrival of the Spaniards. I will come back to the significance of the Indigenous conceptualization of the "discovery and conquest," and its significance in the colonial histories of South America and the Caribbean, in chapter 2.

8 The important political-economic factor in the configuration of the colonial matrix of power has been explained by Argentinian economic historian Sergio Bagú, *Economía de la sociedad colonial: Ensayo de historia comparada de América Latina*. Buenos Aires: El Ateneo, 1949. The significance of the global transformation in land appropriation has been described by German political theorist Carl Schmitt, *The Nomos of the Earth in the International Law of the Jus Publicum Europaeum* [1950], trans. G. L. Ulmen. New York: Telos Press, 2003. Notice that these two shortly preceded O'Gorman's thesis on the invention of America. For a study of international law, colonial expansion, and land appropriation from a perspective opposite to Schmitt's (that is, the perspective from the geo-political space of colonial histories and sensibilities, closer to Bagu and O'Gorman in revealing the politics of knowledge), see Siha N'Zatioula Grovogui, *Sovereigns, Quasi Sovereigns, and Africans*. Minneapolis: University of Minnesota Press, 1996.

9 Zapatista National Liberation Army, "Manifesto from the Lacandon Jungle," January, 1994. English translation in J. Beverley, J. Oviedo, and

M. Aronna, eds., *The Postmodernism Debate in Latin America*. Durham, NC: Duke University Press, 1995, pp. 311–13.

10 As is well known, the idea of dependency was introduced by Argentinian economist Raúl Prebisch, in the late 1950s, to explain why Third World countries could not develop economically like the First World countries. Prebisch was not a Marxist, but a liberal economist from the Third World. The idea was taken up by a group of sociologists and economists mainly in Brazil, Chile, Peru, and Mexico, and transformed into "dependency theory," to explain also the power relations between imperial countries like the US and ex-colonies like Latin America. For a summary and update, see Ramón Grosfoguel, "Developmentalism, Modernity and Dependency Theory in Latin America," *Nepantla: Views from South*, 1/2 (2000), 347–74.

11 Bartolomé de Las Casas, *Apologética Historia Sumaria* (c.1552). México: Universidad Autónoma de México, 1967, vol. II, pp. 637–54.

12 Two and a half centuries later, Immanuel Kant was updating Las Casas. The Turks were the common ground, but Kant was looking at the barbarians in the North West: "Since Russia has not yet developed definite characteristics from its natural potential; since Poland has no longer characteristics; and since the nationals of European Turkey never have had a character nor will ever attain what is necessary for a definite national character, the description of these nationss may properly be passed over here" (Immanuel Kant, *Anthropology from a Pragmatic Point of View*, trans. Victor Lyle Dowdell. Carbondale: Southern Illinois Press, 1996, p. 233). "Barbarous habits" in Las Casas became "national characters" in Kant, and the measuring stick against which to rank people according to their degree of reason and their limitations in grasping the beautiful and the sublime.

13 The reader should keep in mind that there is no such a thing as "Latin America" at this point of World History, only the colonies of Spain's and Portugal's empires in the Indias Occidentales and, for some contemporaries, in America or in the New World.

14 "Abya-Yala" is a Kuna Indian word meaning "Place of Life." Today it has been adopted by the Indigenous people from Chile to Canada to mean "Continent of Life," co-existing with what the Europeans called "America." The co-existence of two names is only a problem for Europeans who believe that there is a one-to-one relation between a word and the object that the word names. Naming was crucial for European colonization of the mind, since they "appropriated" the continent by denying existing names and giving it a name that fitted into the Christian cosmology.

15 Isidore of Seville, *Etimologiarum sive originum: Libri X*, ed. W. M. Lindsay [1911], repr. London: Oxford University Press, 1957.

16 Gerardus Mercator, c. 1540, has "India Nova" as the name for what will become America: www.henry-davis.com/MAPS/Ren/Ren1/406C.htm. Abraham Ortelius mapped the fourth part of the world in his famous "Orbis Universalis Terrarum." www.artbeau.com/images_world/Ortelius_World_z.jpg.

17 St Augustine, *Concerning the City of God against the Pagans* (first printed 1467), trans. Henty Bettenson, intro. John O'Meara. London: Penguin, 1984. Italics added.

18 O'Gorman's "invention" instead of "discovery" is a case in point. Haitian historian Michel-Rolph Trouillot made a similar point by shifting the geography and the geo-politics of knowledge and showing that the "silence" around the Haitian revolution prevented the full story from being told, and therefore let the Eurocentric version of the revolution pass as the full story (Michel-Rolph Trouillot, *Silencing the Past: Power and the Production of History*. Boston: Beacon Press, 1995). Sibylle Fischer took Trouillot a step further by showing that silencing was in fact disavowing, meaning that the Haitian Revolution was indeed "recognized" but at the same time "negated" (Sibylle Fischer, *Modernity Disavowed: Haiti and the Cultures of Slavery in the Age of Revolution*. Durham, NC: Duke University Press, 2004). "Disavowal" is a fundamental mechanism in the production and reproduction of the colonial and imperial difference in the sixteenth, nineteenth, and twenty-first centuries, a process that maintains the hegemony of the Western imaginary. (Remember, the imaginary formed around Greek and Latin and the six modern European imperial languages, disavowing, precisely, the potentiality of all other languages and their respective epistemologies – that is, their knowledge potential –in the making of the world order.)

19 On the world commercial circuits before 1500, see Janet Abu-Lughod, *Before European Hegemony: The World System, A.D. 1250–1350*. New York: Oxford University Press, 1989. For the emergence of the Atlantic commercial circuit, see Walter D. Mignolo, *Local Histories/Global Designs: Coloniality, Subaltern Knowledges and Border Thinking*. Princeton, NJ: Princeton University Press, 2000.

20 www.nativeweb.org/pages/legal/indig-romanus-pontifex.html.

21 http://usuarios.advance.com.ar/pfernando/DocsIglLA/Requerimiento.htm.

22 Anibal Quijano, "Coloniality of Power, Eurocentrism, and Latin America," *Nepantla: Views from South*, 1/3 (2000), 533–80.

23 Abu-Lughod, *Before European Hegemony*, p. 355.

24 Abu-Lughod, *Before European Hegemony*, pp. 361–3.

25 "Orientalism," as popularized by Edward Said since 1978 (in his *Orientalism*. New York: Vintage Books), but already being debated in north Africa and in French before then (see Abdelkebir Khatibi, "L'orientalisme desorienté," in *Khatibi, Maghreb pluriel*. Paris: Denoel, 1983, pp. 113–46), couldn't have been conceived without a previous idea of "Occidentalism." "Occidentalism," however, and contrary to "Orientalism," was not an object of study but *the* locus of enunciation.

26 For the most recent critical revisiting of the "idea" of Europe, see Roberto Dainotto, *Europe (in Theory)*. Durham, NC: Duke University Press, forthcoming. Dainotto shifts the epistemic center of knowledge grounded in eighteenth-century France, England, and Germany that produced the idea both of the Orient and of the South of Europe. He locates the epistemic gaze in the history of the South and questions the assumed neutrality of the geo-politics of knowledge from where the Orient and the South were defined and categorized. Furthermore, this historical moment witnessed the concurrence of the division of the world into four races and the rearticulation of the sixteenth-century idea of four religions (Christianity, Judaism, Islam, and "the rest"). See Tomoko Masuzawa, *The Invention of World Religions: Or, How European Universalism was Preserved in the Language of Pluralism*. Chicago: University of Chicago Press, forthcoming. Thus, you can see that the "idea of Latin America" cuts across the secular continental racialization attributing one skin color per continent and the religious rearticulation of the ratio between religion and continents.

27 Fernando Coronil, "Beyond Occidentalism: Toward Nonimperial Geohistorical Categories," *Cultural Anthropology*, 11:1 (1955), 52–87; and Walter Mignolo, "Post-Occidentalismo: el argumento desde America Latina," *Cuadernos Americanos*, XII/1 (1998), 143–66.

28 Samuel Huntington, *The Clash of Civilizations and the Remaking of the World Order*. New York: Simon and Schuster, 1996. See chapter 3 for more on Huntington.

29 Sun Ge, "How Does Asia Mean?" *Inter-Asia Cultural Studies*, 1/1 (2000), 13–47, 1/2 (2000), 320–41. The end of the Cold War put the question of continental divides onto the geo-political agenda. In Asia, Sun Ge is not an isolated case. See for further discussions: Wang Hui, "Imagining Asia: A Genealogical Analysis," www.lse.ac.uk/collections/LSEPublicLecturesAndEvents/pdf/20040512Hui.pdf; and Jang In-

sung, "Discourse on East Asia in Korea and Asian Identity," www.waseda-coe-cas.jp/e/symposium0312/sympo03-s2jang-e.pdf.

30 See Walter D. Mignolo, *The Darker Side of the Renaissance: Literacy, Territoriality and Colonization*. Michigan: University of Michigan Press, second edition, 2004, chapter 5.

31 Sun Ge, "How Does Asia Mean?" p. 14.

32 Sun Ge, "How Does Asia Mean?" p. 14.

33 Said quoted by Sun Ge, "How Does Asia Mean?" p. 13.

34 Sun Ge, "How Does Asia Mean?" p. 13.

35 Sun Ge, "How Does Asia Mean?" p. 14.

36 V. Y. Mudimbe, *The Invention of Africa: Gnosis, Philosophy and the Order of Knowledge*. Bloomington, IN: Indiana University Press, 1988; and *The Idea of Africa (African Systems of Thought)*. Bloomington, IN: Indiana University Press, 1994. In Africa, there is also a debate going on over the historical assumptions of continental divides prompted by neo-liberal imperialism. After Mudimbe, see Achille Membe, "At the Edge of the World: Boundaries, Territoriality and Sovereignty in Africa," *Public Culture* 12:1 (2000), www.newschool.edu/gf/publicculture/backissues/pc30/mbembe.html.

37 See Walter Mignolo, "The Geopolitics of Knowledge and the Colonial Difference," *South Atlantic Quarterly*, 101/1 (2000), 57–97.

38 Enrique Dussel, *Philosophy of Liberation* [1977], trans. Aquilina Martinez and Christine Morkovsky. Eugene, OR: Wipf and Stock, 1985.

39 Hector A. Murena, *El pecado original de América*. Buenos Aires: Editorial Sudamericana, 1954, p. 163.

40 Anibal Quijano and Immanuel Wallerstein, "Americanity as a Concept; Or the Americas in the Modern World-System," *ISSA*, I:134 (1992), 549–56.

41 Quijano and Wallerstein, "Americanity as a Concept," p. 549.

42 I have to apologize to readers who dislike jargon. I am trying to avoid it as far as possible, but there are limits and this is one of them. If I did not introduce this concept, I could not get out of the frame of mind that current and non-jargonistic language shut me inside. Consider this concept, as well as that of coloniality, as the key that opens the door to show you a view that was blocked by a huge black gate and an even bigger black fence. We should note that the idea of historico-structural heterogeneity itself arose not in discussions and reflections on the French or Industrial Revolutions by European or US scholars, but from the experience of the colonial discovery/invention/construction of America as analyzed by Peruvian sociologist Anibal Quijano.

2 *"Latin" America and the First Reordering of the Modern/Colonial World*

1 Eric Williams, *Slavery and Capitalism*. Chapel Hill, NC: University of North Carolina Press, 1944, p. 32.

2 Immanuel Kant, "What is Enlightenment"? [1792], in Peter Gay, ed. and intro., *The Enlightenment: A Comprehensive Anthology*. New York: Simon and Schuster, 1954, p. 384. Eduardo Mendieta observed that "self-imposed maturity" is a more standard translation of Kant's *Unmudigkeit*.

3 Arturo Ardao, *Génesis de la idea y el nombre de América Latina*. Caracas: Centro de Estudios Latinoamericanos Rómulo Gallegos, 1993, p. 19.

4 Ardao, *Genesis*; see also, by the same author, *América Latina y la latinidad*. Mexico: Universidad Nacional Autónoma de México, 1993.

5 For the emergence of the Creole consciousness in the Spanish colonies, see Sam Cogdell, "Criollos, Gachupines, y 'plebe tan en extremo plebe': Retórica e ideología criollas en *Alboroto y motín de México de Siguenza y Góngora*," in Mabel Moraña, ed., *Relecturas del Barroco de Indias*. Hanover: Ediciones del Norte, 1992, pp. 245–80; and for the Creole consciousness in the Portuguese colonies see Lucía Helena Costigan, "La cultura barroca y el nacimiento de la conciencia criolla en el Brasil," also in Moraña, *Relecturas del Barroco de Indias*, pp. 303–24.

6 Waman Puma de Ayala is one example among many. See chapter 3.

7 Bolívar Echeverría, *La modernidad de lo Barroco*. México: Editorial Era, 1998, p. 82 (italics added).

8 It may be a little confusing for the reader not familiar with the history of political theory to face these definitions of republicanism and liberalism. On the basis of current experience, the original definitions of republicanism and liberalism sound upside down. Or, if we pay attention to the administration of George W. Bush, we may realize that "neo-liberalism" is indeed a coordination of both: free trade and individual enterprise with a strong state controlling national security, foreign policy, and military control over the world. But not only that: the legacy of secular republicanism and liberalism is being coordinated with secular conservatism (i.e., an ideology based on the moral values of Christianity). That is to say, it is an interesting fusion of the church and the state, disguised by a secular and ambiguous discourse in which state centralization goes together with a strong push for commercial

and free trade. What really is at stake in this complex picture is liberal support for individual freedom. Individual freedom is being curtailed on several fronts: by the control justified in the name of national security (e.g., racial and geo-political control of immigration) and by the control justified by the administration's moral values (e.g., control of gender and sexuality by banishing gay marriage).

9   For nineteenth-century Argentina, see Natalio Botana, *La tradición republicana: Sarmiento, Alberdi y las ideas politicas de su tiempo*. Buenos Aires: Editorial Sudamericana, 1984. And for a larger view of nineteenth-century Latin America, see José Antonio Aguilar and Rafael Rojas, eds., *El republicanismo en Hispanoamérica: Ensayos de historia intellectual y politica*. México: Fondo de Cultura Económica, 2002.

10   Quoted in Miguel Rojas Mix, *Los cien nombres de América Latina: Eso que descubrió Colón*. San José: Editorial Universitaria de Costa Rica, 1991, p. 352. For a recent explorations of the consequences of Bilbao's observation, see Walter D. Mignolo and Madina Tlostanova, "The Logic of Coloniality and the Limits of Postcoloniality," in Revathi Krishnaswamy and John Hawley, eds., *The Postcolonial and the Global: Connections, Conflicts, Complicities*, University of Minnesota Press, forthcoming.

11   Quoted by Rojas Mix, *Los cien nombres de América Latina*, p. 350.

12   Leopoldo Zea, *The Role of America in History* [1957], ed. and intro. Amy A. Oliver, trans. Sonja Karsen. New York: Rowman and Littlefield, 1992.

13   Rodolfo Stavenhagen, "Class, Colonialism and Acculturation," *Studies in Comparative International Development*, 1:7 (1965), 53–77; Pablo Gonzalez Casanova, "Internal Colonialism and National Development," *Studies in Comparative International Development*, 1:4 (1965), 27–37.

14   Immanuel Kant, *Observations on the Beautiful and the Sublime* [written 1763], trans.. John. T. Goldhwait. Berkeley: University of California Press, 1960, esp. section IV.

15   Norman E. Whitten, Jr, and Diego Quiroga, "Ecuador," in Minority Rights Group, ed., *No Longer Invisible: Afro-Latin Americans Today*. London: Minority Rights Publications, 1995, 287–318.

16   Santiago Castro-Gómez, p.c. based on his current research on racial configurations in Colombia in the seventeenth century.

17   Nelson Maldonado-Torres, oral presentation in the undergraduate seminar "The Clash of Empires," co-taught by Ebrahim Moosa and Walter D. Mignolo, Duke University, spring, 2004.

18   Fanon observed: "It is not because the Indo-Chinese has discovered a culture of his own that he is in revolt. It is because 'quite simply'

it was, in more than one way, becoming impossible for him to breathe" (Frantz Fanon, *Black Skin, White Masks* [1952], trans. Charles Lam Markmann. New York: Grove Press, 1967, p. 226); and Anzaldúa in the same vein noticed that "The U.S.–Mexican border *es una herida abierta* where the Third World grates against the first and bleeds" (Gloria Anzaldúa, *Borderlands/La Frontera*. San Francisco: Aunt Lute Books, 1987, p. 25).

19 Jules Michelet, *Histoire et philosophie* [1831]. Paris: Denoel, 1900, pp. 73–4.

20 Rémi Brague, *Europe, la voie romaine*. Paris: Gallimard, 1992.

21 Brague, *Europe*, p. 40.

22 Brague, *Europe*, p. 53.

23 Juan Bautista Alberdi, *Bases y puntos de partida para la organización nacional* [1852], Buenos Aires: La Cultura Argentina, 1915. Notice how Alberdi is placing himself in Greece where the Egyptians moved to, and how the same law "moved" the Egyptians to Greece and "moved" the Greeks to civilize Italy.

24 Quoted in Ardao, *Génesis*.

25 Quoted in Ardao, *Génesis*, pp. 153–67.

26 Quoted in Ardao, *Génesis*, p. 54.

27 Quoted in Ardao, *Génesis*, p. 165.

28 Zea, *The Role of America in History*, pp. 121–36. Not by chance, the same issue has been rethought by a scholar based in Galicia. See Ángeles Huerta González, *La Europa periférica: Rusia y España ante el fenómeno de la modernidad*. Santiago: Universidad de Santiago de Compostela, 2004.

29 Aims McGuinness, "Searching for 'Latin America': Race and Sovereignty in the Americas in the 1850s," in Nancy P. Appelbaum, Anne S. Macpherson, and Alejandra Rossemblat, eds., *Race and Nation in Modern Latin America*. Chapel Hill, NC: University of Carolina Press, 2003, pp. 87–107.

30 McGuinness, "Searching for 'Latin America,'" p. 99.

31 G. W. F. Hegel, *The Philosophy of History*. Buffalo: Prometheus Books, 1991, p. 81 (italics added).

32 Spanish conservative José Donoso Cortés published in France in 1852 (that is, the same year Karl Marx published *The Eighteenth Brumaire of Louis Bonaparte*) a book titled *Catholicism, Liberalism, Socialism*.

33 I am using here the same word, "colonialism," in two distinct contexts (or universes of discourse, to use an expression from analytical philosophy). In one context, colonialism is the complementary sphere of imperialism as a historical project. I am also using "imperialism/

colonialism" to talk about empires based on capitalist economy and located in the Atlantic (Spain, Holland, France, England, and the US) in the past five hundred years. During that period, there were various imperial and different colonial historical moments, in the Americas, in Asia, and in Africa. My premise is that there is no imperialism without colonialism; colonialism is constitutive of imperialism as coloniality is of modernity. On the other hand, I am also using "colonialism" as the hidden or disguised ideology of the modern/colonial world – of Christianity and the monarchic Spanish Empire during the sixteenth and seventeenth centuries (disguised as "conversion" and as "Castilanization"); and of secularism and the nation-state empires (e.g., those of England, the US, the Soviet Union), disguised as the civilizing mission, socialism and the dictatorship of the proletarian class, or market democracy. Briefly, imperialism/colonialism are both historical projects (Spanish imperialism/colonialism is different from British and US). At the same time, the three of them are connected through the *rhetoric of modernity* (salvation, progress, well-being for all) and the *logic of coloniality* (racism that justifies exploitation, oppression, marginalization, appropriation of land, control of authority).

34 Jorge Larrain, *Identity and Modernity in Latin America*. London: Blackwell, 2000, p. 67.

35 Frantz Fanon, *The Wretched of the Earth* [1961], trans. Constance Farrington. New York: Grove Weidenfeld, 1991, p. 61.

36 Michel-Rolph Trouillot, *Silencing the Past: Power and the Production of History*. Boston: Beacon Press, 1995.

37 Anibal Quijano, "Coloniality of Power, Eurocentrism and Latin America," *Nepantla: Views from South*, 1/3 (2000), 533–80.

38 Lewis Gordon, *Existentia Africana Understanding Africana Existential Thought*. New York: Routledge, 2001, pp. 159–60.

39 Gordon, *Existentia Africana*, pp. 159–60 (italics added).

40 Boaventura de Sousa Santos, "The World Social Forum: Toward a Counter Hegemonic Globalization," www.ces.fe.uc.pt/bss/documentos/fsm_eng.pdf.

3 After "Latin" America: The Colonial Wound and the Epistemic Geo-/Body-Political Shift

1 See *Global Trends 2015*, http://www.cia.gov/nic/NIC_globaltrend2015.html#link13h.

2   By "epistemic" I simply mean the principles, conceptualization, and normativity of knowledge as they have been naturalized, for example, in the disciplines (e.g., the social sciences and the humanities). The "shift" I am explaining has been taking place in the Third World and in the intellectual production of "minorities" in the US. The biography and the geo-graphy of racialized communities are reclaiming their right to know and to criticize imperial knowledge, responding to the imperial devaluation of non-Western knowledge underway for the past five hundred years.

3   Sylvia Wynter, "1492: A New World View," in Vera Lawrence Hyatt and Rex Nettleford, eds., *Race, Discourse and the Origin of the Americas: A New World View*. Washington, DC: Smithsonian Institution, 1995, pp. 5–57. For further and more recent development of these ideas, in dialogue with the modernity/coloniality research project, see her "Unsettling the Coloniality of Being/Power/Truth/Freedom," *New Centennial Review*, 3:3 (2003), 257–337.

4   Santiago Castro-Gómez, "La hubris del punto cero: Biopolíticas imperials y colonialidad del poder en la Nueva Granada (1750–1810)," manuscript, 2003.

5   Frantz Fanon, *Black Skin, White Masks* [1952], trans. Charles Lam Markmann. New York: Grove Press, 1967, pp. 17–18.

6   Fanon, *Black Skin*, p. 18.

7   I highlight the paradigm of co-existence (an-other language, an-other thinking, an-other logic) in my *Local Histories/Global Designs: Coloniality, Subaltern Knowledges and Border Thinking*. Princeton, NJ: Princeton University Press, 2000, pp. 313–38; and also in the "Prefacio a la edición Castellana," *Historias locales/diseños globales: Colonialidad, conocimientos subalternos y pensamiento fronterizo*. Madrid: Editorial Akal, 2003.

8   V. Y. Mudimbe, ed., *The Surreptitious Speech: Présence Africaine and the Politics of Otherness* [1947–87]. Bloomington: Indiana University Press, 1992, p. xvii.

9   Padget Henry, *Caliban's Reason: Introducing Afro-Caribbean Philosophy*. New York: Routledge, 2000.

10   Henry, *Caliban's Reason*, p. 3.

11   Henry, *Caliban's Reason*, p. 3.

12   Henry, *Caliban's Reason*, p. 3.

13   Samuel Huntington's Anglo identity politics, and his fear of Hispanic/Latinos/as, is developed in *Who Are We? The Challenges of America's National Identity*. New York: Simon and Schuster, 2004, particularly ch. 9. As the reader will remember, Huntington is a political theorist,

at Harvard University, who during Bill Clinton's presidency wrote *The Clash of Civilizations and the Remaking of the World Order* (New York: Simon and Schuster, 1996), which, in retrospect, looks more like an announcement of things to come than a political analysis. In these two books, Huntington set Islam against Western Civilization and Latinos/as against Anglos in the US.

14 Bibliography on Haiti is gaining ground. For my argument, the following are relevant: Michel-Rolph Trouillot, *Silencing the Past: Power and the Production of History*. New York: Beacon Press, 1995; Susan Buck-Morss, "Hegel and Haiti," *Critical Inquiry*, 26:4 (2000), 821–65.

15 Some of the work being done in northwest of Ecuador, in collaboration with the Universidad Andina Simón Bolívar, can be seen in Juan García Salazar, ed. and prologue, *Historia de Vida Papá Roncón*. Quito: Fondo Documental Afro-Andino, 2003. He is the leading figure of Afro-Ecuadorian work toward reactivating history and inscribing an-other epistemology in the geo-politics of knowledge. See also the collaborative article by Catherine Walsh and Edizon León (the leading figure of the younger generation), "Afro-Andean Thought and Diasporic Ancestrality," paper delivered at the meeting of the Caribbean Philosophical Association, "Shifting the Geography of Reason," Barbados, May, 2004.

16 Frantz Fanon, *The Wretched of the Earth* [1961], trans. Constance Farrington. New York: Grove Weidenfeld, 1991, pp. 39–40.

17 Walter Mignolo, "The Zapatistas' Theoretical Revolution: Its Historical, Ethical and Political Consequences," *Review*, XXV:3 (2002), 245–74.

18 In personal conversation, Catherine Walsh and Edizon León pointed out Waman Puma's derogatory attitude to African people. While this should be critiqued, we should not lose track of his double critique. Las Casas made the same mistake, although he corrected himself; and Marx foresaw the development of a European-type bourgeoisie in India as a necessary step toward the socialist revolution. All three thinkers remain exemplars of critical consciousness in spite of their racial blindness. Furthermore, in the case of Waman Puma the colonial difference in subalternity should be noticed. The idea of "Latin" America was constructed with Indians as a problems and Afros as an absence.

19 For a rationale of the politics of language and epistemology (that is, for an argument why and how to shift the geo- and the bio-politics of knowledge), see the argument by Otavalo intellectual and activist

175

Ariruma Kowii, "Barbarie, civilizaciones e interculturalidad," in Catherine Walsh, ed., *Pensamiento crítico y matriz (de)colonial*. Quito: Universidad Andina and Abya-Yala, 2005, 277–96.

20 Luis Macas, reappointed president of CONAIE in April 2004, secretary of agriculture of Lucio Gutierrez for 204 days, and president of Amawtay Wasi, has written several pieces in which the concept of "interculturalidad" is played with and made to interact with concepts that are celebrated by the state (like democracy) and that are used to do exactly the opposite of what they claim. Making "interculturalidad" and democracy interact, for example, provides a new departure, a delinking from the closed circle of Western political theory. See, among other examples, Luis Macas, http://icci.nativeweb.org/boletin/63/macas.html on "interculturalidad" and economy; Macas, http://conaie.nativeweb.org/conaie5.html. For a scholarly analysis of the concept of "interculturalidad" in dialogue with concurrent theories (the "modernity/coloniality project) and in contradistinction to perspectives from modernity, even progressive ones, see Catherine Walsh, "Interculturalidad and Coloniality of Power: An 'Other' Thinking and Positioning from the Colonial Difference," in R. Grosfóguel, J. D. Saldívar, and N. Maldonado-Torres, eds., *Coloniality of Power, Transmodernity and Border Thinking*, Duke University Press, forthcoming.

21 Vine Deloria, Jr, *Custer Died for Your Sins: An Indian Manifesto* [1969]. Norman, OK: University of Oklahoma Press, 1988, p. 11.

22 See Luis Macas, http://icci.nativeweb.org/boletin/19/macas.html; http://icci.nativeweb.org/boletin/33/presentacion.html. Catherine Walsh, from the Universidad Andina Simón Bolívar (Quito), has done an enormous amount of work with the Indigenous community and Indigenous intellectuals, and has contributed to our understanding both of what is at stake now in the Indigenous movement in relation to the process of epistemic decoloniality, and of the meaning of "interculturalidad" within Indigenous discourses (in contradistinction to the use of the terms in the discourses of the state). See her "Bases teórica para la (re) construcción del movimiento Indígena," paper presented at a meeting of Indigenous leaders of Ecuador, convoked by Luis Macas (Quito, July 2004, mimeo); and "Interculturalidad and the Coloniality of Power: An 'Other' Thinking and Positioning from the Colonial Difference," in R. Grosfóguel, J. D. Saldívar, and N. Maldonado Torres, eds., *Coloniality of Power, Transmodernity and Border Thinking*. Durham, NC: Duke University Press, forthcoming.

23 For a panoramic view of Amawtay Wasi in the history of the Western university, from the Renaissance to the corporate university, including the colonial expansion since the sixteenth century and the foundation of colonial universities, see Walter D. Mignolo, "The Role of the Humanities in the Corporate University," *Nepantla: Views from South*, 4:1 (2003), 97–120. Recently, the report on the Universidad Intercultural was published under the title *Aprender en la sabiduría y el buen vivir/Learning Wisdom and the Good Way to Live*. Paris and Quito: UNESCO, 2004. The publication is not easy to access and I have not yet been able to consult it.

24 Notice that I am identifying theology, egology, and organology as three different faces (with cumulative effects) of modern epistemology, from the Renaissance, the Enlightenment, and the end of World War II and the beginning of the Cold War. Norbert Winner's *Cybernetics*, which initiated the organological epistemic framework, was published in 1948.

25 See the collective document prepared by the Instituto Científico de Cultural Indígenas (the institution where the work toward the creation of Amawtay Wasi was concentrated), http://icci.nativeweb.org/boletin/19/uinpi.html.

26 Mignolo, "The Zapatistas' Theoretical Revolution."

27 See the reproduction of it in the postface.

28 Among many others, see: Pablo González Casanova, "The Caracoles," www.memoria.com.mx/177/gonzalez.htm; Raúl Ornelas, "La autonomía como eje de la resistencia zapatista: Del levantamiento armado al nacimiento de los Caracoles," in Ana Esther Ceceña, ed., *Hegemonías y emancipaciones en el siglo XXI*. Buenos Aires: CLACSO, 2004, pp. 133–74. This book was already in production when the Zapatistas' "Red Alert" was issued, followed by further public statements. For a summary, see www.leftturn.org/Articles/SpecialCollections/ZapatistaRedAlert.aspx.

29 James Lockhart, "Double Mistaken Identities," in Lockhart, *Of Things of the Indies: Essays Old and New in Early Latin American History*. Stanford, CA: Stanford University Press, 1999, p. 99.

30 The challenge for the progressive post-soviet turn in Spanish and Luso American states (Hugo Chávez in Venezuela, Lula da Silva in Brazil, Nestor Kirchner in Argentina, and Tabaré Vázquez in Uruguay) is to take seriously the Indigenous concept of "interculturalidad" and turn the plate around. Otherwise, if the management of the state continues to be on the Euro-American model only, it will continue to perpetuate imperial violence and manipulation. The way to "other possible worlds"

can today hardly come from republican, liberal, or Marxist models (e.g., in South America, the Creole and the "Latin American" ethos). Elements of these modern models should be incorporated or included in the perspectives offered by the Indigenous and Afro ethos that sustain delinking projects (political, economic, ethic, epistemic) put forward and carried on by men and women dwelling in that ethos.

31 However, the recent project toward the "Union Sudamericana" challenges the very idea of Latin America from the state itself and not only from civil/political society. See the postscript to this chapter.

32 Arturo Escobar, "Worlds and Knowledges Otherwise: The Latin American Modernity/Coloniality Research Program," *Cuadernos del CEDLA*, 16, 31–67. In connection with this, see too the web dossier to which Escobar's title refers, www.jhfc.duke.edu/wko/contact.php.

33 Huntington, *The Clash of Civilizations*, p. 46; italics added.

34 See note 13 for details.

35 Walter D. Mignolo, "Huntington's Fear: Latinidad in the Horizon of the Modern/Colonial World," in R. Grosfoguel, N. Maldonado-Torres, and J. D. Saldívar, eds., *Latino/as in the World-System*. Hendon, VA: Paradigm, 2005.

36 For the challenge to the national ideology of mestizaje by Aymara leader Felipe Quispe, see Javier Sanjinés C., *Mestizaje Upside-Down*. Pittsburgh: University of Pittsburgh Press, 2004. For the fierce reactions of Creoles and Mestizos in the Caribbean to the fears provoked by the Haitian Revolution, see Sibylle Fischer, *Modernity Disavowed*. Durham, NC: Duke University Press, 2004.

37 There are always exceptions, and one is José Maria Arguedas in Peru, whose mental and psychological move to embrace Indigenous cosmology, and to become himself Indian, ended up in a tragic suicide. "Mestizos" only in blood, but not in mind, are less prone to put their lives at stake.

38 Mexican philosopher, historian and sociologist (1882–1959). His classic book, *La raza cósmica*, was first published in 1927.

39 José Vasconcelos, *La raza cósmica/The Cosmic Race*, trans. and intro. Didier T. Jaén with an afterword by Jozeba Gabilondo. Baltimore and London: Johns Hopkins University Press, 1997, p. 37.

40 After a lecture in which I addressed Anzaldúa's take on Vasconcelos, the audience – composed of Latin Americanists rather than Latinos/as – focused on Vasconcelos, even though the talk was on Anzaldúa. It was indeed a revealing example of the blindness of the "Latin" American frame of mind and the legacies of colonialism and internal colonialism at work. The charge was that I was simplifying Vasconcelos;

that he is a more complex and open-minded philosopher, aware of the importance of Asian (Indian and Chinese) philosophy and thoughts. I can grant all that. However, Vasconcelos worked within the "Latin" (and male) racial and epistemic framework I described in chapter 2, whereas Anzaldúa was tearing that apart, while creating a geo- and bio-political space of knowledge. While Vasconcelos, like any other "Latin" thinker from South America, was anchored in European traces ("subjective understanding," Vasconcelos's impossibility of locating himself in the "original" history of Afros and Indians, instead of in the "original" history of Europe), Latinos/as in the US cut that umbilical cord. And that is the radical spatial (and decolonial) epistemic break introduced by Anzaldúa vis-à-vis the "Latin" American notion of mestizaje and, in particular, of Vasconcelos's "la raza cosmica." Colombian writer Manuel Zapata Olivella (self-identified as Afro-Colombian, and seen as Latino in the US because Spanish and not English is his national language) twisted Vasconcelos's dictum in yet another direction in his autobiographic and reflective book *Levántate mulato! "Por mi raza hablará el espíritu"* (Bogotá: Editorial Letras Americanas, 1990, pp. 235–7). I owe this insight to Colombian intellectual Santiago Arboleda.

41 Gloria Anzaldúa, *Borderlands/La Frontera*. San Francisco: Aunt Lute Books, 1987, p. 99.

42 Anzaldúa, *Borderlands/La Frontera*, p. 100.

43 Anzaldúa, *Borderlands/La Frontera*, p. 101.

44 Anzaldúa, *Borderlands/La Frontera*, pp. 100–1.

45 I would like to underline that my entire argument should be considered as the contribution that the modernity/coloniality project is making to shifting the geography and geo-politics of knowledge. I am writing the dissenting "Latin" American genealogy of thoughts (Bilbao, Martí, Mariátegui, dependency theory, theology/philosophy of liberation on which the modernity/coloniality project is grounded) and as a Hispanic following the lead of thinkers like Gloria Anzaldúa and Americo Paredes. For an overview of Anzaldúa's legacy and links with women activists in South América, see Sonia Saldívar-Hull, *Feminism on the Border: Chicana Gender Politics and Literature*. Berkeley: University of California Press. For Américo Paredes's contribution, see Ramón Saldívar, *The Borderland of Cultures: Américo Paredes, Social Aesthetics and the Transnational Imaginary*. Durham, NC: Duke University Press, 2005.

46 Boaventura de Sousa Santos, "The World Social Forum: Toward a Counter Hegemonic Globalization," www.ces.fe.uc.pt/bss/fsm.php;

Emir Sader, "Por qué y qué en Porto Alegre?" in Sader, *La Venganza de la Historia: Hegemonía y contra-hegemonía en la construcción de un Nuevo Mundo possible*. Buenos Aires: CLACSO, 2002, pp. 75–94; José María Gómez, "De Porto Alegre a Mumbai: El Foro Social Mundial y los retos del movimiento altermundialista," in Ana Esther Ceceña, ed., *Hegemonías y emancipaciones en el siglo XXI*. Buenos Aires: CLACSO, 2004, pp. 173–96.

47 Walter D. Mignolo and Freya Schiwy, "Double Translation: Transculturation and the Colonial Difference," in Tullio Maranhao and Bernhard Streck, eds., *Translation and Ethnography:The Anthropological Challenge of Intercultural Understanding*. Tucson: University of Arizona Press, 2003, pp. 3–29.

48 Abel Posse, "Unión Sudamericana: ser o no ser," *La Nación*, December 21, 2004, p. 25; italics added.

49 Isaac Biggio, www.bigio.org/nota.asp?IDNoticia=2328.

50 Noted Egyptian sociologist Samir Amin published his well-known book *La Déconnexion* (Paris: Editions La Découverte) in 1985. It was translated into English with the title *Delinking: Towards a Polycentric World*. London: Zed Books, 1990.

Postface: After "America"

1 For this inverted map, see www.ceciliadetorres.com/jt/jt.html; www.public.asu.edu/~aarios/resourcebank/maps/page4.html.

2 A case in point is Neil Smith, *American Empire: Roosevelt's Geographer and the Prelude to Globalization*. Berkeley: University of California Press, 2003.

3 The Second Summit of the Indigenous People of the Americas took place in Quito, Ecuador, in July 2004, just one week before the first meeting of the Social Forum of the Americas. In that Summit, it was accepted by the overwhelming majority of Indigenous peoples, from the Mapuches in Chile to the Fourth Nation in Canada, that their dwelling place is Abya-Yala and not Latin America. www.rebelion. org/sociales/040321zhingri.htm.

4 Sociologist Agustín-Lao Montes (University of Massachussets, at Amherst) is currently conducting a research project on "Afro-Latinidades" in the US, and literary and cultural critique Gertrude Gonzáles de Allen (Spelman College) is finishing a book on Manuel Zapata Olivella (Colombia), Nelson Estupiñan Bass (Ecuador), and Quince Duncan (Costa Rica).

5 Mexican president Vicente Fox devised the Plan Puebla-Panama (PPP), an eight-billion-dollar package that would create a development corridor from the Mexican state of Puebla through the country of Panama. It is being promoted under the guise that it will bring the people of these areas out of poverty by creating new economic opportunities for them, as well as for big business. Furthermore, it is said to promote trade, tourism, education, and the protection of the environment. But remember that the corridor goes through areas with a high Indigenous population and rich lands. Furthermore, it goes through the domain of the Zapatistas. Briefly, the PPP looks like an official project of land expropriation and the political control and subjugation of Indigenous people.

6 Gloria Anzaldúa, *Borderlands/La Frontera*. San Francisco: Aunt Lute Books, 1987, p. 102.

Index